Multilingualism

Multilingualism

Multilingualism

Larissa Aronin
Trinity College Dublin
and Oranim Academic College of Education, Israel

David Singleton
Trinity College Dublin

John Benjamins Publishing Company
Amsterdam / Philadelphia

 The paper used in this publication meets the minimum requirements of the American National Standard for Information Sciences – Permanence of Paper for Printed Library Materials, ANSI z39.48-1984.

Library of Congress Cataloging-in-Publication Data

Aronin, Larissa.
  Multilingualism / Larissa Aronin, David Singleton.
    p.   cm. (IMPACT: Studies in Language and Society, ISSN 1385-7908 ; v. 30)
Includes bibliographical references and index.
1. Multilingualism. I. Singleton, D. M. (David Michael) II. Title.
P115.A74   2012
404'.2--dc23   2011046459
ISBN 978 90 272 1870 4   (Hb ; alk. paper)
ISBN 978 90 272 1871 1   (Pb ; alk. paper)
ISBN 978 90 272 7498 4   (Eb)

John Benjamins Publishing Co. · P.O. Box 36224 · 1020 ME Amsterdam · The Netherlands
John Benjamins North America · P.O. Box 27519 · Philadelphia PA 19118-0519 · USA

*This book is dedicated to the kindness
and courage of Larissa's sister, Anna,
and David's brother, Peter*

Table of contents

Acknowledgments IX

CHAPTER 1
Introduction 1

CHAPTER 2
Multilingualism: Some preliminary considerations 11

CHAPTER 3
Multilingualism as a new linguistic dispensation 33

CHAPTER 4
The Dominant Language Constellation (DLC) 59

CHAPTER 5
Multilinguality and personal development 77

CHAPTER 6
Language development in multilingual conditions 99

CHAPTER 7
Classifications of multilinguals, multilingual contexts
and languages in multilingual environments 117

CHAPTER 8
A multilingual monolith? 145

CHAPTER 9
Towards a comprehensive view of multilingualism 163

CHAPTER 10
Concluding thoughts 187

Bibliography 191
Language index 221
Name index 223
Subject index 227

Acknowledgments

We should like to thank four people for their help in making this book a reality. First and foremost, we wish to acknowledge the patience and encouragement of our John Benjamins Commissioning Editor, Kees Vaes, who never stopped believing in the project. Second we need to recognize our indebtedness to our two John Benjamins reviewers, whose comments and suggestions were absolutely invaluable in the process of enriching and tightening our final draft. Finally we want to express our warm gratitude to Faina Furman for her assistance in preparing the manuscript.

CHAPTER 1

Introduction

What this book is about

This book is about multilingualism as a contemporary reality and a field of knowledge in its own right. It is clearly not the only publication available addressing the phenomenon of multilingualism. On the contrary, a large number of treatments of the topic have appeared in recent years, which induces us to raise a number of questions. Why it is that multilingualism is currently felt to be such an important issue? What kinds of relationships are being tracked in the abundant literature on multilingualism between individual lives, societies and the global community? What are the reasons being suggested for the way in which multilingualism has come to loom so large in perceptions of contemporary society? How has our understanding of multilingualism advanced in the midst of the research and debate which at present surrounds it? What is our view of the nature of the multilingualism which now confronts us, and do the view and the reality differ from what went before? And finally, what role has globalization had in the rise of multilingualism in the world? Such questions are underlying leitmotivs of the present volume, which is founded on the premise that multilingualism stands in urgent need of the most comprehensive consideration possible.

What is multilingualism? Terminology and definitions

Perhaps the first question that needs answering is: what do we mean by multilingualism? Basic though it may be, this is not, in fact, an easy question to answer; the definitions of multilingualism, and also of bilingualism, are many and wide-ranging. They are rooted in diverse theoretical and practical perspectives and emphasize different aspects of using and learning languages.

One major issue in this connection relates to levels and breadth of proficiency in the languages in question. Should we reserve the label bi- or multilingual for persons whose proficiency is native-like and balanced across both/all their languages and across the range of language skills – i.e., understanding and producing speech, reading and writing – or should we be less demanding in our application of these terms? Might we, for example, be prepared to qualify as bilingual the Russian engineer who with fluency and understanding reads technical articles in English but is unable to pronounce what he reads? Can we conceive of attributing multilingual status to the Spanish opera singer who performs consummately in Italian, German and French but is unable to converse in any of these languages?

Some definitions suggest that in order to count as a bi-/multilingual a person has to make frequent use of both/all the languages at his/her disposal. The trouble is, of course that different researchers may define frequency and indeed use in different ways. Much the same kind of difficulty attaches to the evocation in some definitions of fluency and of communicatively successful use of the languages in question. How fluent is fluent? Is making a purchase in the market place – using limited vocabulary and gestures, and relying on the goodwill of the stallholder eager to sell his product – categorizable as communicatively successful language use? And who is to decide on these questions?

Some researchers take a narrow stand on the above discussion points. Others take a broader view. Narrow definitions, more limiting and demanding, tended to prevail in research of some decades ago and still probably represent the "person-in-the-street" perspective. In 1933 Bloomfield (1933: 56) defined bilingualism as "native-like control of two or more languages". For Braun (1937: 115) multilingualism had to involve "active, completely equal mastery of two or more languages". Interestingly, taking its lead, no doubt, from such academic views, the 1961 edition of the *Webster Dictionary* defined *bilingual* as "having or using two languages especially as spoken with the fluency characteristic of a native speaker; a person using two languages especially habitually and with control like that of a native speaker". It is to be noted that such definitions constantly refer to the monolingual norm, requiring from the bilingual a level of proficiency in both languages comparable to that of monolingual native speakers of the languages in question.

At the other end of the scale we find a very liberal interpretation of bilingualism and multilingualism. Edwards's somewhat tongue-in-cheek representation of this interpretation is as follows: "[i]f, as an English speaker, you can say *c'est la vie* or *gracias* or *guten tag* or *tovarisch* – or even if you understand them – you clearly have some command of a foreign tongue" (Edwards 1994: 55). Members of the "*c'est la vie* camp" (Edwards 1994: 56), i.e. of those who espouse a rather wide definition of bilingualism and multilingualism are more numerous in our times than in the early to mid twentieth century. But already in 1952 Hall (1952: 14) considered a person who had "at least some knowledge and control of the grammatical structure of the second language" to be a bilingual. Diebold (1961) recognized what he called "incipient bilingualism" in speakers of the Huave language in Mexico although they had only "passive knowledge of Spanish".

Both of the above extremes can be helpful theoretically in setting out definitional possibilities but are less useful at a practical level. With regard to the narrow approach, it is generally acknowledged that very few people have really mastered two or more languages to an equal level of across-the-board native-likeness. As for the very wide definition of bi-/multilingualism, it is difficult to see what this contributes, given that in very many countries of the world it would encompass virtually the entire population. This last remark is by no means intended to devalue the importance of even a small amount of knowledge of additional languages, which may, of course, constitute a first step on the road to a more narrowly defined bi-/multilingualism. Receptive and other limited kinds of knowledge of additional languages may enhance metalinguistic awareness and have a significant preparatory value for further language acquisition (Jessner 2006).

Between the two extremes one encounters an extensive array of definitions. For example, according to one proposed by Titone (1972: 11), bilingualism is "the individual's capacity to speak a second language while following the concepts and structures of that language rather than paraphrasing his or her mother tongue". Macnamara (1967) for his part, characterizes as a bilingual anyone who possesses some proficiency in any one of the four language skills (i.e., listening comprehension, speaking, reading or writing) in a language other than his/her mother tongue. Current perspectives on bilingualism and multilingualism tend away from the very narrow view. While different researchers continue to define these terms in different ways, the application of the very demanding criterion of balanced, native-like proficiency in both/all of a bi-/multilingual's languages is no longer a feature of discussion in this area (see e.g. ten Thije 2007).

To complicate matters further the concept of *mother tongue* or *native language* is itself problematic. It traditionally carried connotations of origin, denoting the first language spoken as a child, the language of one's mother, one's family, one's home and of the wider community in which one lived; but already in 1981 Skutnabb-Kangas pointed out that there was more than one way of characterizing this notion, other possible dimensions of its definition relating to high degrees of proficiency, functionality, identification, and automacy (Skutnabb-Kangas 1981: 18–20). These days, it is by no means unusual for a person to take some time and to think very hard before responding to the question 'what is your native language?' Increasingly, popular usage applies such terms to a person's strongest language or the language considered by the individual as his/her most important language, whether or not this was the language originally encountered as the parental or home language. Moreover, whatever the order of acquisition, the language perceived as the first language may or may not be the language of the wider community.

Another issue of relevance in the context of defining the terms *bilingualism* and *multilingualism* is the question of the relationship between the phenomena which they denote. Do bilingualism and multilingualism constitute essentially the same phenomenon, with the latter just perhaps exhibiting a little more complexity than the former, or are there fundamental qualitative differences between them? Here again consensus is lacking; researchers see the interrelation between bilingualism and tri-multilingualism in a variety of ways.

The once dominant scholarly perspective – still frequently encountered – treated multilingualism as a mere extension of bilingualism. Weinreich, for instance, wrote (1953:5):

> …the practice of alternatively using two languages will be called here BILINGUALISM, and the persons involved BILINGUAL. Unless otherwise specified, all remarks about bilingualism apply as well to multilingualism, the practice of using alternatively three or more languages.

Likewise, Haugen (1956:9) referred to multilingualism as "a kind of multiple bilingualism". Mackey too used *bilingualism* as a cover term for all forms of multilingualism (1957:51)

> … if we are to study the phenomenon of bilingualism we are forced to consider it as something entirely relative. We must moreover include the use not only of two languages, but of any number of languages. We shall therefore consider bilingualism as the alternate use of two or more languages by the same individual.

We find a similar approach in the work of Baetens Beardsmore (1986:3): "the term bilingualism does not necessarily restrict itself to situations where only two languages are involved but is often used as a shorthand form to embrace cases of multi- or plurilingualism". Correspondingly, the study of multilingual acquisition is often considered to fall within the domain of second language acquisition research – on the basis that "[s]econd language acquisition (SLA) will normally stand as a cover term to refer to any language other than the first language learned by a given learner or group of learners" (Sharwood Smith 1994:7).

Thus, in much academic discussion bilingualism and multilingualism are interchangeable notions. A fairly recent (and widely cited) book on bilingualism has the following to say on the matter:

> The word 'bilingual' primarily describes someone with possession of two languages. It can, however, also be taken to include the many people in the world who have varying degrees of proficiency in and interchangeably use three, four or even more languages.
>
> (Li Wei 2000:7)

A rationale underlying such interchangeability of multilingualism and bilingualism is supplied by Baetens Beardsmore:

> There is no evidence to suggest that the fundamental principles affecting language usage are any different whether two, three or more languages are being used by one and the same speaker, and the major question is whether they differ significantly from the cases where only one language is being used.
>
> (Baetens Beardsmore 1986: 3)

Of late, it has to be said, Baetens Beardsmore's confident assertion has been called into question. There is, of course, absolutely no doubt that bilingualism and multilingualism share many similarities. This is true at the psycholinguistic level but also at the sociolinguistic level. With regard to the latter, for instance, the same kinds of global and local sociolinguistic conditions are causing both bilingualism and multilingualism to spread. On the other hand, much recent writing on this topic insists that there are very good reasons to recognize that multilingualism has "characteristics of its own" (Hoffmann 2001b: 3). One can cite in this connection the longstanding indications suggesting a better performance on the part of bilinguals as compare with monolinguals in third language learning, that is, apparently demonstrating a language-learning advantage where a multiplicity of languages is involved. Ringbom's (1987) research relating to Finnish-Swedish bilinguals learning English as a third language, for instance, and Thomas's (1988) investigation of the learning of French as L3 by English-Spanish bilinguals point precisely in this direction.

Current research in this domain begins by emphasizing the quantitative distinction between multilingualism and bilingualism and the greater complexity and diversity of the factors involved in acquisition and use where more than two languages are involved (Cenoz 2000; Hoffmann 2001a, 2001b; Herdina & Jessner 2002). Thus, it is pointed out that not only do multilinguals have larger overall linguistic repertoires, but the range of the language situations in which multilinguals can participate, making appropriate language choices, is more extensive. Herdina & Jessner (2000b: 93) refer to this capacity as "the multilingual art of balancing communicative requirements with language resources". This wider ability associated with the acquisition of more than two languages has also been argued to distinguish multilinguals in qualitative terms. One dimension of such a qualitative difference is clearly of an experiential nature: bilinguals and multilinguals differ as to the nature of their experience in learning languages, the latter having passed along a more varied route (Cenoz 2003). A further qualitative distinction seems to lie in the area of strategies. Kemp (2007), for example, reports that multilingual learners' learning strategies differ from those of monolingual students learning their first foreign language. She also notes more variation in multilinguals' use of strategies. Yet another difference between multilinguals and bilinguals has to do with cross-linguistic interaction. Studies going back to the 1970s (e.g. Kellerman 1977; Sjöholm 1976, 1979) and continuing down to the present day (e.g. De Angelis & Selinker 2001; De Angelis 2005; De Angelis & Dewaele 2009; Singleton 1987, 2006; Singleton & Little 2005) have shown that, in dealing with gaps in their knowledge of a given additional language, multilinguals draw not only on their native or strongest language but also on other additional languages at their disposal. Obviously this latter variety of resource expansion is not available to bilinguals.

For the above kinds of reasons there is an increasing tendency for researchers to be more careful in their use of the terms *bilingualism* and *multilingualism* (cf. e.g. Aronin & Hufeisen 2009a; Kemp 2009). Nor is this simply a matter of abstract terminological niceties. If it is the case, as it seems to be, that there are qualitative distinctions between the phenomena of bilingualism and multilingualism, this patently needs to be taken into account in designing relevant empirical studies and interpreting their findings. For example, a 'second language' acquisition study involving a sample that mixed monolingual foreign language acquirers with bilingual foreign language acquirers would risk running into the problem of confounding variables. At the more practical level of language teaching, it would seem sensible to envisage that curriculum design, teaching/learning environment, teaching/learning methodology and other components of the enterprise should take account of whether the initial state of the learners is monolingual, bilingual or multilingual (cf. Hufeisen & Neuner 2004).

Whereas previously, as we have seen, bilingualism was taken to be the starting point for discussion in this area, with multilingualism being treated as a more complex subcategory, increasingly it is now multilingualism that is perceived as the point of departure. Thus, for example, Herdina & Jessner consider bilingualism as "only one possible form of multilingualism, albeit a common one". They view multilingualism as "a varied phenomenon ranging from monolingual acquisition (the acquisition of a foreign language based on the command of one language) through balanced bilingualism, to the command of three or more languages, to name but a few stages of the multilingual continuum" (Herdina & Jessner 2000b: 84; cf. Crystal 1997: 253). A similar approach assigning the overarching role to the notion of multilingualism can be seen in a recent definition offered by Franceschini:

> The term/concept of multilingualism is to be understood as the capacity of societies, institutions, groups and individuals to engage on a regular basis in space and time with more than one language in everyday life.

> Multilingualism is a product of the fundamental human ability to communicate in a number of languages. Operational distinctions may then be drawn between social, institutional, discursive and individual multilingualism.
>
> (Franceschini 2009: 33–34)

This last approach to the multilingualism/bilingualism distinction is on the whole the one we adopt in this book. That is to say, unless the context indicates otherwise, when we use the terms *multilingualism* and *multilingual*, we apply them in a broad, inclusive sense, in such a way that they include the concepts of bilingualism and bilingual within their respective ambits. There are, however, moments in the discussion, as is evident already from the foregoing, where we wish to distinguish between *bilingualism/bilingual* (where two languages are involved) and *multilingualism/multilingual* (where more than two languages are involved). The formulation of descriptions and arguments at such junctures make clear that this kind of differentiation is intended. The terms *trilingualism/trilingual, quadrilingualism/quadrilingual*, etc. are used where the reference is to situations involving a precise number of languages above two.

A further terminological refinement is derived from the work of Hamers & Blanc (1989, 2000) who distinguished between bilingualism as an individual attribute – for which they coined the term *bilinguality* – and societal bilingualism – for which they retained the term *bilingualism*. Along the same lines, Aronin & Ó Laoire (2004) coined the term *multilinguality*, defining it (p. 17) as "a personal characteristic", restricting *multilingualism* – by analogy with the Hamers & Blanc's usage – to societal multilingualism. In the present text we broadly (but not necessarily dogmatically) adopt the Hamers & Blanc/Aronin & Ó Laoire distinctions in this connection. An additional term that often appears in the literature of bilingualism and multilingualism is *plurilingualism*. This is used – especially in Francophone research publications – sometimes as a synonym for multilingualism, but sometimes with specific reference to individual multilingualism (what we have labelled above *multilinguality*), as opposed to *multilingualism*, understood as the phenomenon of the use of many languages in a given society. We ourselves make no use of the term *plurilingualism* here. A final terminological distinction that needs to be noted is between *simultaneous* bilinguality or multilinguality, which refers to situations where a child is exposed to two or more languages at the same time from infancy onwards and *sequential* or *consecutive* bilinguality or multilinguality, which refers to situations where an additional language or additional languages are acquired later in childhood (some researchers take the age of three as the dividing line) – or indeed in adolescence or adulthood (cf. Baker 2006: Chapters 5 and 6).

The structure of the book

In the present chapter we have discussed some definitional issues and given some indications about the nature and scope of the book.

In Chapter 2 we discuss the phenomenon of human language in general, and explore mono-, bi-, and multilingual perspectives on language.

In Chapter 3 we address the rise of multilingualism in the world and try to account for it. The chapter makes the claim that the current situation constitutes a new world dispensation and that, as such, it requires to be approached in new ways with new research tools. It goes on to discuss, on the one hand, the challenges posed by multilingualism to societies and how they try to cope with such challenges, and, on the other, the very wide range of assets and possibilities offered by multilingualism and the ways in which societies are making use of its potential benefits.

Chapter 4 defines and illustrates the notion of *Dominant Language Constellation* (*DLC*) and discusses the role of such constellations in the new world dispensation. It then sketches some significant DLCs of the contemporary world and explores their functioning and influence within societies. The chapter describes the effects of the DLC in respect of such domains as social adaptation, daily routine, career opportunities and decisions, and relationship choices. In other words, an attempt is made to accumulate and examine evidence referring to all aspects of the individual's life path that are identifiable as being influenced by his/her DLC. To further illuminate the discussion, the chapter includes some personal stories of multilinguals.

Chapter 5 provides a comprehensive treatment of the concept of multilinguality. The chapter subsequently compares and contrasts the present conception of multilinguality with conceptions of individual multilingualism and discusses the emerging tendencies regarding individual multilingualism. In addition, it describes some most significant models of multilingual acquisition and processing.

Chapter 6 explores language development under multilingual conditions. It begins by considering the kinds of situations where a child grows up with more than one language at his/her disposal; and then scrutinizes the particularities of the process of acquiring two or more languages. The chapter goes on to explore the extent to which the languages at a multilingual's disposal are integrated or separate and finally attempts an evaluation of the advantages and disadvantages of multilinguality.

Chapter 7 reviews existing classifications of multilinguals, which tend to be based on the numbers of languages and specific languages known by multilingual individuals and on their levels of proficiency in these languages, and attempts to broaden the scope of the classificatory apparatus by proposing an approach which not only takes into consideration linguistic and psycholinguistic facts but also brings sociolinguistic perspectives to bear on the categorization process. This latter approach takes account, for example, of the fact that while some multilinguals use one or more of their languages principally or solely in specific situations (the home, the workplace, religious settings, etc.), others use all their languages across a wide range of functions and activities.

Chapter 8 addresses the question of whether knowledge of two or more languages constitutes a monolith in terms of acquisition and processing or is separable into different entities. The chapter surveys a range of psycholinguistic and neurolinguistic evidence in this context and argues that, while the multilingual's language knowledge can, in terms of dynamic interconnection and interplay, be seen as holistic 'multicompetence', there is no question but that the competencies associated with different languages known to an individual are at some level and in some sense differentiable and differentiated by the individual in question.

Chapter 9 attempts to relate the societal, political and educational facts of multilingualism to the complex nature of multilingualism. Recourse is had in this context to the concepts and analytical approaches of complexity science, which, in its claim that perspectives associated with the study of complexity in one area of investigation may also shed light on other areas, seems to offer the hope of generating new and predictive insights with regard to the complexities which characterize multilingual communities and to the individual multilingual's possibilities, constraints and choices. The chapter sets out to sketch a research programme which might generate testable predictions in respect of not only the prospects for particular patterns of language use in specific circumstances but also the progress/decline of particular aspects of language proficiency in the multilingual language user.

Finally, Chapter 10 offers a brief recapitulation of the content of previous chapters.

CHAPTER 2

Multilingualism

Some preliminary considerations

Human language, communication in other species and multilingualism

Let us begin our exploration of multilingualism with some first thoughts about language in general. Language may be conceived of from at least three different points of view. We can think of language in terms of its being a uniquely human possession; we can see language as a tool; and we can consider language as an ability.

Language as a unique human possession

Human language is a truly an "extraordinary institution" (Cooper 1973:3). We rightly never cease to marvel at its complexity, its versatility and its universality. The vast majority of human beings master language to a sufficiently high level to interact within personal and social relationships, to express and comprehend emotions and thoughts, to communicate and absorb detailed information, to share complex ideas, to tell and understand jokes, to drop and pick up on hints etc, etc. Communication systems used by other species have nowhere near as extensive or as flexible a range of functions and potentialities.

The comparison of human languages with other communication systems is a fascinating topic with a long history (see e.g. Russell & Russell 1973:161). Following Hockett (e.g. 1963), Aitchison (1998:27ff.) discusses a number of design features of human language, exploring their presence in non-human communication. These are listed and briefly commented on below in line with Aitchison's discussion.

Use of the vocal-auditory channel
This attribute, the use in communication of sounds made with the vocal organs which are received by a hearing mechanism, is clearly not unique to humans, being shared by a wide range of species – from chaffinches to dolphins. Moreover, just as human languages can be broken down into basic functional sound-units,

so non-human systems can each be analysed into a number of basic distinctive units. It is worth saying that the vocal-auditory channel is the normal and overwhelmingly dominant modality of communication, but not an indispensable design feature of human language as such, and that other modalities – sign languages, writing systems – are under various circumstances – deployed in human linguistic communication

Arbitrariness

In human language most of the signs used are neutral rather than motivated by the nature of the meanings they communicate. Thus, there is no particular connection between the meaning 'dog' and the word *dog*, as is demonstrated by the fact that this meaning is rendered as *собака* in Russian, *chien* in French and *Hund* in German. Even in that small number of cases where the meaning of the sign does influence its form – as in the instance of *cuckoo*, where the name of the bird derives from the sound it makes – there remains a certain arbitrariness in the forms of such signs, as is illustrated by the fact that they vary from language to language; thus *cuckoo* corresponds to *кукушка* in Russian, to *coucou* in French and to *Kuckuck* in German. Arbitrary signs are not specific to human language; for example, herring gulls seemingly irrelevantly pluck at grass as an indication that they are threatening attack.

Semanticity

Units of human languages denote objects, actions, processes, qualities, etc. It is unclear whether or not animal signals are semantic in this sense. For example, a vervet monkey chattering in the presence of the snake may be referring to the snake or may be warning of danger in a more general way. Semanticity, accordingly, may or may not be an attribute peculiar to human language.

Cultural transmission

Human languages are passed on from one generation to the next. The role of teaching in animal communication seems to vary from system to system, but teaching certainly does have a part to play in many cases. Birdsong, for instance, has to be learned by each generation, sometimes in some of its aspects, sometimes almost wholly, depending on the type of bird in question. On this basis, human beings cannot be said to be unique in transmitting their communication system to their children.

Duality (or double articulation)

Human languages are organized into two levels – the level of meaningless units (sounds, letters, etc.) and the level of meaningful units (words, phrases, etc.).

Many non-human communication systems, as has already been indicated, share this trait, being composed of basic units, in themselves without significance, which combine into larger units which then do function as signals. Birdsong is a good example of this. Duality cannot then be considered to be a species-specific feature of human language.

Displacement

'Displacement' is the term applied to the capacity of human language to refer to entities and experiences far removed in place and time. Von Frisch's (e.g. 1962) research shows that the honeybee 'dances' when returning to the hive after discovering a new source of honey – a dance which is able to indicate to the other bees the distance and direction of the source. This is clear evidence that displacement is not confined to human language, although in non-human systems there may be limits on the degree of displacement possible; for example, in the case of the honeybee the distance parameter will be constrained by the number of kilometers a bee can actually fly. Human displacement is much less constrained.

Structure dependence

Human language is organized structurally, not linearly. That is to say, grammatical operations in language are sensitive to structural relationships rather than just the sequence of units in a sentence. For example, in the sentence *Watching those squirrels stealing nuts from birdtables really amuses me* the form of *amuses* is determined by is subject, the singular verbal noun *watching*, despite the fact that seven words, including three plural nouns, stand between them. Apparently, no definite example of this kind of structure-dependence has been to date discovered in any non-human communication system, which seems to imply that it structure-dependence is a distinctive feature of human language.

Creativity (or open-endedness or productivity)

An aspect of human language much emphasized in recent years is that which enables us to produce and understand an indefinite number of utterances which we may never have heard, read or used previously and which have a flexible relationship to stimuli and contexts. This is generally seen to be in stark contrast to non-human communication systems. Marshall's words of nearly forty years ago (1970: 234) are still generally regarded as valid:

> The most striking difference between animal signs and language behaviour are to be found … in the rigid stereo-typed nature of the former and the fact that they are under the control of independently specifiable external stimuli and internal motivational states.

One further feature of human language which has recently been under discussion is that of *recursivity* (see e.g. Bickerton 2009; Hauser, Chomsky & Fitch 2002) or 'discrete infinity':

> The core property of discrete infinity is intuitively familiar to every language user. Sentences are built up of discrete units: There are 6-word sentences and 7-word sentences, but no 6.5-word sentences. There is no longest sentence (any candidate sentence can be trumped by, for example, embedding it in "Mary thinks that …"), and there is no nonarbitrary upper bound to sentence length.
>
> (Hauser et al. 2002: 1571)

Parker (2011), however, disputes the notion that recursivity has any kind of special status as *the* distinguishing property of human language. She offers three empirically grounded reasons for her viewpont: (i) the fact that recursion is neither unique to language in humans, nor unique to the human species; (ii) the fact that human language is characterized by a number of features which have been claimed to set it apart, and which are independent of recursion (see above), and (iii) the fact that, according to her account at least, recursion may not even be necessary to human communication.

What then can we conclude about the uniqueness of human language on the basis on the above? While there are many features shared by human and non-human communication, in respect of at least two attributes – structure-dependence and creativity – human language appears to stand apart from non-human communication systems, and on a third criterion – that of semanticity – human language may also be distinct, although in this instance there is less certainty. In sum, those who argue that language is specific to the human species have substantial evidence in support of their case.

As well as comparing features of human language with those of non-human communication systems, some researchers have actually tried to teach human language to other species, notably higher apes. The earliest endeavours in this direction (Hayes 1951; Kellogg & Kellogg 1933) were disappointing, chiefly, it seems, because the attempt was made to teach the apes to talk, which they are not equipped physiologically to do. Later ventures in this domain relied instead on sign language and the manipulation of tokens or button pressing. Some of these are briefly outlined and assessed below.

Washoe. In the 1960s, a female chimpanzee named Washoe was trained to communicate in American Sign Language by researchers Allen and Beatrice Gardner (see e.g. Gardner & Gardner 1969, 1971). After 51 months of training Washoe had acquired 151 signs and was producing what appeared to be her own combinations of words. These included *dirty Roger* and, in reaction to seeing a swan on a lake, *water bird*. This looked very much like creativity. However, the researchers themselves admitted that these word combinations might have been a delayed imitation of the signing behaviour of her human companions rather than genuinely creative linguistic communication. Washoe seemed to have problems with the ordering of signs, which may relate to an inability to cope with the patterned nature of language – although other explanations are possible: the inherently freer nature of signed languages, the relaxed, unconstraining approach of her trainers in this regard and the possibility that word order fluctuation was just a transitional phase (Aitchison 1998: 37f.).

Sarah. Sarah was another female chimpanzee. She was trained by David Premack (see e.g. Premack 1970, 1971), and in her case the training was very strict. She lived in a cage and was taught to manipulate tokens – each representing a word – on a magnetic board. She in due course came to understand 100 words and a range of relationships between them. For example if presented with the symbols for QUERY CUP EQUAL SPOON ('Is the cup the same as the spoon'), she could correctly answer with the symbol for NO. Some commentators have raised doubts as to whether what Sarah learned was actually language. However, whatever it was it was impressive and at least language-*like*.

Nim Chimpsky. Nim Chimpsky was a male chimp who in the 1970s took part in a Columbia University study led by Herbert Terrace (see e.g. Hess 2008; Terrace 1979, 1983) involving instruction in a sign system. Nim learned about 125 signs and even used them in novel combinations: MORE EAT NIM; BANANA NIM EAT; TICKLE ME NIM; BANANA ME EAT BANANA). Nim was raised in the Terrace family and household as if a human child, but the Terraces noticed certain differences between his utterances and those of human children. Thus, between the ages of two and four years the percentage of full or partial imitations produced by Nim increased from 38% to 54%, which is the converse of what happens in humans, who imitate less as they mature. It was also noted that Nim did not initiate conversations and seemed not to be able to turn-take. Terrace concluded that "Nim's signing with his teachers bore only a superficial resemblance to a child's conversations with his or her parents" (Terrace 1983: 57) – a conclusion, let it be said, which is hotly disputed by other researchers.

Kanzi. Kanzi (see Savage-Rumbaugh & Lewin 1994) is a bonobo (pygmy) chimp who has been the subject of extensive and very detailed study by Sue Savage-Rumbaugh, for many years a sceptic in relation to apes' use of 'language'. Kanzi grew up from birth onwards in an environment where he was communicated with in spoken words and via a language board (featuring arbitrary symbols – lexigrams – which could be pointed to convey object, actions etc.). Kanzi's response to these conditions was to begin to use the language board to communicate with his human companions. His accomplishments are impressive in terms of his ability to understand aspects of spoken language and associate it with lexigrams and his ability to understand simple grammatical sentences. There is also some evidence that he may have invented novel vocalized words. On the other hand, as Goldin Meadow (1996) points out in her review of the above-cited book, Kanzi as a language learner differed markedly from the language-learning child. For one thing he needed a great deal of input, whereas human children entirely deprived of linguistic models (such as profoundly deaf children with no access to sign language) will struggle to use any means available (gesture, etc.) to communicate quite difficult concepts. Another point made by Goldin-Meadow is that, whereas humans produce a great deal of 'chat' in terms of comments on their circumstances, comments accounted for only 4% of Kanzi's recorded communications.

When Washoe died in 2007 aged 42, the obituaries together with her photograph appeared in many newspapers as well as on Internet news sites. She was described as 'a daughter of the community', and 'a polite, cheerful person', the implication being that in all respects (including language use) she was essentially human. As we have seen, however, some serious doubts surround the question of the relationship between the language abilities of higher apes and the human language capacity. Moreover, the fact that apes like Washoe have been celebrated merely for learning to use something like human language to communicate – after intensive training – in fact highlights the exceptionality of such cases; human toddlers achieve much more quite routinely, which, at the very least, seems to indicate that humans are better equipped than apes for this particular task.

Tomasello (Tomasello 1999, 2008; Tomasello & Call 1997) situates the particularity of human use of language within his discussion of the human evolution of the ability to 'identify' with conspecifics, leading to an understanding of them as intentional and mental beings like the self. This, he suggests, made possible new forms of cultural learning and sociogenesis, which led to cultural artifacts and behavioural traditions that have accumulated modifications over historical time. For him, it is the fact that human children grow up in the midst of the consequential socially and historically constituted artifacts and traditions, which underlies the language capacity – enabling them "to acquire and use … cognitive representations in the form of linguistic symbols (and analogies and metaphors constructed from these symbols)" and to "internalize certain types of discourse interactions into skills of metacognition, representational redescription, and dialogic thinking" (Tomasello 1999:10).

Turning back to the question of bilingualism and multilingualism, here we find another distinction between humans and other animals. In the natural state each non-human species clearly operates with a single communication system, whereas in human society most individuals have more than one language or language variety at their disposal. In the case of domesticated animals, some elements of the human code may be added through training. For example, a dog may be taught to respond to the command *sit!* Also, as we have seen, apes may be trained to add a large range of elements of human language to their own systems. However, one can note again that in such cases rather special training is necessary and that such instances are departures from the norm, whereas bi-/multilingualism in humans is entirely routine and normal.

Language as a tool and language as ability

With regard to the other two above-mentioned facets of human language, language as a tool and language as an ability, these have long been studied by a range of scientific disciplines. *Language as an ability* has been a source of long-standing interest to neurobiologists, neurolinguists, psychologists, and psycholinguists. Neurobiology and neurolinguistics study the neural bases of language: the areas of the brain, the human brain mechanisms and the neural processes underlying language comprehension and production. Psychology and psycholinguistics are concerned with the psychological dimension of the real-time processes which make possible the acquisition and use of language. The findings of these disciplines are drawn on by a range of other disciplines – such as language acquisition studies and the educational sciences.

Issues relating to such areas as immigration, acculturation, social identity and ethnicity, especially as dealt with in the domains of sociolinguistics and the sociology of language, are all connected with *language as a tool*. Researchers in these fields investigate the functions of languages and their role for individuals and groups, approaching language in the perspective of a tool for survival and for sustaining human society. Language in this optique is considered to be instrumental, for example, in the negotiation and renegotiation of identity, in personal development, in maintaining well-being, in attaining educational and career goals, in carrying out and disseminating research, and also for working towards peaceful coexistence.

Concerning multilingualism, Edwards (2007:462) sees this as vital part of the "social life of language". The idea of an intimate connection between language arrangements and the development of human society can be seen in Gumperz's claim that "[c]ommunity bilingualism, speech stratification, or major stylistic variance seems to become possible only as the economic base expands to allow economic stratification" (Gumperz 1971:106). Aronin (2005), for her part, has suggested that not only economic, but more generally the social nature of language and ideas about it roughly parallel stages of societal evolution and organization, varying under changing historical circumstances (see Table 1).

Table 1. Stages of societal organization and language patterns (after Aronin 2005:9)

Stage of societal organization	Language crucial as
Tribal	A Language
Nations/states	The Language
Globalization: centralization and localization	Languages

In a very simplified and schematized manner this table seeks to suggest that in the earliest communities, **a** language was essential as a tool of communication and cognition at a micro level for the development of each individual and society. The fact that a language was being used at all distinguished people from animals (see above). Later, historical changes led to the establishment of nation-states. In very many of such cases a particular language or language variety from among those used within a nation's borders was selected to play a unifying role. For example, in France, the language variety of the Paris region – the regional variety known as Francien in its medieval form – was from the Renaissance period onwards gradually promoted and, especially after the French Revolution, imposed as the language of the French national territory (cf. Singleton 1992; Lodge 1993). Without such a consolidating tool, political and economic development in a country such as France might have been more difficult. In modern times, in the wake of globalization and widespread migration, a group of two or more languages rather than one single language often meets a society's and an individual's fundamental needs in respect of communication, cognition and identity. For example, in recent years a Polish diasporic community has established itself in Ireland, some members of which already consider themselves to be 'Irish Poles', most members of which need to make use of both Polish and English in their daily lives, and schoolgoing members of which also have at least educational contact with the Irish language (cf. Singleton, Skrzypek, Kopečková & Bidzińska 2007; Singleton, Smyth & Debaene 2009).

On the African continent, the conception expressed in the table also valid, but in a different way, since, as the researches of African sociolinguistics have long insisted, along with clear similarities with the rest of the world, and European countries in particular, African multilingualism has developed in its own particularities (see e.g. Brann 1981; Makoni & Meinhof 2003; Anchimbe 2007). In particular with regard to the stages adumbrated in the above table, we can say that although many African tribal groups have always been multilingual, the multilingual arrangements in question have had an inner cultural significance and have not been crucial for the life of the tribe. The post-colonial and contemporary language re-arrangements, with the colonial languages' (English, French, Spanish, Portuguese and German) and the African languages' actively redefining their roles, present a new stage, a quantitatively different set of patterns of multilingualism, embedded in globalization processes.

Societal awareness of language and languages

The amount of knowledge concerning human languages and their use which has accumulated over the millennia is of course massive. Societal awareness of and perspectives on language and languages in both scientific terms and at a practical level can, in a rather general and rough-and-ready way, be seen as falling into three stages: monolingual, bilingual and multilingual (in the narrow sense). The stages in question have absolutely nothing to do with the number of languages in use in given societies but rather reflect social conditions and world-views and the language arrangements associated with these. We should certainly not be understood to be claiming that the so called monolingual stage is characterized by the use of a single language in a given context, or the bilingual stage by the use of just two languages. Nor do we imply that the stages are neatly discrete. It is very much the case that investigations into language in a monolingual mode continue during the current stage, which we would wish to describe as multilingual (in the narrow sense of relating to more than two languages), and, in fact, during the present stage there is more bilingual research going on than multilingual research. What the proposed diachronic tripartition is meant to relate to is the nature of socially significant arrangements and trends in awareness.

The 'monolingual stage' of societal awareness in respect of language

Language has aroused philosophical interest throughout human history. We shall have things to say about the more distant past elsewhere in the book, but if we stay for the moment relatively close to our own times, we can point to a benchmark at the end of 19th century when Gottlob Frege, the originator of analytic philosophy invented his 'concept notation' or '*Begriffsschrift*' (Frege 1879 [1972]) stating that his aim in this venture was "to free thinking from the fetters of language by pointing up the logical imperfections of language" (cited Beaney 2006:61). In the twentieth century language became a rather celebrated focus of interest in philosophy, attaining a particularly prominent place in the domains of logic and the philosophy of science. It should be noted that the philosophy of language tended to ask "general questions about language as such" rather than about specific languages (Lacey 2001:172) and that the general questions posed by the philosophy of language are ultimately concerned with issues other than language issues. In

Cooper's words, "philosophers became interested in language for what they could get out of it for philosophy" (Cooper 1973:4).

Those thinkers who were specifically concerned with exploring and reflecting upon language knowledge, language use and language acquisition in their own right – theoretical and philosophical linguists such as Saussure (e.g. 1916), Bloch & Trager (e.g. 1942), Whorf (e.g. 1956), Chomsky (e.g. 1957), Katz (e.g. 1972) – tended to ignore complications arising from the fact that a given individual might have more than one language and more than one language competence at his/her disposal. This kind of phenomenon was treated as abnormal, peripheral, 'fringe', even though in fact it represents the most frequent case. Thus it was that when, as recently as 1992, Vivian Cook started preaching the idea of 'multicompetence', the notion that in the typical instance a language user has competence in a number of languages and that these competencies systematically interact with each other, his views were even at that late stage treated by many theoretical linguists as suspect. He differs notably from the orthodox Chomskyan perspective on this matter. Cook & Newson (2007:222) comment:

> Chomsky too often talks of bilingualism proper as simply the extreme end of a continuum of grammatical variation inherent within all speakers. 'To say that people speak different languages is a bit like saying they live in different palaces or look different, notions that are perfectly useful for ordinary life, but are highly interest-relative. We say that a person speaks several languages, rather than several varieties of one, if the differences matters for some purpose or interest'.
>
> (Chomsky 2000a:43–44)

The kind of philosophical and language-theoretical ambience alluded to above and the ways in which, correspondingly, language arrangements tended to be viewed, talked about and indeed legislated for in society, may be appropriately labelled as 'monolingual', since the focus tended to be very much on *a* language.

The 'bilingual stage' of societal awareness in respect of language

There came a point, of course when the facts of bilingualism could not be ignored and forced themselves into the spotlight. From this point onwards bilingualism became a salient issue in areas such as politics, economics and the cognitive sciences, and began to raise questions in relation to a wide range of discussions and reflections – social, psychological, ethical, educational, and many more. Accordingly, the individual and societal aspects of bilingualism started being seriously investigated. It is of course impossible to set the exact time limits for this stage but one can note that a number of seminal and interest-provoking contributions in this perspective were already being published early in the twentieth century and that it is possible to discern a real upsurge of interest and research in bilingualism from 1960s and 1970s onwards.

Widely cited among early studies of bilingual development are those of Ronjat (1913) and Leopold (1939), both of which were based on diary records and both of which related to *simultaneous* bilingual development or *bilingual first language acquisition* (BFLA) – where two languages are acquired from infancy – as opposed to *successive* or *sequential* bilingualism, where the second language is added when the first is already to some extent established. Ronjat (1913) described the simultaneous acquisition of French and German by his son, Louis, until he was about five. The parents used the strategy of '*une personne, une langue*' – 'one parent, one language' – which was successful, according to Ronjat, in bringing Louis to a mastery and appropriate separation of the two languages. Leopold (1939), for his part, gave an account of the simultaneous acquisition of English and German by his daughter, Hildegard. In this case, although these parents had also adopted Ronjat's '*une personne, une langue*' approach, Hildegard passed through a stage when she used words from both languages in the same utterances, which was interpreted as evidence of confusion of two languages.

Core questions (cf. e.g. McLaughlin 1978: 91ff.) which arose from these and subsequent case studies (e.g. Bergman 1976; Chimombo 1979; Saunders 1982; Taeschner 1983), as well as from studies of groups of early bilinguals (e.g. Genesee 1989/2000), include the following:

1. Are the process of acquiring two languages from infancy and the time taken to acquire two languages from infancy the same as those associated with the acquisition of only one language?
2. Does one common language system develop or do two distinct language systems develop?
3. Does the acquisition of two languages from infancy impair or advantage the child's linguistic and cognitive development?

These questions are still with us and we shall return to them in detail in later chapters.

A broader perspective on bilingualism – including sociolinguistic dimensions – was provided by studies conducted by such researchers as Uriel Weinreich, Einar Haugen, Charles Ferguson, Joshua Fishman and John Gumperz. As a result of such research, a picture was established of bilingualism in geographically, socially and experientially diverse populations using various combinations of languages. Some brief snapshots of some of the research in question follow.

Uriel Weinreich's *Languages in Contact* (1953) deals insightfully with psycholinguistic, grammatical and sociolinguistic aspects which continue to be relevant today. Among these is the issue of *interference* understood by him as "[t]hose instances of deviation from the norms of either language which occur in the speech of bilinguals as a result of their familiarity with more than one language, i.e. as a result of language contact" (Weinreich 1953: 1). The term *interference* comes from the terminology of behaviourist psychology and is clearly negative in both sense and connotation. The term *transfer*, also a behaviourist coinage, allows for distinction to be made between *negative transfer* (i.e. *interference*) and *positive transfer* (i.e. facilitation), all of these terms now having moved beyond the confines of their behaviourist definitions (cf. Odlin 1989). Other terms which have more recently been used in this context and which do not have a behaviourist pedigree are *cross-linguistic influence* (Sharwood Smith & Kellerman 1986), *cross-linguistic operation* (e.g. Singleton 1996) and *cross-linguistic interaction* (e.g. Herdina & Jessner 2002), this last expression seeking specifically to signal the fact that the interplay between a bilingual's languages is bilateral. A further lasting contribution from Weinreich is his oft-cited classification of bilinguals into *subordinative bilinguals* (whose access to semantics when using to their second language is represented as indirect, proceeding via first language forms), *compound bilinguals* (both of whose linguistic codes are represented as having direct semantic access but as sharing a common semantic system), and *co-ordinate bilinguals* (who are represented as having both two separate linguistic codes and two separate semantic systems). These different kinds of bilingualism were associated by Weinreich with different kinds of acquisitional experience, but recent psycholinguistics has also begun to establish them as different acquisitional stages (cf. Singleton 1999).

Einar Haugen for his part published in 1953 a highly influential study of Norwegian-English bilinguals in the United States under the title *The Norwegian language in America; A Study in Bilingual Behavior*, which made a major contribution of this book to bilingualism studies through its wide-ranging and very useful account of cross-language borrowing phenomena. Another important aspect of Haugen's work was his origination of the *ecological approach to language* and his invention in 1971 of the term *ecology of language* to refer to attempts "to see language in relation to its human environment" (Haugen 1987: 27). The term, the concept and the approach have been widely embraced since and have found especial application to situations where more than one language is involved and to language teaching contexts (Hornberger 2009).

Charles Ferguson (1959) brought into the spotlight the phenomenon of *diglossia,* that is to say, the co-existence and alternating use of two historically and structurally related language varieties in a speech community. Ferguson's definition of a diglossic situation runs as follows:

> A relatively stable language situation in which, in addition to the primary dialects
> of the language (which may include a standard or regional standards), there is a
> very divergent, highly codified (often grammatically more complex) superposed
> variety, the vehicle of a large and respected body of written literature, either of
> an earlier period or in another speech community, which is learned largely by
> formal education and is used for most written and formal spoken purposes but is
> not used by any sector of the community for ordinary conversation.
>
> (Ferguson 1959: 336)

The former variety is known labelled by Ferguson the *Low* (*L*) variety and the latter the *High* (*H*) variety. An example of diglossia referred to by Ferguson, and by many others since, is that of the Arabic-speaking world. In each Arabic-speaking country two varieties of Arabic are in use: on the one hand, the High, or *fusha* variety, which is used in formal situations such as religious occasions, political speeches, news broadcasts and lectures, as well in written discourse, and, on the other, the Low, demotic (i.e., popular, familiar, intimate) variety, that is, the local vernacular (Kuwaiti Arabic, Lebanese Arabic, etc.) which serves as the medium of everyday communication. While the latter is acquired naturalistically as mother tongue, the *fusha* literary or 'written', 'formal' Arabic requires formal schooling. The High variety is held in high esteem because it is perceived as including the classical variety in which the Quran is written as well as that in which a centuries-old literature has been clothed; its modern manifestation, Modern Standard Arabic, retains a clear relationship with the classical form of Arabic. Demotic Arabic, on the other hand, derives its Low status from the fact that its use requires no educational experience and no command of literacy skills, and that it is not associated with high cultural activity or artifacts.

Joshua Fishman (1967) extended the concept of diglossia from Ferguson's definition linking it to historically related linguistic varieties by applying it to the alternating use of completely different languages. Fishman's essential criterion for a diglossic situation was that in such situations language varieties exhibited a clear separation of social functions, *compartmentalization* and for him typological relatedness was irrelevant in this connection. He suggested the following four ways in which individual monolingualism, individual bilingualism and societal diglossia (in his broader definition) operate in communities: (1) with both bilingualism and diglossia (e.g. Guarani-Spanish bilingualism in Paraguay); (2) with diglossia but without bilingualism (e.g. the use of classical and colloquial Arabic in Egypt); (3) with bilingualism but without diglossia (e.g. German-English bilingualism in Germany); and (4) (very rare) with neither diglossia nor bilingualism (e.g. monolingual parts of the USA). Another important concept also put forward by Fishman was the concept of *domain* of language behaviour (Fishman

1964, 1965/2000). This evolved from the need to account for patterns of language choice in bilingual communities whereby the use of particular languages in stable bilingual contexts is habitually associated with specific topics, settings and groups of interlocutors, that is, different domains of use. Fishman defined a domain as a "cluster of social situations typically constrained by a common set of behaviour rules' and as a 'social nexus which brings people together for a cluster of purposes' (1965: 75, 1965/2000: 94). Fishman maintains that the use of one language rather than another in such situations is far from being a random matter of momentary inclination, and he offered an exposition of the topical, situational and group regulations of language choice.

> Domains are defined, regardless of their number, in terms of institutional contexts and their congruent behavioral co-occurrences. They attempt to summate the major clusters of interaction that occur in clusters of multilingual settings and involving clusters of interlocutors.   (Fishman 1972: 441)

Fishman identified five domains: family, education, employment, friendship, government and administration. His concept of domain provides a way of abstracting general regularities from actual language choice and his domain analysis permits the illumination of language choice-patterns in various institutional contexts in a multilingual society.

John Gumperz studied bilingualism from an ethnographic and sociolinguistic perspective. He examined linguistic repertoires, speech variation and speech communities, and he was interested in the relationship between linguistic categories and social categories. His research on the languages of India, on code-switching in Norway, and on conversational interaction led him to new insights in the realm of sociolinguistics. Out of his work, and his collaboration with Dell Hymes, whose work dealt with languages of the Pacific Northwest, was born the *ethnography of communication,* a new framework for analysing how speakers signal and interpret meanings in social interaction (1982a, 1982b). Since his death in 2009, Hymes's work has been increasingly revisited by scholars. He is widely remembered for his use of the term *communicative competence* (Hymes 1972) to encompass the entirety of the knowledge the language user needs in order to communicate, in contradistinction to the narrow, essentially grammatical notion of competence espoused by Chomsky. This concept of communicative competence has had a major role in a wide variety subdisciplines of linguistics and sociolinguistics, including their most 'applied' domains.

As research into bilingualism continued to thrive though the 1970s and 1980s and into the 1990s, new waves of work appeared which strove to raise the level of understanding of bilingualism with a view to making some impact on prevailing attitudes and practices in society and improving relevant aspects of language education. Consciousness about bilingualism was widely raised by the still influential monuments of bilingualism studies produced at this time by such writers as Hugo Baetens Beardsmore (*Bilingualism Basic principles*, 1984, 2nd edn. 1986), Josiane Hamers & Michel Blanc (*Bilingualité et bilingualisme*, 1983; English translation, 1989, 2nd edn. 2000), Suzanne Romaine (*Bilingualism*, 1989, 2nd edn. 1994), and Tove Skutnabb-Kangas (*Bilingualism or Not*, 1981).

Developments in second language research at the psycholinguistic level also fed into the ferment of interest in bilingualism. While some definitions of bilingualism insist on the criteria of simultaneity of acquisition and balance between the two languages in terms of competence and use, other definitions admit of varying kinds and degrees of bilingualism. In this latter perspective, developments in second language research are clearly pertinent to bilingualism research. An example of a concept arising from second language research that bilingualism researchers took note of was that of *interlanguage*. The term was coined by Larry Selinker (1972), but the essential notion was first developed by Stephen Pit Corder (1967) under the name *transitional competence* and was also discussed by William Nemser (1971), who came up with the label *approximative system*. The underlying idea in all three cases is that learner's language is systematic at every its stage as he/she progresses through increasing levels of proficiency in the target language, however remote some of these stages may be from the target system. A further aspect of this concept is its implication that there is a sense in which the learner's language is intermediate between the source language (the learner's mother tongue) and the target language, which relates to the fact that in moving towards the target language, the learner continues to draw on the resources of the source language. On this view, the learner's 'errors' are significant in providing evidence of the state of the learner's version of the target language system – showing where the learner is along the 'interlanguage continuum', in demonstrating the systematicity as well as the dynamism of learner language and in shedding light on the ways in which learners try out the items regularities they have assimilated from the target language – sometimes misapplying them in various ways. Although the early discussion of interlanguage has been in many ways superseded by subsequent research and reflection, the basic characterization of learner language as systematic, dynamic and driven by interaction with target language input while continually referring to the source language, is still regarded as valid, and as still having much to offer bilingualism studies and specifically to the study of sequential bilingualism.

Another second language issue which was focused on within bilingualism studies was the age factor. It is undeniable that a relationship exists between age and success in second language learning: for the most part, in situations of immersion in the second language, younger beginners are observed in the long run to reach higher levels of attainment than older beginners. The precise nature of the relationship between age and second language learning, however, has for decades been a matter of controversy. The main point of contention relates to the question of whether (i) there exists a specifically language-related maturationally constrained period which is species-wide and absolute in its effects at the offset of which language learning becomes more arduous and less successful in its outcome (cf. Lenneberg 1967), or (ii) the observed age-related diminution in language learning capacity and success results from the impact of other factors, including cross-linguistic factors, input factors and general biological and cognitive decline (cf. Singleton & Ryan 2004). This issue is of obvious relevance to sequential bilingualism, relating as it does to the question of whether the age at which the bilingual encounters his/her second language determines the level of proficiency which it is possible for him/her to reach.

A further matter in which both second language acquisition research and bilingualism research have shared an interest is that of *code-switching*. We have already referred to alternation between languages/language varieties at a societal level. *Code-switching* is applied to such alternation at what one might call the micro level – that is, "the alternate … use of two or more languages in the same conversation" (Milroy & Muysken (1995:7). This phenomenon is a central issue in second language research and bilingualism studies and its study is complicated by the fact that, because it has been perceived by various researchers as encompassing different forms of bilingual behaviour, including, for example, the communication strategy of resource expansion via borrowing and the language deficit of language confusion symptomized in language mixing. Accounts of code-switching phenomena have also been investigated at different levels – notably, at the 'intra-sentential' level (i.e., focusing on switches within the sentence) and 'inter-sentential' codeswitching (i.e., focusing on switches between sentences) (see e.g. Clyne 1967, 1987/2000, 2003; Milroy & Muysken 1995; Poplack 1980, 1987; for recent discussion see e.g. Gafaranga 2009; Maneva 2004).

Neuroscience has also increasingly had a role to play in second language acquisition and bilingualism research. A recent book on this area of research describes it as "a rapidly growing field of study, touching on a range of theoretical questions" and as associated with 'excitement' and a 'sense of momentum' (Indefrey & Gullberg 2006:7). Indeed there is absolutely no doubt that neurolinguistics is one of the areas in linguistics which is attracting most interest at the present time. Neuroscientists – starting with Wilder Penfield, the groundbreaking Canadian neurosurgeon and researcher of the early to mid-twentieth century – have for decades volunteered insights of relevance to this area, and these insights have sometimes found their way into mainstream discussion. However, the recent advent of brain-imaging technology, with its promise of the possibility of finally making the link between the psychological and the physical dimensions of cognition, has now rendered the appeal of the neurosciences all but irresistible to researchers in the language acquisition/processing domain. Traditionally the neuroscientific input was based on a close analysis of data from subjects suffering from various kinds of language disorder or deficit associated with brain damage resulting from injury or brain surgery as well as with procedures exploring hemispheric dominance in the undamaged brain (e.g. dichotic listening tests). Thus, using such approaches, Paradis (e.g. 1978) explored the issue of language disorders in a bilingual context, and a wide variety of researchers, following in the footsteps of Gloning and Gloning (1965; cf. Goral et al. 2002), investigated questions of the laterality of language functions in the brain – both aphasic and normal – where more than one language was involved (see e.g. Albert & Obler 1978; Hyltenstam & Obler 1989).

With regard to brain-imaging methodologies, two major technologies have been used in recent times: Positron Emission Tomography (PET) and Functional Magnetic Resonance Imaging (fMRI). Both technologies image the brain in a dynamic way, thereby making it possible to detect changes over time. Almost all right-handed and most left-handed subjects are shown by brain-imaging to exhibit language-related activation that is strongly lateralized to the left hemisphere (Matthews, Adcock, Chen, Fu, Devlin, Rushworth, Smith, Beckmann & Iversen 2003). However, interpreting the images generated by these technologies is fraught with difficulty, as experimental tasks typically activate many different areas of the brain simultaneously. Moreover, different modes of language use – e.g. speaking versus reading – seem to involve the activation of different areas of the language centres (Scott, Blank, Rosen & Wise 2000). Complex neural networks are activated by tasks involving even single words; when words are combined into phrases and sentences the networks become still more complex, owing to the activation of many pragmatic and affective as well as linguistic areas.

One of the major questions to arise in relation to research dealing with bilingualism was whether the bilingual was advantaged or disadvantaged as compared with the monolingual. Early treatments (e.g. Pintner & Keller 1922; Saer 1923) – and some more recent research (e.g. Oller & Eilers 2002) – suggest the latter, the disadvantage being seen as connected with competition between the languages. Jakobovits (1970) cites research by Macnamara (1966) and others suggesting that bilingual development is associated with linguistic and academic deficits. Other research showed bilinguals faring at least as well as their monolingual peers. For example, Padilla and Liebman studied the language development of three English-Spanish bilingual children and arrived at the conclusion that "[i]n spite of the linguistic 'load' forced on them due to their bilingual environments. [the children] were acquiring their two languages at a rate comparable to that of monolingual speaking children" (Padilla & Liebman 1975: 51). Actual bilingual *superiority* emerges from Peal & Lambert's (1962) study, which, in Jakobovits's words, "shows that French-Canadian children in one bilingual setting in Montreal who have developed a good grasp of English are superior in both verbal and non-verbal intelligence to their French-speaking monolingual peers" (Jakobovits 1970: 58).

Hamers & Blanc, for their part, (2000: 89) note that advantages for bilinguals have been found in relation to a whole range of further abilities. Research shows that bilinguals are more likely than monolinguals to have understood that linguistic signs are arbitrary and that an object and its attributes are to be distinguished from its label (see e.g., Bialystok 1987; Ben Zeev 1977; Ianco-Worrall 1972), and that they exhibit more sensitivity to semantic and grammatical relations and regularities (see e.g. Bialystok 2001, 2002). Such attributes may be related to the fact that bilinguals may have words in each of their languages for a given object or idea, and that corresponding words in their languages may have different ranges of senses and different connotations. For example, the word for 'blue' in German – *blau* – can also mean 'drunk' or 'gay' (in the sexual orientation sense), whereas *blue* in English can also mean 'pornographic' or 'obscene' (as in *blue movie, blue language*). Thus bilinguals need to be more adept than monolinguals at negotiating diversity of meanings, associations and images, and this presumably requires them to be psychologically more flexible and creative.

The greater communicative demands on users of more than one language imply more awareness of language resources and more control over such language resources, and this seems to have cognitive consequences. Further cognitive advantages have been found for bilinguals in areas beyond the linguistic domain such as Piagetian conservation tasks and visual-spatial abilities (see e.g. Diaz & Klinger 1991) and in the capacity to solve problems based on conflict and attention (such as sorting cards by colour and then re-sorting by shape) (Bialystok 1999). One should not ignore either the social dimension of the advantages of bilingualism in terms of the wider possibilities it offers for communication in the family and in the community, on an international scale and at inter-community levels. Li Wei (2000: 23) connects these to the enhancement of mutual understanding and the amelioration of relationships. Baker (1993) talks about bilinguals' *communicative sensitivity*, referring to the proposition that bilinguals are "more attuned to the communicative needs of those with whom they talk" and have "two or more worlds of experience" (Li Wei 2000: 23). Clearly, such dimensions of bilingualism have implications for general enjoyment of the social dimension of life and also for employability.

How is one to reconcile the seemingly contradictory results regarding the effects of early bilingualism? Cummins (1984: 101) draws attention to the prejudice against bilingualism which existed at the time when many of the studies with negative results were carried out and also (*ibid.*: 103) emphasises the methodological deficiencies of early studies; noting that the "[f]ailure to control for factors such as SES [socioeconomic status], urban-rural differences and language of testing render [*sic*] most of the findings uninterpretable." One might add that unrealistic expectations that all bilinguals should behave as if two monolinguals in the same person – the so-called *double monolingualism hypothesis* – might have played a role. In addition, Cummins refers to Lambert's (1975) point that the early studies mostly focused on sequential bilingualism in immigrant or minority children whose first language was effectively being replaced by the language of the majority population. This point remains valid for more recent studies showing negative effects for early sequential bilingualism, almost all of which "have been conducted in Western cultures with children of minority groups schooled in the majority language" (Hamers & Blanc 2000:93). The bilingualism of this kind of situation Lambert calls 'subtractive', in contrast to the 'additive' sequential multilingualism achieved by children whose first language is not threatened with replacement by other languages. 'Subtractive' situations are posited as leading to the impoverishment and ultimately the suppression of the first language, and are argued to be not particularly effective at promoting L2 proficiency either, resulting, according to some, in a kind of 'double semilingualism' (see e.g. Skutnabb-Kangas 1981:248–263). Cummins notes (1984:107) that most studies showing advantages associated with bilingualism have been carried out in 'additive' situations.

A valuable concept which was developed within bilingualism studies but which subsequently found application in multilingual contexts was Grosjean's (1985) notion of a *language mode*. According to Grosjean, while a monoglot speaker has no option but to communicate in his/her one and only language, an individual who has two languages at his/her disposal has three possibilities – to use the L1 (say, Greek), to use the L2 (say, English – to interlocutors who do not know Greek), or to alternate between the two languages (if communicating with someone who knows both these two languages). In the first two cases the individual is likely to be in monolingual mode, with the particular language in use having clear hegemony of activation and switches between languages being rare; in last case the individual is in bilingual mode in the sense that both languages are highly activated and both may appear in the individual's output. According to Grosjean, the language mode phenomenon constitutes a continuum and "bilinguals differ among themselves as to the extent they travel along the language mode continuum; some rarely find themselves at the bilingual end (the other language is never very active) whereas others rarely leave this end (the other language is always very active)" (Grosjean 2001:17).

More broadly, Grosjean's (1989, 1992) conception of bilingualism differs markedly from some conventional views. For him bilingualism is not an exceptional condition but the norm. In his perspective, being bilingual does not necessarily mean knowing two or more languages equally well. He recognizes that, depending on a person's experience, needs and interests, two languages known to an individual may have associated with them similar or different degrees of proficiency, similar or different patterns of communicative purposes, and similar or different domains of use. Grosjean has always insisted that the bilingual is a unique kind of language-user, who should be studied in his/her own right as such, rather than constantly by reference to the monolingual. Such a view is clearly rich with implications for the educational sphere, where within given instructional or testing situations may be present bilinguals of varying degrees of balance, stability and breadth of diversity of use of specific languages, and of varying kinds of experience and preference in respect of different language modes.

Cook has become prominent in the sphere of bilingualism/multilingualism studies for his conception of *multicompetence* (1991, 1992, 1993, forthcoming b) and his scrutiny of the notion of *native speaker*. According to Cook, those with a knowledge of more than one language possess a special quality distinguishing them from those who have mastered only one language – namely, multicompetence, defined as "knowledge of two or more languages in the same mind" (Vivian Cook's website: <http://homepage.ntlworld.com/vivian.c/SLA/Multicompetence/MCEvidence.htm> accessed December 1, 2011) and "the compound state of mind with two grammars" (Cook 1992:557–558). Multicompetent language users are claimed by Cook (1992) to differ from monolinguals in terms of the nature of their linguistic knowledge, in terms of their metalinguistic awareness, and in terms of their cognitive processes. Cook's (1992) account portrays multicompetence as manifested in ready codeswitching between languages, in the sharing across languages of lexical reference points, in highly interconnected processing across languages, in joint usage across languages of the same areas of the brain, and in the building of academic proficiency in one language on pre-established academic proficiency in another. Both Grosjean and Cook take a *holistic perspective* on bilingualism and considering it not only from a psycholinguistic point of view, but also from a societal standpoint. In this optique the difference between a monolingual and bilingual relates also to the sociological dimension of the matter, i.e. the ability of bilinguals to function "*in more contexts*", the ways in which bilinguals "create their own linguistic means in order *to master particular communicative situations*" (Hoffmann 2001a: 19), the *communicative versatility* of those with additional languages. Such holistic understanding of bilingualism casts doubt on the notion of basing an approach to the processing of language on the ideal of the monolingual native speaker (Cook 1993:245). Problematizing the fundamental yardstick hitherto provided by the monolingual native speaker, though slow to be accepted as legitimate, in the long run resulted in a general re-evaluation of norms pertaining to both the linguistic and the social domains of language use.

Research on bilingualism and bilingual experience (and subsequently on the case of knowledge and use of more than two languages) gradually took account of the fact that the bi-/multilingual language user was not to be evaluated in terms of 'perfect' or 'native-like' command of the languages at his/her disposal but rather in terms of degrees of functionality in any given language environment.

With regard to explanatory models, since the 1960s bilingualism studies have developed a number of innovative frameworks and perspectives, spurred on by advances in second language acquisition and processing research (see e.g. Hamers & Blanc 1983), in which domain by 1997 it could be stated that "over 40 separate theories exist … and many more models have been developed and are still under construction" (Larsen-Freeman & Long 1997: 227, cited in Marx & Hufeisen 2003). Most of these models were elaborated during what we here call the "bilingual stage" of societal language awareness. For example, in the 1980s Green (1986, 1993) came up with the activation/inhibition model according to which bilinguals do not switch one of their languages off when using the other, but rather both languages remain active, each exhibiting a different level of activation at any given moment depending on whether or not it is being deployed. Also in the 1980s Levelt (1989), proposed a speech processing model for monolinguals, but which was subsequently applied to bilingual situations (e.g. de Bot 1992). Levelt's account divides the speech production process into four distinct steps: message generation, grammatical encoding, phonological encoding and articulation and suggests that language production includes the coordinated work of five modules: the conceptualizer, the lexicon, the formulator, the monitor system and the articulator.

The current, 'multilingual beyond bilingual stage' of societal awareness of language

The last two decades may be characterized as the 'multilingual beyond bilingual' decades, since the multiple acquisition and use of languages has very much come to the fore as an object of scrutiny both in the academic sphere and in terms of general interest throughout communities (Auer & Li Wei 2007; Aronin & Hufeisen 2009c; Cenoz & Genesee, 1998; Cenoz & Jessner 2000; Cenoz, Hufeisen & Jessner 2001; Edwards 1994; Extra & Yağmur 2004a; Herdina & Jessner 2000a, 2002; Hoffmann 2001; Paulston 1994; Pattanayak 1990; Skutnabb-Kangas 1995; Turell 2001). The fact that multiple language users are currently very visible in most countries and regions may not in itself explain the triggering of such attention, given the existence throughout history of the phenomenon of multilingualism. The difference in the contemporary world may be that the deployment of multiple languages is a quintessential, indispensable feature of the world landscape. In this connection we need to examine the process generally known as globalization with a view to shedding some light the interrelationships between this process and the dramatic changes which are observable in language behavior. This process and the current linguistic dispensation will be discussed in the next chapter and in what follows.

CHAPTER 3

Multilingualism as a new linguistic dispensation

The globalization phenomenon

We have already mentioned globalization a number of times in previous chapters. The globalization phenomenon is widely agreed to be a major determinant of the shape of multilingualism as we experience it in the modern world. Accordingly, in order to understand the distinctive features of contemporary multilingualism, it is necessary to take a close look at the global changes that have taken place in recent times and to explore the influence they have had on language distribution and patterns of use in our present-day world.

Globalization and language use

Our current day-to-day existence and social behaviour – constantly, of course, accompanied by the use of language – differ markedly from those of previous generations. The most apparent global transformations are connected with time-space dimensions, the interrelationship between the local and the global, geographical and social mobility, the transcendence of territorial and social boundaries, technological breakthroughs and the intense focus on identity issues. The changes that have taken place are probably already widely taken for granted. Still, these shifts are remarkable and they warrant an attentive review in the present context. We shall briefly discuss these various dimensions in a little more detail in what follows.

Time, space and technology

Vast numbers of the Earth's inhabitants have the everyday experience of using the fruits of the recent unprecedented technological progress, which, among other benefits, permit instantaneous, 24/7/365 interaction. Thanks to e-mail, e-chat, blogs and social networks such as Twitter and the various functions of mobile telephones, IPads and other gadgets, we are always available and can constantly be in contact with anybody anywhere.

This notorious 'tyranny of the moment' (Eriksen 2001), dubbed by Cilliers (2005) life in an eternal present, can be seen to manifest itself in our 24-hour society. Working times and locations are increasingly deregulated and scattered (cf. Garhammer 1995; Breedveld 1998). *Flexibilization*, the phenomenon of the "reduction of rigidly institutionally timed events" (Southerton 2003:7) – e.g. 'flexitime', allows employees to work at unregulated convenient hours. Of course, large numbers of people still, as before, work strict hours, and their recreational activities take place at traditional times. But flexibilization nevertheless exists in varying degress both as a possibility and reality of us, and this represents an important shift.

Despite such shifts, a widespread predisposition to stay with traditional time regimes has been noted by several researchers (Flaherty & Seipp-Williams 2005). The predominant pattern still appears to correspond to the custom-honoured rhythms of the working day and week. Baker et al. (2003) found that the preferred times for work and leisure activities remain within the conventional frames. For example, evenings and weekends are the times of choice for families and friends to get together. Similarly, Flaherty & Seipp-Williams (2005:42) found clear patterns of e-mail use by students and teachers at a university in the USA in terms of the temporal flow of e-mails in weekly, daily and hourly cycles. They concluded on the evidence that the volume of e-mail per hour and per day is structured by socio-temporal rhythms.

The distinction between home and the workplace and between worktime and private leisure/consumption time is increasingly collapsing (Cilliers 2005; Southerton 2003:6). As a result, even the apparently positive fact that large numbers of people now have markedly more leisure time than formerly is associated with increased time pressure and time dissonance (Waterworth 2003:47). Southerton explains that as consumption is more available to people than before, they are tempted to engage in more and more diverse kinds of consumption/leisure activities, which actually put considerable demands on their time. In consequence, they feel hurried and stressed. Chunks of uninterrupted time diminish, and people continually engage in 'multitasking' (Southerton 2003:7).

The current situation may lead us to believe that contemporary life is lived exclusively in *instantaneous time*, that is, a time whose passing can barely be observed. Thus, for example, the popular microblogging web application, Twitter, allows for almost instantaneous commentaries, from a multiplicity of perspectives, on events as they unfold in 'real time'. However, in fact contemporary humankind employs various kinds of time which underlie social reality, although it is true that the range of social times inhabited by contemporary humankind is dramatically different from the social time of previous epochs. It is interesting to note that the French sociologist of knowledge Georges Gurvitch (1894–1965) maintained that varying perceptions of social and psychological time attest to different kinds of social reality (Gurvitch 1964: 14). Already the Ancient Greeks perceived a difference between chronological and kairological time. The latter, so called after the god of time, Kairos, is associated with opportunity and chance, and, unlike chronological time, is connected with nature, the reality of the here and now, need and inclination rather than with what hour of the day it is (Levine 1997; Thackara 2005). Babies and animals can be said to live in kairological time, sleeping when they are tired and eating when they are hungry.

Fernand Braudel (1902–1985), one of the foremost French historians of the postwar era, studied large-scale social change over long periods of historical time. He drew distinctions between slow time, intermediate time, and fast time for different kinds of historical developments – e.g. climate change, economic cycles and battles (Braudel 1969). Braudel makes the point that the individual may have consciousness of and agency over 'fast' processes, while 'intermediate' processes and 'slow' macro processes are not discernible to the individual and not open to individual agency. At the beginning of the 20th century the time-zones were synchronized, and these days most of the globe lives according to clock-time, but this does not mean that time has become 'settled'. Urry (2000: 105) notes that "new technologies appear to be generating new kinds of time which dramatically transform the opportunities for, and constraints upon, the mobilities of peoples, information and images". Linguistic processes, being a dynamic part of social reality, also take place within varying time regimes. Most linguistic communication these days is instantaneous – or quasi-instantaneous. Slow time is the domain of certain aspects of language change – though, again, not all, as the rapid invention and dissemination of new technical terms testifies – and also represents the perspective of those working to maintain or revive heritage languages. Thus, it takes the lifetimes of one or more generations of migrants to stop using the language they brought with them and to shift to the host language, and then at least the lifetime of a generation to begin again to raise young speakers of the heritage language of the community. With specific regard to multilingualism, at the level of individual language use, switching languages to meet the needs of the situation is in the main an instantaneous or quasi-instantaneous affair. At the societal level, whilst the technological changes and shifts in population which favour multilingualism are not instantaneous, they are hardly glacial either.

The issue of time is entwined with that of space, and the concept of *timespace* has gained currency (cf. Sklair 1999; Cilliers 2005; Bauman 1999; Urry 2003). As a result of technological advances of various kinds we have seen a dissociation of time and space from specific social reference (cf. Avgerou 2002: 98). Hence the widespread use of expressions such as *global village* and *spaceship earth*. Paul Virilio, one of the most significant contemporary French cultural theorists of post-modernity, best known for his writings about technology as it has developed in relation to speed and power, pointed out in an interview with Chris Dercon that time-space compression represents an essential facet of contemporary life: "[t]oday we are entering a space which is speed-space... This new other time is that of electronic transmission, of high-tech machines, and, therefore, man is present in this sort of time, not via his physical presence, but via programming" (Dercon 2001:71). Time and space compression and extension are manifested in the changes relative to how people feel about it, what Urry calls a transformed "structure of feeling" (Urry 2003:124).

Mobility and flux, borders and exclusions

Mobility appears to be the most obvious nexus between timespace and languages. Many researchers see mobility as a primary trait of present-day existence. The significance of mobility and the new perceptions and functioning of timespace with respect to multilingualism can be seen, for example, in the sociolinguistic restructuring associated with emerging multilingual and multicultural societies resulting from the processes of migration. Thus, these days Chinese, Arabic, Ukrainian and Swahili are commonplaces on the streets of London, Paris, Berlin and Amsterdam. Newspapers in Russian and Russian shops are now easy to find in the towns of Canada, Germany, Ireland and Israel. The multilingual cities described in the reports assembled in Extra & Yağmur (2004a) serve further to illustrate the point. These new spaces represent the modern circumstances of global mobility, where people increasingly often find themselves intermixed with others from differing cultures, traditions, memories and civilizations.

Blommaert argues (Blommaert 2010; Blommaert & Rampton 2011) that globalization has changed the face of social, cultural and linguistic diversity.

> Due to the diffuse nature of migration since the early 1990s, the multiculturalism of an earlier era (captured mostly, in an 'ethnic minorities' paradigm) has been gradually replaced by what Vertovec (2007) calls 'super-diversity'. Super-diversity is characterised by a tremendous increase in the categories of migrants, not only in terms of nationality, ethnicity, language, and religion, but also interms of motives, patterns and itineraries of migration, processes of insertion onto the labour and housing markets of the host societies, and so on (cf. Vertovec 2010). The predictability of the category of 'migrant' and of his/her sociocultural features has disappeared.
>
> (Blommaert & Rampton 2011:2)

It is often the case that when we think about movements of population we tend to think of the present day or of recent history, but the fact is that we humans have always been on the move – before even we began to speak. The "Out of Africa" model of our earliest origins posits extensive migration of early humans, on the basis of a persuasive genetic evidence deriving from mitochondrial DNA (mtDNA) studies (see, e.g. Ingman 2001). Migration dates are debated by archaeologists, but the fact and importance of these migrations are not. Recent anthropological thinking suggests that early human migrations were the vehicle constituent in the process of the evolvement of anatomically modern humans (*homo sapiens sapiens*). To be noted is that the first members of the Homo genus, including *homo habilis*, who, according to some accounts, migrated from Africa to Asia and Australia, were not yet able to speak in the way modern humans do, since they were anatomically incapable of articulate speech. Scientists testify that "[t]he two earliest *homo* species were … capable of only short, slow, unmodulated speech patterns, not of articulate speech, which is the systematic arrangement of significant vocal cords" (Fischer 2004: 37).

Moving closer to our own era, medieval history (see e.g. Holmes 2001) and early modern history (see e.g. Betteridge 2007; Schilling 2008) present us with evidence of significant movements of individuals, populations and goods around Europe – from the land-hungry wanderings of the Vikings to the post-Reformation displacements occasioned by religious conflicts (cf. Le Goff 1964). Chaunu (1966) describes the ways in which improving transport in Europe increasingly facilitated the flow of people and trade, resulting in some places in remarkable economic effects. Of course, the reasons for mobility throughout the history of humankind overlapped and coincided with the reasons for mobility in our own times: people have always moved, essentially, in search of sustenance, in search of security, and in search of a better life.

On the other hand, there are differences between earlier mobility and what is happening now. Recent and current migration processes are more intense, and more crucially intertwined with the fabric of society. They are also more visible, receive more attention and have more serious consequences ascribed to them. The International Organization for Migration estimated the number of international migrants as 214 million in 2010 in its *World Migration Report* (2010). An especially interesting feature of current migration is noted by Chinchilla (2005), who discussing her observations on international migration based on Central American experience cites evidence that "transnational ties among recent emigrants are more intense than those of their historical counterparts (2005: 170) and that "[r]ecent innovations in transportation and communication have made possible a density and intensity of links not seen before" (2005: 175).

The social topology of structure (communities, groups, states) is amidst this intensity of interaction being replaced by the fluid social topology of networks (Friedman 1999; Urry 2000). People are now very often grouped on bases other than traditional societal groupings (e.g. nation, class, gender, ethnic distinctions or states). L. Friedman (1999) writes of the emergence of 'horizontal groups' taking the place of the previous fixed collectivities and coming together as e.g. stamp collectors, pizza lovers, academics, celebrities, vegetarians, etc. on the bases of wide-ranging and mutable criteria such as hobbies, disabilities, preferences, professional interests – as opposed to the previously strictly fixed criteria of origin, class and gender, etc.

The elements of the new social topology are linked by languages in different ways from previous patterns. A particular focus of current discussion is the issue of identity. In the contemporary world identity is recognized as compounded and multifaceted, negotiable and negotiated, fluid and transient (Bauman 1999; Bendle 2002; Doepke 1996; Giddens 1991; Williams 1989). Identity issues confronting migrants are typically perceived in the terms of 'ethnic identity', 'national identity', 'group identity' and 'cultural identity' (see e.g. Fishman 1989, 1999; Paulston 1994; Weinreich 2000) in all of which concepts 'language' and 'languages' clearly play a vital role. The identities of both indigenous and migrant populations fluctuate. Migrants may undergo language shift, that is, acquire a new language and abandon their mother tongue, but all populations in a society experiencing in-migration tend to reposition the various languages at their disposal. Migrants undergo a more radical experience of the fluxiveness of the modern world than host populations. Their self-concepts fluctuate in the crossing from one culture to another where they have to accommodate themselves to a new environment. Maines (1978) holds that the migration of 'selves' (or identities) usually follows a different schedule from that of their actual bodies. Horenczyk expresses this idea in the comment that "selves arrive 'later' than bodies" (Horenczyk 2000: 14). Obviously, these 'selves' are modified and expressed through language to a crucial extent (cf. Kouritzin 1999). Languages travel and 'settle' in new countries together with people, and, like people, often undergo various changes in the process.

It is noteworthy that everything in contemporary society and the contemporary environment that Urry (2000: 3) refers to as mobile and fluid has a connection with language, and the kind of social fluidity treated by L. Friedman (1999) in terms of the 'horizontal society' is also language-related. In sum, multilingualism, being a result of mobility, as well as being itself characterized by fluidity, fits current societal arrangements perfectly. With regard to migration, it is clear that this has a major impact on patterns of language use. Thus, Extra & Yağmur note (2004b: 26) that "[a]s a consequence of socio-economically or politically determined processes of migration and minorization, the traditional patterns of language variation … have changed considerably." An instance of this can be found in Ireland, where alongside a 'traditional' (numerically small) bilingual population using Irish and English in their daily lives there have since the beginning of the century come to be tens of thousands of individuals operating in Polish and English, Mandarin and English, Russian and English, etc. (cf. Singleton 2007b).

It would obviously be a mistake, however, to see the causes of diversity of culture and language in populations and in contexts of work, education and leisure as relating only to migration. Certain processes taking place within particular countries and relating to populations which do not fall into the category of migrants are also involved in promoting diversity. Non-migrants are not necessarily definable as static. They too may be subjected to pressures towards mobility, of a variety of kinds, orientations and scale.

Personal mobility is an especially popular topic of investigation in the context of the discussion of identity. Individuals may perceive radical transformations in their milieu and consequent shifts in affordances (roughly speaking opportunities or possibilities for action and change; see further discussion in Chapter 9) as accruing from the crossing of boundaries of various kinds (social, linguistic, physical, etc.). The resultant reshaping of identity is widely discussed in the sociological, psychological and educational literature. The manifestations of mobility in all its dimensions, in terms of flow, change and mixture, as well as in terms of boundaries and exclusions account for much of the fuzziness, unpredictability, diversity and complexity we experience in our world.

Both integrating and disintegrating processes are present in every dimension of social life. The dual nature of globalization is expressed in the term *glocalization*, referring to the fact that alongside border- and culture-transcending developments, we are also experiencing a renewed focus on local dimensions and preoccupations. The concept of glocalization captures our understanding of the contemporary world as multifarious and non-homogeneous, arising from a multitude of diverse local values, behaviours, symbols and activities. Not everything is fluid; there are borders and exclusions. Not everything is globalized, there are many localized developments. In all of this we see the polarized dichotomies of local/global and progressive/detrimental, in which both local and global may be seen as either objectionable or desirable (see Blommaert 2010 on locality and periphery). This polarization is reflected in the controversies surrounding such issues as language policy and education, the role and place of English and other international languages, and the fate of lesser used languages. A further aspect of the local/global nature of globalization is the so-called *niched* nature of globalization phenomena.

Clearly, all of the foregoing places multilingualism in the thick of the globalization process. The expansion of multilingualism is not only a result of the globalization phenomenon (Fishman 1998) but is also playing a supporting and intermediary role in the economic, political and cultural processes of globalization (Maggipinto 2000), since most of the dimensions of globalization – cultural, communicative, economic, political and even ecological (Chase-Dunn 1999) – can be carried through only with the involvement of languages in their contemporary pattern of arrangement.

Recognition of the ubiquity of contemporary multilingualism

The extent to which multilingualism is now being recognized as a ubiquitous phenomenon is remarkable. One aspect of this is the increase in the number of languages recognized as such in the modern world. In this context we need to be aware that, for reasons outlined below, it is in fact impossible to count exactly how many languages are in existence. First, there are no purely linguistic criteria according to which one can distinguish *languages* from *dialects*. There are clearly socio-political factors which come into play in labelling a given linguistic variety a language: association with a powerful political entity, association with a rich literature and set of cultural traditions, association with a large number of users, etc.

The criteria of mutual intelligibility between language varieties also features in this discussion, but it yields no final arguments. In mutually unintelligible cases such as Italian and Korean we seem clearly to be dealing with two different languages. On the other hand, in the instance of the Norwegian, Swedish and Danish, mutual intelligibility appears not to preclude the categorization of these varieties as distinct languages. There are some well-known examples of varieties which to all intents and purposes are linguistically one but which have been split asunder because of politico-historical factors. One can cite in this connection the case of Romanian and Moldovan (both Eastern Romance) as well as that of Hindi and Urdu (both derived from Hindustani). Subsequent to division, such sundered languages tend to develop separately, often acquiring different scripts. Thus, Moldovan is written in Cyrillic, while Romanian is written in Roman script; Hindi, one of the official languages of India is written in the Devanāgarī alphabet, while Urdu, the official language of Pakistan, is written using Arabic script. In time, the divided language varieties separate more – with the inclusion of different lexical items, divergent structural modifications and other changes.

In such cases there is a consequential increase in the number of languages on record. Increases may also result from the conferral of the status of language on various kinds of language varieties – e.g. world Englishes, pidgins, urban dialects – which previously did not have this status. Typically, the visibility of a particular language variety which is being promoted or revitalized eventually leads to its being given – unofficially or officially – the status of a language, adding to the language count. On the other hand, lesser used languages are dying by the month. Quantifying languages in this mix and melée of circumstances is obviously a challenge! Deciding when a given language has definitively died is itself fraught with problems. What is the criterion to be used for language death, for example? Does a language have to be down to its last hundred elderly speakers. Does there have to be proof of the demise of the last speaker of the language in question? One notes also that a language may not be known well enough by anyone to serve as a means of communication in all the spheres of life; should we class such an dysfunctionally known language as dead?

All of the above challenges having been acknowledged, there may nevertheless be some utility in referring to current accounts of the number of languages in the world. This number is estimated at between 5,000 and 14,000, depending on modalities of definition. One frequently quoted figure is approximately 6,000 (Graddol 1997; Valdés accessed December 1, 2011, *Ethnologue* accessed December 1, 2011). Around 1,200 of these languages are standardized (Fishman 1998). The current high estimations of the global number of languages as compared with earlier estimations are due to several factors. One is the relatively recent reappraisal, in the light of social and political developments, of what should be labelled as a language. Afrikaans, for instance, was in the past considered to be a variant of Dutch, whereas it is now recognized as a separate language. Creoles, which used to be stigmatized, are, for their part, no longer seen as corrupt versions of their source languages, but rather as languages in their own right. Some are given official recognition. Thus, Tok Pisin, the creole spoken in northern mainland Papua New Guinea, is one of the official languages of that country (and the most widely used). The increase in the number of recognized languages also owes something to developments in the perception of World Englishes: Indian English, Irish English, African American Vernacular English (AAVE), etc. are not infrequently treated as quasi-distinct languages. Yet another factor is the reinvigoration of languages in decline – examples being the revival of Hebrew, and the revitalization of Basque, Catalan, Māori and Welsh.

It is frequently noted that monolingualism is characteristic of only a minority of the world's population. Trudgill & Cheshire (1998: 1), among many others, claim that "in most parts of the world monolingual people are the exception rather than the rule" (see also e.g. Baker & Prys Jones 1998: 134; Graddol 1997; Herdina & Jessner 2002; Tucker 1998). This has clearly been true for millennia, but it is now, as it were, truer than ever. If one looks, for instance at historically multilingual countries, such as Switzerland, with its four official languages (German, French, Italian and Romansch), one finds that such countries are now more multilingual than previously. It is noteworthy that, as a result of migration, Switzerland these days has many more languages spoken within its frontiers than would have been mentioned in traditional accounts (Lüdi 2008). Other countries that used to be regarded as monolingual or bilingual now have sizeable populations of users of multiple languages. In this context we have already referred to the case of Ireland, which was once seen as – at most – bilingual. Addressing a conference of the Royal Irish Academy in Dublin in February 2006, Ireland's then Minister of Education, Mary Hannifin, reported that, whereas ministers visiting Irish schools used to be greeted in Irish and English, she herself had recently been welcomed at a particular primary school in a total of 24 languages. *The Irish Times* (March 25, 2006) citing research conducted by academics at the National University of Ireland, Maynooth, referred to Ireland as a land of over 167 languages <http://www.irishtimes.com/newspaper/frontpage/2006/0325/1142365526361.html>.

The new linguistic dispensation

Scale and significance

Current developments in multilingualism go beyond the mere addition of further elements to individuals' stock of linguistic knowledge or the mere augmentation of numbers of languages, multilinguals, and multilingual countries. The scale and significance of such developments amount to a global pattern. They have reached a point where, we believe, they can be seen as assimilable to politico-economic aspects of globalization, global mobility and 'post-modern' modes of thinking. It is to emphasize this point that in previous publications and publications we, alongside other researchers (Fishman 1998; Maurais 2003), have applied the concept of 'new world order' to the current sociolinguistic situation (cf. Aronin 2007; Aronin & Singleton 2006).

The term *world order* is used predominantly in political science, where it is defined as "patterned human activities, interaction regularities or practices evident on a world scale" which "have both motivating or dispositional elements, environmental-geographic contexts, and associated outcomes and effects" and are "multidimensional" and "dynamic" (Alker et al. 2001). Such regularities are seen as affecting units of various kinds (nations, firms, parties, interest groups, class or status groups, armies, churches, communities, etc.) and as involving conscious and unconscious relationships between units and with social and natural environments.

In relation to the present discussion, a patterned regularity is discernible in a range of pertinent facts – including the following: multilingualism is spreading to all parts of the world; English has become a world *lingua franca*; and patterns of language use are, as noted earlier, dramatically diversifying. In Africa, for instance, a number of international languages of wider communication – English, French, Portuguese, Spanish, Italian and German – have become established on this already multilingual continent. In parallel, the roles of regional lingua francas such as Amharic in Ethiopia and Afrikaans in the South Africa, are threatened and modified both by language policies and by the *de facto* situation: "[a]ttempts are made to eliminate or minimize vertical power differentials between local and regional languages" (Heugh under review). One thinks also of the diversification associated with smaller communities of language users in various walks of life and various ages, such as young users of so-called Rinkeby Swedish in Stockholm, adolescent urban Turkish-speaking immigrants in double-diglossia areas of West Berlin, triglossic speakers of the Casablanca variety of Moroccan Arabic (Bardel, Falk & Lindquist under review; Dittmar & Steckbauer under review; Ennaji under review). Diversity is discernible also in the fact that in modern times language patterns have changed so significantly that sets of languages, rather than single languages, now often perform the essential functions of communication, cognition and identity for individuals and communities (Aronin 2005).

Bull (1977: 20–22, 67–71, 97; see also Bull & Watson 1984) defines *world order* as "those patterns or dispositions of human activity that [achieve and] sustain the elementary or primary goals of social life among mankind as a whole". Multilingualism fits this definition perfectly. On the other hand, because of the association of the expression *new world order* with particular (in many cases particularly objectionable) kinds of political ideologies and regimes, it has the potential of being interpreted as having sinister connotations. Accordingly, we have proposed (Aronin & Singleton 2008a; see also Aronin, Fishman, Singleton & Ó Laoire under review) the substitute term *new linguistic dispensation*. The reality to which this term applies embraces, in our understanding, language ideologies and policies, language education in all its dimensions, and the patterns of language use of communities and individuals. It also encompasses the systemic development and evolving status of the full spectrum of extant and emergent language varieties.

'Historical multilingualism' vs. 'current multilingualism'

Of course, it is no part of our argument, as is made clear above, that multilingualism itself is a new phenomenon. It has self-evidently been with us throughout history (see e.g. Adams & Swain 2002; Braunmüller & Ferraresi 2003). There are, however, a number of differences between what one might call historical multilingualism and that which we experience around us in the world today. Just as we consider mobility a special and characteristic feature of the contemporary globalized world, even though we recognize that mobility existed in all times, so it is our understanding that multilingualism has received a new impetus in the current environment.

The fact of people and groups of people using multiple languages does not *per se* imply a multilingual society, any more than the existence of slaves in the modern world means that we live in an age of slavery. The crucial difference between current and 'historical' multilingualism lies in the degree to which multilingualism is or was integral to the construction of a specific social reality; to put it another way, the difference between the two is to be found in the degree to which virtually every facet of human life depends on multilingual social arrangements and multilingual individuals. Whereas vital societal processes and salient characteristics of contemporary society are inseparably linked with multilingualism, 'historical' multilingualism was largely supplementary to the development and maintenance of previous societies.

By way of example, in ancient Egypt, where a number of languages were in use for various purposes, the most important and socially valued linguistic ability was the *skill of writing*. The Papyrus of Ani, c.1300 BC (below), may serve as an illustration in this connection. The papyrus depicts Thoth, the god of Letters, as a scribe recording measurements of weight.

(Thoth, god of Letters, appears in this picture as the baboon atop the scales post, and again as an ibis-headed official)

Figure 1. The Papyrus of Ani, c.1300 BC (anonymous)

The papyrus illustrates the significance and the centrality of *writing skills* (rather than the mastery of several languages) for politics, religion, agriculture and economy in ancient Egypt. In a civilization that believed in the magical power of written or drawn signs, the caste of scribes played a key role in the centralized and rigid hierarchy of ancient Egypt (Hagen & Hagen 2003: 13–14). Having skills in a number of languages was useful in Egypt in those times too, but such skills were not valued in the same way as simply being able to write.

In contrast to contemporary sociolinguistic arrangements, in which a constellation of languages is increasingly frequently a prerequisite for global society's functioning and progress (cf. Aronin 2005), previous social arrangements typically required only a given additional language, a particular aspect of language-related knowledge or a number of specific language skills for sustaining economic, political and religious systems. In contrast to the linguistic needs that characterized such 'historical' multilingualism, today a variety of languages, language skills and areas of linguistic competence in various combinations are often requisite. This can be illustrated by reference to languages of wider communication (such as English and Spanish in the Americas, Hindi in India, and Kiswahili (Swahili) and Lingala in African countries), without which many features of contemporary life would be unimaginable: the diffusion of common values and practices, international cultural activities, services, university education, literature and fashion; likewise, cross-border trade, capital flow, product chains, and labour mobility.

Arising from these underlying differences there are a number of clearly observable differences in the way multilingualism manifests itself in historical and contemporary times (see Table 1). These can all be seen as differences of *degree*, but degree in different dimensions, as can be judged from the following (non-exhaustive) inventory.

We do not wish to suggest that the statements made in Column 2 never hold true in the modern world but rather that the statements made in Column 3 are in quantitative terms more representative and that such quantitative differences have reached a point where one is entitled to speak of a qualitative change.

Let us now look in a little more detail at the differences sketched in Table 1. With respect to (1), the origins of languages in a multilingual community's repertoire, in the past such languages tended to originate from locations which were geographically close. Clearly, this was not *always* the case. Thus, the Greeks took their language to India (Fussman 1996; O'Brien 1994) from the fourth century B.C.; two millennia later the British repeated the trick in India more extensively and duratively with English (cf. Crystal 2003: 46–49). However, the diffusion of English is no longer tied to Britain's colonial past and multilingualism involving English is present in cultures and amidst languages far removed not only geographically but also historico-politically from the historical source of English and

Table 1. Distinctions between historical and contemporary multilingualism

	Historical multilingualism	Contemporary multilingualism
1. Contiguity of origin	In the past where two or more languages were widely used the languages in question tended to originate in contiguous areas/nations/tribes.	In the contemporary world a particular area may be characterized by the use of languages of a wide diversity of origins, including very distant origins.
2. Class	In some societies in the past the use of more than one language was mostly confined to particular social strata.	In contemporary societies the use of more than one language is increasingly spread though the entire social range (obviously in some places more than others).
3. Geographical location	In the past the use of more than one language was very often a feature of particular types of geographical locations (border areas, regions having their own local language varieties, towns on trade routes, imperial administrative centres, etc.)	In the contemporary world the use of more than one language is becoming an increasingly ubiquitous phenomenon.
4. Medium	In some societies in the past the use of additional languages was mostly confined to the written medium.	In contemporary societies the use of additional languages is rarely confined to the written medium.
5. Ritual	In some societies in the past the use of additional languages was principally associated with ritual purposes.	In contemporary societies multiple language use is rarely confined to ritual purposes.
6. Profession	In some societies in the past the use of more than one language was associated with particular trades and professions.	In contemporary societies the use of more than one language is typically spread across a range of professional groups.
7. Spatio-temporal aspects	In the past multilingual communication tended to be face-to-face or over modest distances and, in its written form, could be quite slow.	In the contemporary world most multilingual communication is instantaneous and such communication routinely takes place over vast distances.

indeed from all centres of English native-speaking population. As with English, so with many other languages.

Concerning (2), the restriction of multilingualism to particular social strata, this can be illustrated by the way in which knowledge and use of Greek alongside Latin in the Roman Republic was confined principally on the one hand to slaves and workers of Greek origin and on the other to an educated social elite (see e.g.

Swain 2002). Whilst it is certainly not unknown for particular languages in modern societies to be primarily associated with migrants, the migrants in question these days increasingly cover a broad social spectrum. For instance, Polish immigrants in Ireland work in shops, bars and restaurants but also in the educational sector, in the IT industry and their own businesses. As for the association of multilingualism with educated social elites, the fact that education – and initiation into additional languages – is progressively available to all social categories means that the notion of a multilingual educated social elite is constantly being eroded.

The association (3) between multilingualism and particular localities can be illustrated by the case of the border city of Vyborg – now in Russia, but formerly Swedish and Finnish – which had a centuries-long history of quadrilingualism, the languages involved being Finnish, Swedish, German and Russian (see Tandefelt 2003). While such local blossoming of multilingualism – underlain by very local factors – is to be found in today's world too, contemporary multilingualism is very far from confined to particular places. Virtually *any* reasonably sized urban centre in Europe in the current era, for example, can be expected to be characterized by some degree of multilingual language use.

With regard to (4) the use of additional languages being confined to the written medium, an example of this is the continued use and study of written Sumerian in Babylonia after its existence as a spoken language had been ended by the spread of Akkadian (Kramer 1963; Starr 1991:46ff.). The use of Latin in Medieval and Renaissance Europe resembles the Sumerian case. Obviously, ancient languages continue to be studied in our own times, but we have been able to find no precise modern parallel to the above-cited instances.

Turning now to (5) multilingualism in ritual situations, in the Dublin of the early 1960s three languages were in wide use: English, Irish and Latin. English was the majority language of everyday communication; Irish was encountered by most Dubliners in education, in street signs, in a small number of columns in newspapers and magazines, in a few radio and television programmes and in the opening sentences of speeches given by anyone with a public profile. Latin was encountered by some in the classroom but by all Catholics in the liturgy of their church. In the last case, the dominant use of the language was clearly ritual. The use of Irish too – in politicians' speeches, in bilingual signage etc. – can be seen as at least partly ritual. Compare this with the situation in contemporary Dublin: English remains the majority language of communication; the use of Latin as a hieratic language has largely fallen away; ritual uses of Irish in speeches, etc., remain, but Irish is much more present in the media – including the broadcast media – than previously. In addition, a multiplicity of other languages are now present in the city in absolutely non-ritual mode, so that the conversations one hears when shopping in O'Connell Street are in such languages as Polish, Mandarin and Russian as well as in English.

In relation to (6) multilingualism being linked in the past to particular trades and professions, one can cite the instance of shipwrights and port officials in Medieval England, who were, according to Trotter (2003) not only conversant with the languages of England (English, Anglo-Norman and French) but were also "used to terminology drawn from all over the known world" (Trotter 2003: 28). It is still the case that people working in areas associated with international travel often master a range of languages, but, since every area of trade, as well as every area of technology, construction, the arts, scientific research, law, journalism, and the rest may have an international or intercultural dimension, it is difficult these days for any professional activity to stand completely aloof from multilingualism.

Let us end by looking at (7) the spatio-temporal dimension of multilingualism. In the past non-face-to-face communication tended to be in writing and non-immediate. One example is multilingual inscriptions; for example, "[t]he record of the achievements of the early Sassanian king Shapor I (241–272) is carved on a stone wall … and written in … Persian (the original text), Parthian, and Greek" (Cotton, Millar & Rogers 2002: 45). Another example is the use of more than one language in official documents – such as the use of Norwegian and Low German in the documents of the Hanseatic League emanating from Bergen in the fourteenth century (Nesse 2003). The telecommunication systems of the modern world, on the other hand, mean that complex interactions, in speech or writing, sometimes in quasi face-to-face mode, sometimes involving more than two participants, can take place without any kind of noticeable time-lag in any number of languages.

Two trends

Researchers generally agree on two trends broadly characterizing today's world linguistic situation (see e.g. Fishman 1998; Maurais 2003). One is the wide diversification of recognized languages in use (see above), which is accompanied, on the other hand, by a troubling decline in the vigour of many languages – to the point where many are simply disappearing (Crystal 2000; Dalby 2003). The other is an unprecedented spread of the use of English (Crystal 1985, 2003; Fishman 1998; Graddol 1997, 2006).

These two trends can be seen to be developing simultaneously and appear to be in contradiction with each other. On the one hand, the globalization of trade and manufacturing is promoting the globalization of English. On the other hand, economic regionalization is promoting regional languages. Fishman comments on the situation in the following general way:

> English has become the leading international language, in economic and political spheres, and is becoming the language of high society and of the young. At the same time, however, regional languages are also making considerable headway, thanks to new social interaction and economic backing from their governments.
>
> (Fishman 1998)

In relation to the first trend, it is common knowledge that English is now the dominant language of world communication, trade, diplomacy and upward social mobility (cf. de Swaan 1988a, 1988b, 1999, 2001) and that more and more people are accordingly motivated to master it. In many parts of the world this results in 'multilingualism with English' (Hoffmann 2000; Jessner 2006; Ó Laoire & Aronin 2005), and has led to a situation where the number of non-native users of English exceeds its native speakers by a ratio of 3:1 (Crystal 2003:69). Unsurprisingly, the hegemony of English is often referred to in highly pejorative terms; *linguistic genocide, killer language* (see e.g. Skutnabb-Kangas 2000, 2001) and even *glottophagy* ('language cannibalism') are among the expressions that have been deployed in this context. On the other (cf. e.g. Chiti-Batelli 2003), there is the perspective which represents English as the Great Facilitator – enabling international trade, fostering international and intercultural communication and empowering individuals in their personal, educational and career development.

With regard to the second trend – the increase in the number and diversity of languages in use worldwide – this, as has been noted, is to a high degree driven by the revitalization and revaluation of languages previously in decline by, for example, giving previously stigmatized languages official recognition, encouraging the use of certain languages in domains from which they were previously excluded, and using the educational system to raise the status of languages of perceived lower standing (see e.g. Jones 1981; Mar-Molinero 2000; Ó Riagáin 1997). The result in many cases is that a particular lesser used language is used more – typically alongside a more widely used language. Thus, for example, according to Jones (1981) in Wales there have in recent times been more people than previously using Welsh alongside English.

Language diversity, especially given the proliferation of recognized languages discussed earlier, poses numerous practical challenges with respect to ethical, cultural, financial and other considerations. In education, for example, it has to be decided whether to increase (and if so, by what extent) the number of languages specified as compulsory or optional elements of school curricula. Should heritage languages be revived and taught, or should the concentration be on languages of wider communication? Should additional languages be taught merely as school subjects alongside other subjects or should they deployed as languages of instruction? To what levels of proficiency should they be taught and which of the four skills (listening, speaking, reading, writing) should be focused on?

Where decisions are taken to support local, immigrant and heritage languages within given communities, there are bound to be obstacles to the implementation of such a policy, given the numbers of languages likely to be involved. Such obstacles will almost certainly be financial and organizational in nature. They may have socio-political dimensions as well; for instance, a large section of a particular population may resist the allocation of resources to the maintenance of lesser used languages. Even speakers of the languages in question may have practical concerns about certain language revitalization policies. Thus, Safont Jordà (2007) reports that "Catalan speakers were a bit reluctant about the inclusion of their language in their children's school curricula" (p. 93) when a bilingual model in which some school subjects would be taught in Catalan was proposed to them. Finding pedagogical materials in the languages concerned (textbooks, grammars, dictionaries, etc.) may also pose challenges, which may be especially acute where a given language community does not have a long history of widespread literacy. In addition, human resource issues may present difficulties; it is not always straightforward to recruit properly qualified teachers of specific languages. A further consideration is that official support may not suffice to prevent the decline or even loss of languages from a country or region if countervailing factors are strong. For example, in Ireland, despite constant (and multidimensional) state support for the Irish language over more than eighty years, the situation of the language continues to deteriorate (cf. Singleton 2007b). In other words, the flourishing of multiple languages seems to require more than governmental encouragement – obviously, at the very least, real interest and robust motivation on the part of those involved in the learning of the languages in question.

The properties and developmental directions of the new linguistic dispensation

The intricate interplay of the two above-outlined trends of current multilingualism accounts for distinctive *specific qualities* inherent in the new linguistic dispensation (that is, current multilingualism). The new dispensation can be characterised as *suffusive, complex* and *liminal*. These three characteristics (each separately and all together) in turn lead to *specific developments* (key processes and phenomena) in the realities of global societies (Aronin & Singleton 2008d) (see Figure 2). We shall discuss the properties and developments in more detail below.

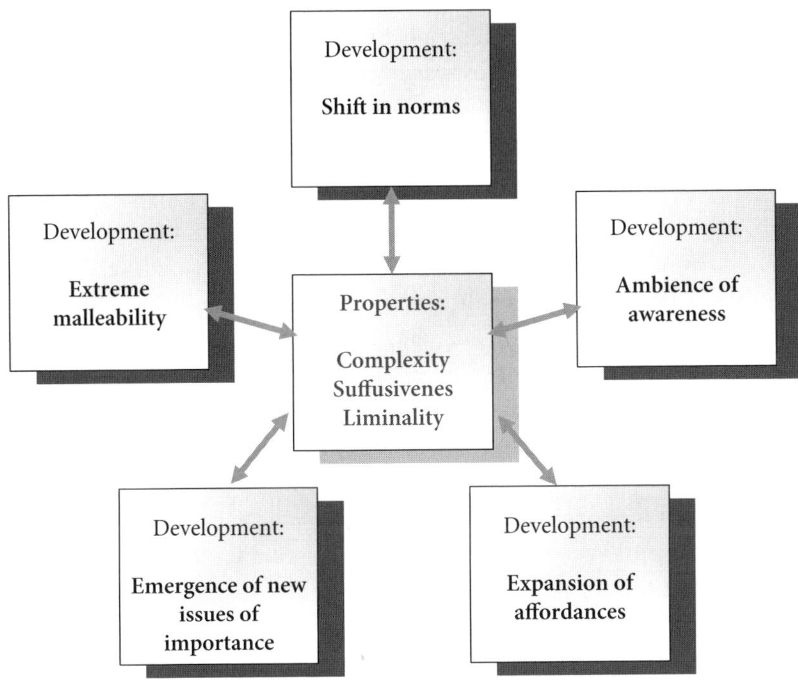

Figure 2. Properties and developmental directions of the current global linguistic dispensation (after Aronin & Singleton 2008d)

Suffusiveness

The *suffusive* attribute is manifested in the way in which language-related phenomena (in particular English-related phenomena) pervade so many aspects of our lives. Probably less obvious but deeply significant is the degree to which multilingualism is integral to the construction of contemporary social reality. Contemporary multilingualism is suffusive in the sense that it permeates the world in terms of the existence of multilingual populations, multilingual spaces, and activity domains (e.g. business) where multilingual practices prevail. In fact, virtually every facet of life in the present era depends on multilingual social arrangements and multilingual individuals.

Of course persons speaking just one language in a multilingual society can very often survive quite well. For example, an elderly Russian-speaking immigrant to Israel who has not mastered Hebrew and who does not know English can cope through Russian in selected banks, hospitals, post offices, etc. and she can have access to newspapers and cultural events in Russian. But this is a case of the *management* of particular situations. Clearly, knowing the other languages of the environment would be the norm, simply because knowing these other languages renders life easier and yields a great variety of tangible benefits.

Complexity

The property of *complexity* can readily be seen in the dynamic, polymorphous nature of current multilingualism, with its many interweaving levels and forms. Complexity in this context is readily discernible (and not just to researchers) in the practices of child-rearing, in language teaching, in everyday language use, in the multiplicity of languages meeting in particular locations, and in individuals' personal experience of languages. Such complexity makes it impossible to provide a plausible account of multilingualism based simply on an aggregation of its various parts. When we look closely at multilingual phenomena we are confronted – at both the psycholinguistic and the sociolingustic levels – with a great multiplicity of agents (varying numbers of languages, variability among multilinguals in terms of modes of use and levels of mastery, an immense range of interaction-types, etc.) and apparent unpredictability. The resultant perception is of fuzziness, irregularity, fragmentariness, even near chaos (cf. Aronin & Singleton 2008b; Larsen-Freeman 2002).

Complexity is the subject matter of complexity science, which has proved to be effective in arriving at solutions in fields as varied as medicine, traffic organization, and financial services (Waldrop 1992; Kaneko & Tsuda 2001; Capra 2005), and whose techniques, ideas and solutions can, we believe, be fruitfully transferred to multilingualism studies. A more detailed account of how complexity methods and concepts may be used in reference to multilingualism will be given in Chapter 9.

Liminality

Finally, we turn to the property of *liminality*. The term derives from the Latin word for 'threshold' – *limen*. *Liminal* is defined by the Oxford English Dictionary as "[o]f or pertaining to the threshold or initial stage of a process". The Merriam-Webster Dictionary defines it as "[o]f or relating to a sensory threshold", "barely perceptible" and "of, relating to, or being an intermediate phase or condition".

Before spreading to other fields. the term was used in anthropology in connection with coming-of-age rituals, denoting the specific period in life where an individual is in the process of entering into a new status in the community: "the midpoint of transition in a status-sequence between two positions" (Turner 1974:237). Our usage of the concept overlaps with its ethnographical sense. The concepts we refer to are for a period liminal – that is, are initially not noticeably but then increasingly visibly taking on a new status and quality which allows them to be clearly perceived and taken account of. While the ethnological understanding of liminality emphasizes the idea of 'betwixt and between', in our discussion of liminality in multilingualism, while we certainly include this meaning, we particularly focus, on the next stage of liminality, which is emergence.

The term *liminality* is occasionally applied in the literature to linguistic and cultural transitions of individuals (e.g. Quist & Jørgensen 2007). In the present context we use *liminality* to advert to the fact that many processes and phenomena connected with language and languages seem recently to have become discernible or noticeable, the realization of their importance deriving perhaps from the challenge of recent linguistically connected events and developments and patterns. Examples are numerous and come from all the aspects of multilingualism. Spolsky (1999) provides a clear instance of liminality in his remarks on second/foreign language teaching and learning:

> Those of us concerned with the field of second-language learning have been forced by the ethnic revival and by our new appreciation of language and ethnicity to extend our concerns to embrace the social context in which the teaching takes place.　　　　　　　　　　　　　　　　　　　　　(Spolsky 1999: 182)

Another example refers to the sociology of language: Extra (under review) makes the following point:

> ... there have always been speakers of immigrant languages in Europe, but these languages have only recently emerged as community languages spoken on a wide scale in urban Europe, due to intensified process of migration and intergenerational minorization. Turkish and Arabic are good examples of so-called 'non-European' languages that are spoken and learned by millions of inhabitants of the EU nation states.　　　　　　　　　　　　　　　　　　　　　(Extra under review)

Harjanne & Tella (2008) propose a similar notion to that of liminality. They talk about the idea of transpiring tendencies which they call *weak and strong signals*. Weak signals are conceived as "those barely noticeable signals that surround us and are likely to become important trends or phenomena at a later stage ... signs of the future, foreshadowing emerging developments" (2008: 56). Strong signals they understand as "highly prominent trends" (*ibid.*). In this connection Harjanne & Tella see the ascent of the foreign language to the status of "empowering mediator" as the result of a "chain of conceptual changes", arguing that (2008: 58) "at the beginning, the question was mostly of a weak signal, but which has gradually occupied the centre stage and can now be considered as something that has a major impact on people's conceptions of languages, language proficiency and language teaching".

The three *properties* of contemporary multilingualism, *suffusiveness, complexity* and *liminality,* materialize in the concrete *developments* taking place in the context of the current global linguistic dispensation (Aronin & Singleton 2008d), which we now discuss.

Developments characterizing the new linguistic dispensation

Developments characterizing the new linguistic dispensation include (but in our view are not limited to) shifts in norms, the emergence of new focal issues, an expansion of affordances, an ambience of awareness, and extreme malleability (see above Figure 2). These developments are easily illustrated with respect to the English language, or are particularly salient in this connection, but in fact a vast multiplicity of other languages are affected by these trends. We shall deal with the above-listed developments in turn.

Shifts in norms

Norms have shifted in respect of at least the following aspects of relationships between people and language(s):

- the bi-/multilingual rather than the monolingual language-user is increasingly recognized as the norm (Cook 1992, 1999; Grosjean 1985, 1992);
- native speakers are losing their special status (see e.g. Barbour 2002; Cook 1992; Cheshire 2002); this phenomenon has mostly been commented on with respect to English native speakers, but as a tendency it is not language-specific;
- bi-/multilingual education is common – and not just for elites or specific professions, or in border areas; such education very frequently involves English (see e.g. Björklund & Suni 2000; Cenoz & Gorter 2005; Cenoz 2009; Cenoz & Gorter 2008a);
- the aims of the formal learning and teaching of additional languages are typically formulated these days in terms of communicative goals and tasks rather in terms of the objective of aping native speakers (Cook 1993; Jessner 2006), so that, for example the tolerance range regarding accent has broadened;
- the recognition of the role of language knowledge in defining the life path has increased (this matter will be further discussed in the chapter on Dominant Language Constellations and life-paths);

– the correlations between particular languages and particular geographical/
national/ethnic units have loosened giving way to more dynamic concepts of
network and flow.

New focal issues

Another development is the emergence of new 'hot' topics of discussion in the
language area. These include the following:

– the demarcation of the concept of a language in a world where a myriad of
language varieties are recognized;
– the definition of *native speaker* and determination of the relevance of this notion amidst current multilingual, multivarietal complexity and diversity;
– the ownership of languages of wider communication – notably English;
– the impact of the proliferation of multilingual families;
– issues arising in respect of multilingual identity;
– the expression of emotions in multilingual language use;
– life-long multilingual language learning;
– the respective advantages and disadvantages of native and non-native language teachers in contemporary conditions;
– the fortunes of minority languages in today's highly multilingual
environment;
– the multidimensionality and multidirectionality of cross-linguistic influence
in multilinguals.

Expansion of affordances

The development which we have labelled an *expansion of affordances* (see our
earlier definition of *affordance*, and see further discussion in Chapter 9) is partly
related to the provision of opportunities to acquire English as an international
language (and other languages of wider communication). To have a knowledge of
English is significantly to extend possibilities of all kinds across a very wide range
of domains (see e.g. Ammon 2007). For example, Hoffmann (2000: 5) notes that
"English is a *sine qua non* if one wants to gain access to international electronic information networks". In another dimension, the teaching of and through regional
languages such as Basque, Catalan and Frisian (Cenoz 2009; Cenoz & Gorter
2008a; Cenoz & Jessner 2009; Ytsma 2001) can be seen, *inter alia*, as facilitating
the education of native speakers of the languages in question and furnishing a
range of career opportunities for individuals with a command of such languages.

Ambience of awareness

The development of an ambience of awareness (however flawed sometimes) around language, languages and multilingualism (cf. e.g. Hawkins 1999; Jessner 2006) is well illustrated by the following press item. In October 2003 Reuters (Demick 2002) reported the case of a Korean mother who had a surgical operation – costing approximately €94 – performed on her six-year-old son's tongue. The procedure, known as frenectomy, involves shortening the tongue by one centimetre. It has become increasingly popular in South Korea as more and more parents drag frightened children – almost all under five – into doctors' surgeries. These parents believe that the operation in question will improve their children's ability to differentiate Rs and Ls in the English manner – so that, for instance, *rice* does not come out as *lice* – and thus give them a competitive edge in Korea's English-obsessed society. The doctor interviewed for the Reuters article reported that he performs this procedure about ten times a month. This example is admittedly an extreme one, and we do not wish to claim that tongue-slashing is sweeping the planet. Nevertheless, the example does provide a powerful sidelight on the extraordinary awareness of importance of English in Korea and, by extension, in the wider world.

Malleability

Finally, the development we have dubbed *malleability* refers to the very rapid and often unpredictable changes in the constituents of multilingualism in response to changes in conditions and needs. This applies to such phenomena as the individual's shifting levels of proficiency in his/her languages, the evolving status of particular languages in particular locations, changing rates of frequency of use in respect of specific languages, and developments in relation to the availability of language instruction in respect of given languages. Whereas multilingual situations always have been of their very nature highly transient, the mobility and rapidity of transformation characterizing the contemporary world currently render such transience extreme.

Concluding summary

In this chapter we have suggested that current multilingualism has attained to the scope and significance of a new linguistic dispensation on a world scale. Because multilingualism and globalization are so inextricably intertwined, all the major attributes of the globalization phenomenon characterize multilingualism as well. In this connection we have referred to the ubiquity of multilingualism and the increasing breadth and depth of its effects; we have also noted its relationship to the modifications in human experience those of compression and expansion of time and space, mobility and fluidity, transcendence of territorial and social boundaries, transience and negotiability of identity.

We have further claimed that the crucial difference between current and 'historical' multilingualism lies in the degree to which multilingualism is or was integral to the construction of a specific social reality. Our view is that, whereas vital societal processes and salient characteristics of contemporary society are inseparably linked with multilingualism, 'historical' multilingualism was typically supplementary in nature. We take the line that, in contrast to contemporary sociolinguistic arrangements, in which constellations of languages are prerequisite for society's functioning and progress, previous social arrangements tended to be more local in nature and to require only a particular additional language, language-related knowledge or a number of specific language skills for sustaining economic, political and religious systems.

An additional focus of this chapter has been an exploration of the distinctive characteristics of the new linguistic dispensation in terms of properties and developments. We have proposed complexity, liminality and suffusiveness as the main properties of current multilingualism. We have gone on to suggest that these three properties become manifest in the concrete developments taking place in the current linguistic dispensation. Among the developments are a shifting of norms, the surfacing of new focal issues, an expansion of affordances, the coming into being of an ambience of awareness and a trend towards extreme malleability.

CHAPTER 4

The Dominant Language Constellation (DLC)

Although there exist many places in the world where the linguistic environment is monolingual, on a world scale it is mostly multilingual institutions and communities that enable and facilitate the advance of human society in its current direction. As we have pointed out, recent global transformations have resulted in a situation where not a single language, but rather a set of languages, may frequently be the prerequisite for the functioning of an individual or a society. Clearly, this phenomenon cries out for further examination and discussion. We dub a set of languages on which the life of an individual or a society is dependant, a *Dominant Language Constellation (DLC)*.

What is a Dominant Language Constellation?

For any individual the *Dominant Language Constellation* is the group of his/her most important languages that, functioning as an entire unit, enable him/her to act in a multilingual environment in such a way as to meet all of his/her needs. (For an earlier definition see Aronin & Ó Laoire 2004: 19, 26.) Apart from being an individual matter, a DLC may operate across a whole community. As a social phenomenon, a DLC constitutes a complex of languages shared on a day-to-day basis by an entire community for which and within which it meets, as a set, the essential functions of communication, interaction and identity marking.

This concept relates closely to that of *speech community* (or *language community*) which Bloomfield (1933: 43 characterizes as "the most important kind of social groups". Although there is no very precise consensus on what a speech community is, the notion is a recurrent one in sociolinguistics and the sociology of language. The idea is founded on a social perspective rather than focusing purely on the linguistic aspect. It attempts to provide a framework which connects a language and the people speaking it in a single encompassing unit.

According to the simplest understanding of speech community, it is a category covering a collection of people united by the fact that they use the same language or language variety either from birth or by later adoption. Thus, an aggregate of people who use Modern Standard Arabic in Africa, Asia, Australia and America, or who use Standard French in France, Jamaica, African states and Canada would, on the above definition, constitute a language community, although they are dispersed geographically. A more sophisticated view on speech community holds that a given speech community's members share not only a particular language, but also a set of attitudes, values and expectations associated with the use of this language as well, and that they are likely to be in habitual contact (Mesthrie et al. 2009: 37).

One of the classic definitions of the notion of speech community is that given by Gumperz:

> We will define it as a social group which may be either monolingual or multilingual, held together by frequency of social interaction patterns and set off from the surrounding areas by weaknesses in the lines of communication. Linguistic communities may consist of small groups bound together by face-to-face contact or may cover large regions, depending on the level of abstraction we wish to achieve.
>
> (Gumperz 1968: 463)

The boundaries of a language community, however, defined in this kind of way, present problems. First, the extent to which members of the community share values and linguistic norms is difficult to subject to rigorous criterion-referencing. Second, those who comprise a language community, although sharing the same broad language variety, differ in regard to their *idiolects,* that is their individual language patterns and preferences, the details of which are unique to each individual.

The concept of language community evolved from a monolingual perspective, tacitly suggesting that people in a given community would speak one language, and manifesting roots in the ideology 'one language-one nation', which was an important ingredient in the development of nation-states. It is often the case, though, that a particular language and ethnicity may be spread over several countries. Thus, versions of Arabic are spoken in about 47 countries. It is also the case that within the boundaries of a single country a wide spectrum of ethnicities and languages may co-exist and inter-communicate. For example, Nigeria counts hundreds of ethnic groups speaking some four hundred languages.

To return to our concept of a DLC, its member languages typically fulfill different functions. A DLC very frequently includes languages of different levels of status. It is often the case that an international language, a regional lingua franca, one or more state languages and one or more minority (local or immigrant) languages are involved for example: English/Turkish/Persian in Iran; Southern Min/Hakka/English or Mandarin/Southern Min/an Aboriginal variety in Taiwan; English/Hungarian/German in Hungary; French/English/Dutch or Dutch/

Frisian/English in the Netherlands; Polish/German/English in Australia; Hindi/ Maithili/Bhojpuri in India.

The crucial languages for the Russian-speaking community in Israel (see Figure 1), constituting the DLC allowing Russian speakers to manage their daily lives and their education, are Russian (L1), Hebrew – the official language of the country they have come to live in, and English – the language of higher learning. Hebrew may also be regarded as an ethnic, heritage language in this context, while English – widely used as a second language in Israeli everyday life – may in many instances supplement an as yet imperfect command of Hebrew. A specific individual's or family's language repertoire may include more than three languages. With regard to Russian speakers in Israel, Yiddish may be a fundamental defining constituent of individual or family identity but not an integral part of the wider DLC of the entire Russian-speaking community. A Russian-speaking immigrant may also have come to Israel with knowledge of Latvian, Lithuanian, Ukrainian, Byelorussian, or some other language of a former Soviet Republic or some school-acquired proficiency in German or French. These exceed the bounds

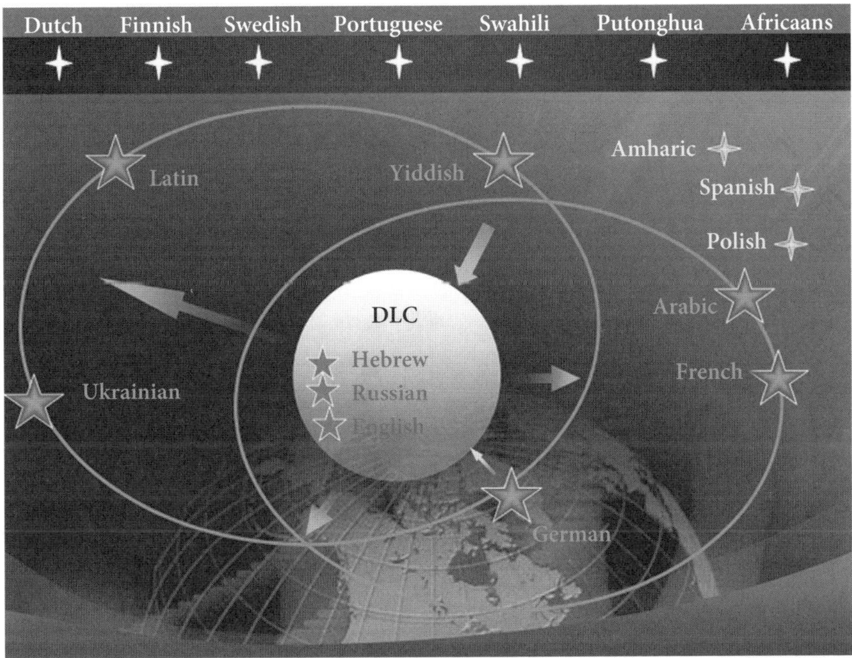

Stars in the inner circle – languages of DLC. Stars on the orbits languages of language repertoire. Stars in the corner: languages encountered in the wider community a person belongs (in this case a country). Stars at the top of the figure: languages a person is merely in some degree aware of.

Figure 1. Dominant Language Constellation and language repertoire

of the broader community's dominant constellation, but it should be noted that it is the community DLC which furnishes the essential tools for communication and which is indeed the basis of community identity (Aronin 2006).

Apart from the languages of the DLC and of an individual's or a family's wider repertoire there may be languages used in the community which a person may perhaps only understand. Or a person may be able to recognize and 'place' the sounds of a community language he/she does not know in any real sense; Russian speakers in Israel may, for instance, be able to recognize the sounds of Amharic (see in Figure 1 the languages in the outer orbits). Alternatively, a person may simply be aware of languages present in his/her environment and may even be planning to learn one of them. Another possibility is that a person may know about the existence of other languages in his/her environment and elsewhere in the world without connecting such languages with his/her own life (see in Figure 1 the languages at the top of the figure).

Language repertoire versus DLC

The notion of DLC is related to, but not the same as that of language *repertoire*. A language repertoire (or verbal repertoire, to use the term deployed by Gumperz 1964: 137–138) is understood as the "totality of linguistic varieties shared by the group as a whole" and as "an individual's particular set of skills (or levels of proficiency) that permit him or her to function within various registers of (a) language(s)" (Schiffman 1996: 42). Later the concept of linguistic repertoire was extended to bilingual situations. For Pütz (2004: 227):

> 'Repertoire' bezeichnet nicht nur die Kompetenzen monolingualer Sprecher, sondern auch im bilingualen Kontext sind die Aspekte des Sprachwechsels (*Code-Switching*) wie auch der Sprachwahl (*language choice*) bedeutsam. … Der Begriff 'Repertoire' lässt sich sowohl auf den individuellen Sprecher wie auch auf die sprachlichen Fertigkeiten einer Sprechgemeinsamkeit anwenden.

> 'Repertoire' not only designates the competencies of monolingual speakers, but in addition in bilingual contexts the aspects of codeswitching and language choice come into play. … The concept of 'repertoire' is applicable both to the individual speaker and to the language capacities of a collectivity sharing a language commonality.   (*our translation*)

While the concept of linguistic (or verbal) repertoire relates to the totality of an individual's or a community's linguistic skills, the DLC concept is concerned with the vehicle languages which stand out as being of prime importance. A range of languages (known either fully or partially, productively or receptively) may be dear to or very proficiently mastered by a speaker or a group, without being essential in that person's or that group's daily life and therefore without being part of that person's or that group's DLC. Another point worth noting is that unlike the notion of language repertoire, which originated from and remains highly relevant to monolingualism, the DLC concept is peculiar to multilingualism. We may say that, while all of the languages of a linguistic repertoire may furnish rewards of diverse kinds to those who know them, only those languages of a repertoire which fulfill functions that are vital for a person or for a community constitute a DLC.

How many languages constitute a DLC?

The number of languages in a constellation seems typically to hover around three, while the repertoire of multilinguals (cf. Ó Laoire & Aronin 2005) may range very widely. It is actually not easy for contemporary developed societies to manage with just one language. On the other hand, deploying more than three languages on a regular basis may also not be particularly common. Håkan Ringbom (personal communication) suggests, for example, that for the functioning of the Finnish national football team three languages – Finnish, Swedish and English – are necessary, but not more. Likewise, a recent study carried out in Ireland and Israel (Ó Laoire & Aronin 2005), demonstrated that, although multilingual participants reported knowing up to 8 languages,

–   the average number of languages that respondents perceived as necessary for their social, cognitive and emotional needs was three;
–   the most frequent number of languages reportedly *spoken* (as opposed to languages *known*) according to these findings was three;
–   from one to three languages were assigned the characteristic of being important by most multilinguals in the study;
–   even the languages in which the multilinguals in the study reported communicating with their pets were languages from their DLC rather than languages from their wider repertoire.

We are not suggesting that three is some kind of magic number, only that out of the whole repertoire of languages known and used by a multilingual only a subset are used intensively and bear the load of the functions necessary to meet the individual's routine needs.

If we look around, we can find ample examples of the fact that in everyday life people tend to use not more than about three (possibly two, possibly four) languages, while other languages in the repertoire are used in response to very particular kinds of demand. In her plenary lecture at the 6th International Conference on Multilingualism and Third Language Acquisition, Franceschini (2009), describing the linguistic situation in the South Tyrol, singled out what she called "predominant linguistic repertoires" – corresponding to what we here label Dominant Language Constellations – of the respective population groups:

> German speakers: L1-South Tyrol dialect / L2 High German / L3 Italian;
> Italian speakers: L1 Italian / L2 High German;
> Ladin speakers: L1 Ladin / L2 South Tyrolean dialect / L3 High German / L4 Italian.

This last example clearly demonstrates that Dominant Language Constellations evolve out of specific needs of specific populations (and individuals) who often share their geographic and political environment with populations for whom other DLCs are vital. A variety of DLCs can co-exist in the same physical space in the same polity.

The characteristic features of a DLC

1. From the foregoing we can derive an important feature of the DLC – its particularity and specificity for each individual and each society. It is this specificity that determines the degree of instrumentality of a given group of languages for the person or society making use of it.

2. The second characteristic feature of the Dominant Language Constellation is the way in which the languages comprising it accommodate to each other. It is obvious that the linguistic qualities and social functioning of a language are not the same in situations where it is used in a constellation as compared to situations where it is used separately, outside such a constellation. A DLC is an instance of language contact, because at the individual level the languages are in one and the same person, subserved by one and the same mind-brain, and inevitably influencing each other in every possible way. Accordingly, each language involved in a constellation differs in both linguistic and social aspects from the same language operating in monolingual circumstances or in another multilingual constellation. This relates closely to our next point.

3. Each DLC is an entity which possesses its own characteristics, its own special identity. Even DLCs composed of the same languages differ widely from context to context depending on the linguistic, political, geographical and societal specificities of the environment in which a given language and a given DLC operate. Consider, for example, the DLC of Ukrainian/Russian/English in the Ukraine and in the USA. The nature of this DLC is clearly not constant

across these environments despite the use of the same set of languages. The differences lie in the 'weight' of each language, the level of mastery of each, and the functions allotted to each. In the Ukraine, English as a foreign language studied at school was for most older adult Ukrainian immigrants to the USA principally a means of cultural enrichment and of enhancing general language and thinking skills, while in America, English is, for these same migrants, a primary means of communication at work, in interaction with social, financial and medical services, in entertainment contexts and with non-Ukrainian friends. Likewise, if one compares the English/Spanish/Catalan constellation in Catalonia in 2008 as compared with 1968, what emerges is a 'gain in weight' for English and especially Catalan, and a 'loss of weight' for Spanish. It should be emphasized also that a DLC is not just the sum of the several languages constituting it; rather, it is an entity that has characteristics and an identity beyond the sum of its parts. Thus, Dominant Language Constellations differ one from the other not so much in terms of the number of languages involved, but rather in terms of the particularities of the languages involved and in terms of the configuration of mastery, of usage and of inter-relationships between them.

4. The number and diversity of DLCs in societies seem almost unencompass-able, but Dominant Language Constellations can certainly be seen as possessing *indexicality* (see Silverstein 2003). Dominant Language Constellations are *indexical*, insofar as they point to, or indicate, some states of affairs with a degree of certainty – such as the geographical residence or origins of their users, the social status of their users, the ethnicity of their users, etc. DLCs are, moreover, ordered within global and local frames; that is, some languages which feature in a DLC clearly figure in the upper reaches of a global hierarchy of importance (English, Chinese, Arabic, Spanish, Russian, French, German, etc.), whereas others are more difficult to 'place', their rating depending on regional, local, historical and cultural considerations (Swahili, Dari, Hebrew, Greek, Italian, etc.). Estimations of the cumulative value of language sets are often unconsciously referred to in societal discourse, but also frequently argued for in respect of the enabling, empowering nature of specific constellations as wholes and of every language in particular constellations. The values that emerge are often consensual, but are perceptibly different in different locations or in different situations or different time-frames. It is impossible to conceive of arranging DLCs into any kind of explicit hierarchy, but indexicality permits the identification of characteristics of a given DLC – its degree of usefulness, prestige, etc. The linguistic composition of DLCs and the inter-relation of their languages, the level of mastery of each of the languages and the configuration of these levels (e.g. L1 fluent; L2 good enough for daily use;

L3 weak) is also indicative of circumstances, qualities, nuances, etc. – details which mirror the dynamics of people's life trajectories. One example of the indexicality of a DLC is the case of a young refugee from Rwanda which is discussed below. DLC indexicality is obviously much more complicated than the indexicality of a single language because a DLC contains two, three and sometimes more languages, each with its points of specificity, and all of these interact and constitute a complexity going beyond a simple arithmetical sum. In addition, societal factors add nuances to the state of affairs that can be 'read' through a DLC. We can thus say that a DLC is an entity with multiple indexicalities.

5. A DLC may fit the situation of a certain individual, may be in harmony with the characteristics of a specific community in a specific location or may have a wider role in the global arena. For example a Dominant Language Constellation of Russian (native language), German (foreign language studied at school) and Czech (acquired later in life) allowed a young man of about 23 – let us call him Dmitri – to secure a job in a small tourist shop in Prague at the beginning of the millennium when a segment of the Russian population were looking for ways of leaving their country and working and settling abroad. Dmitri was pleased with his new life and made good use of both his native Russian and of his German and Czech. This particular constellation was a good basis for working in the Czech Republic where many visiting tourists are Russian speakers or German speakers. The Czech language, being, like Russian, a member of the Slavic language family, was not particularly difficult for Dmitri to develop to a level sufficient for everyday communication. We can speculate that with a DLC including English, Dmitri might have aspired to find work in a more wealthy country and might have earned more, even occupying the same position of a sales-person in a small shop. We shall return to this topic in the next chapter.

6. The nature of Dominant Language Constellations fluctuates. Constellations are often subject to shifts during an individual's life-span. Personal life-events and socio-historical changes may cause some languages leave the DLC, drift into the category of 'languages that happen to be known' and become dormant; other languages may come to the forefront and enter the DLC. By way of illustration we can examine the case of the so called Volga Germans, the ethnic Germans living near the Volga River around the town of Saratov, Southern European Russia. In the eighteenth century Catherine the Great of Russia invited Europeans to immigrate and to farm Russian land. The poor conditions in their home regions at the time prompted large numbers of Germans to take up this invitation, but they held on to their language and culture. Their DLC of those times included particularly well maintained German and

some (often very little) Russian, because they had no commitment to the Russian Empire.

After the Russian Revolution of 1917, the *Autonome Sozialistische Sowjet-Republik der Wolga-Deutschen* (Volga German Autonomous Soviet Socialist Republic) was established, with its capital in the small town of Engels. The republic existed from 1924 till 1942 and during these years, besides maintaining their German as a home and heritage language, the citizens of the area had no choice but to use Russian, the primary language of the Soviet Union, daily, thus having both German and Russian in their DLC. The Russian language became dominant because of the revolutionary and societal ideology of those times.

Subsequent events brought further developments in regard to the Dominant Language Constellation of this community. As Nazi troops advanced into the USSR towards the Volga in 1941, and Stalin became worried about the possibility of Volga Germans collaborating with them, he ordered a 24-hour relocation of the Volga Germans eastwards. After the war, many settled in the Ural Mountains, Siberia, Kazakhstan and Uzbekistan. In the Asian republics of the USSR at that time, alongside the titular national languages, Kazakh and Uzbek, the main language was Russian. The DLC of the ethnic Germans in Kazakhstan and Uzbekistan during that period accordingly consisted of Russian, as the most important language, Kazakh/Uzbek, and German, this last being very often somewhat peripheral. A piece of research conducted in the 1970s (Haarman 1979) revealed that German was rather poorly maintained in this context.

Since the late 1980s many Volga Germans have emigrated to their ancestral homeland of Germany, taking advantage of the German Law of Return. Unsurprisingly, the German language moved back into first place in the DLC of this particular community, and Uzbek and Kazakh moved out of the DLC to the margins of their language repertoire. Russian very often remained as a significant language spoken and read in the homes of the migrants, especially among the older ones (cf. Andreesen 1998).

7. In today's world a DLC traces the life trajectories of individuals, and its composition and the mutual interdependence of its languages define a person's profile much more exactly and in a manner which is closer to life than a language repertoire. Consider the following story, recounted in detail by Blommaert (2008: 3ff.), of an African refugee, Joseph Mutingira. Apart from the message that Blommaert takes from the detail of the story, the narrative can also be regarded as a good demonstration of the difference between language repertoire and DLC, of the crucial practical implications of this difference, and of the instrumental value of DLCs in today's world. Joseph

Mutingira, a refugee from Rwanda, had his asylum application in the United Kingdom refused by the Home Office, largely on grounds of the particular sociolinguistic profile he displayed. Joseph claims he was born in Rwanda and this is disputed by the UK authorities. "He claims to be a Hutu, even though his mother was Tutsi" – Blommaert begins (2008:4). Being taken by his mother to Kenya, Joseph acquired English in an English-medium nursery school and during frequent visits to Nairobi, where they stayed with a friend of his mother's. Although according to Joseph his parents insisted that the children speak English at home in Kigali, Rwanda, and his father forbade the children to socialize with children beyond the wall of the compound they were living in, Joseph also managed to pick up some Kinyarwanda from a family servant. Then, according to Joseph, when he was five (1992) his mother was murdered in Kagali, his house was attacked, his father and other children in the house were killed and the boy jumped out of the window and ran away. The next development of his life trajectory brought Joseph to the house of his uncle in Gisenyi, a town on the border with the Democratic Republic of the Congo (D. R. Congo) where French and Kinyarwanda were spoken. Blommaert points out that Joseph's uncle consistently spoke English with the boy. This uncle was reportedly proficient also in French, Kinyarwanda and Runyankole (this last being a language similar to Kinyarwanda – in which Joseph picked up some proficiency from his uncle). Joseph's Kinyarwanda was very basic when he was interrogated and arrested by Rwandan Patriotic Front government solders for carrying ammunitions and weapons (unknowingly). He was brought to a detention camp on suspicion that he was a foreign 'infiltrant' on the ground of not being fluently proficient in Kinyarwanda. His good Runyankole led others to suggest that he came from across the border. When, at the age of 14 (or 18 in the Home Office account), Joseph applied for the UK immigration, his restricted competence in Kinyarwanda and his fluent Rynyankole resulted in his having Ugandan nationality ascribed to him and to the dismissal of his case as fraudulent, largely owing to his linguistic repertoire.

Blommaert's (2008) report on this case indicates that the young applicant was caught up in the whirlpool of globalization and local events, on account of which his DLC differs from the repertoire expected of a person of his origins. Blommaert argues that Joseph's life history provides many clues about his affiliation and life trajectory that together construct a new sociolinguistic profile, a profile which does not correspond to the traditional national imagination of Rwanda but does fit the realities of Rwanda during and after the 1994 genocide. Blommaert suggests that the sociolinguistic repertoire displayed by Joseph is indicative of *time*, not just of *space*; that it relates to the *history* of a region in the past two decades, not just to the region. On this view, what we are calling DLCs index full histories of peoples and of places.

8. Invoking the DLC construct reveals the 'quality' of multilingual societies by showing some communities or groups as being characterized by a large number of constellations and a wide variety of languages composing such constellations and showing other multilingual communities or groups to be made up of a large number of multilingual speakers but to involve fewer or less variously constituted constellations in circulation. An example of the first type of group would be the one of the authors' classes at the Trinity College which includes students with the following DLCs:

> German/French/English
> Polish/French/English
> Lithuanian/Russian/Polish/English
> Persian/Arabic/English
> Mandarin/Japanese/English
> Mandarin/Southern Min/English

An example of the second type of community type – with many multilinguals but a limited number of languages – would be the Åbo Akademi, the Swedish-speaking university in the Finnish city of Turku/Åbo, where both the staff and student body function according to context and purpose in Swedish, Finnish and English.

Theoretical and practical dimensions of deploying the construct of DLC

The main point underlying a decision to home in on DLCs rather than considering individuals' or communities' entire 'language repertoires' is that, as in any other domain, people do not need to use everything they know. In line with the principle of the least effort (Zipf 1949), in any given context they tend to select the languages which are vital for the management of their lives, and to shelve others which in the context are not of such cardinal importance. Let us consider some theoretical and practical dimensions of deploying the DLC construct.

Researching multilingualism through the prism of a DLC means considering whole sets of languages as units rather than focusing, one by one, on the specific languages used by given individuals or groups. To borrow the terms of complexity thinking, a DLC is an evolving, emergent whole which transcends its parts. Thus, the research focus shifts from the investigation of separate languages to the exploration of their constellations. Managing the constellation purview, taking into consideration all of each constellation's constituents simultaneously as the constellation evolves and functions, obviously differs from dealing with one language at a time. A systematic exploration of the concurrent use of several languages provides advantages in regard to tracing and documenting the uses of these languages. The study of DLCs is replete with opportunities to assemble in a single bank, in an organized, efficacious way, data on multiple languages associated with multiple populations in multiple situations.

Familiarity with specific DLCs makes it easier, moreover, to arrive at efficacious decisions relative to educational choices, political measures and community-oriented planning. For example, a language teaching pedagogy elaborated within the context of a DLC, and which takes account of real circumstances, experience and needs, is likely to lead to more motivated, faster, and less effortful learning. Let us take the example of a Polish linguist, who has native-like command of English, who is working in a university in Southern Texas, and who is currently learning Spanish because it is very present in her environment and therefore useful in her everyday life. A teaching/learning approach with a high probability of success can be devised in this context which makes use of her high degree of linguistic awareness (from her professional research), her familiarity (from Polish) with complex flectional morphology and her knowledge (from English) of thousands of words with Spanish cognates.

The efforts of those wishing to revitalize minority and heritage languages can be more clearly defined and measured in terms of DLC. We may say that their goal is that the language with which they are concerned first enters the DLC of as many individuals as possible and then enters the DLC(s) prevailing in an entire region or country. If this goal is not attained, the effects of their efforts will be regarded as disappointing. For example, the Irish language in the Republic of Ireland, despite decades of endeavours to revitalize it, is a constituent of the DLC of a relatively small proportion of the state's inhabitants; it remains for most a symbolically important but hardly used element in their linguistic repertoire. Catalan and Basque are undoubtedly more advanced in their progress towards figuring in the DLCs of Catalonia and the Basque Country respectively.

The concept of DLC is thus a useful tool for analyzing the state and process of multilingualism; it can be deployed to aid and clarify the identification and representation of language users, circumstances and languages at different stages of their relationships and development. DLCs may be seen as microcosms of the multilingual world order manifest at the level of the individual and the particular community. The DLC notion can also make a major contribution to optimizing practical responses – in terms of language policies and educational measures – to multilingualism.

Possible DLC-based research directions

Several promising research directions incorporating the DLC construct suggest themselves. Initial research might focus on the description of DLCs of multilingual populations; such a description which would serve as a knowledge base enabling various kinds of comparative studies and the establishment of DLC typologies. This in turn would have practical value in terms of informing language planning, language policy, the development of educational and familial models in multilingual settings, and the management of languages in communities.

At a societal level DLC-sharing populations may be mapped according to geography, religious affiliation, ethnicity, and educational or professional community. This kind of mapping could provide answers to questions such as the following. 'What DLCs are to be found in country X?' 'Are the DLCs associated with religious affiliation Y limited in number or widely varying?' 'What are the typical DLCs of ethnic group Z?' Such explorations could generate accounts of DLCs of the world, DLCs of individual continents and DLCs of particular countries, regions and communities. The DLCs of international and supranational populations may also be focused on – e.g. the DLCs of international student bodies of the major universities across the world or the DLCs of elite groups such as EU bureaucrats. Examining the DLCs of given cities is another possibility – can lead to the determination of typical constellations and how these reflect the current sociolinguistic situation and influence the political economic, social, cultural life of the cities in question and the profiles of the individuals using the DLCs concerned. Looking at the DLCs of ethnic groups may contribute to a wide spectrum of areas of inquiry – including, of course, migration studies.

Another starting point of investigation could be languages themselves. We may analyse a DLC according to the languages constituting it: the number of languages; the linguistic distance between the languages in question; the various functions of the different languages; and the levels of mastery of the constituent languages, in terms, for example, of communication skills and literacy. In addition, it would be of interest to examine attitudes towards the different component languages, the order in which they are acquired and relationships of dominance between them.

The investigation of DLCs could also focus on characteristics of their constituent languages. Researching DLCs which include religious languages and heritage languages, or languages which we may call emotionally charged for some of their speakers or for some of those who are addressed in them (see e.g. Pavlenko 2003; Schmid 2004), may yield valuable insights into identity issues regarding multilinguals.

Regarding DLCs including Languages of Wider Communication or super-central languages according to De Swaan's classification (2001), an illustrative example of such a language involved in many DLCs would be Russian. Investigating the DLC profiles of Russian users from Kazakhstan to Ireland would allow linguists, sociolinguists, educationalists and language policy-makers to arrive at informed conclusions as to the respective vitality of each language in DLCs including Russian, and could provide the basis for research-based contributions to the debate (often heated) about whether the Russian language will eventually die out within certain migrant communities and about the extent to which whether it will continue to occupy a stable position as one of the languages of a number of DLCs.

A particularly interesting case is that of languages closely connected to religion. Such as Hebrew, *Leshon HaKodesh*, 'the Holy Tongue'. Some Ultra-Orthodox Jews in Israel, where Hebrew is the official language of the state, insist on reserving Hebrew for the domain of the sacred, taking the view that Hebrew should be reserved for religious study and prayer only. They therefore speak Yiddish rather than Hebrew in their everyday life. By this, among other things, they contribute to the maintenance of Yiddish. Classical Koranic Arabic is used for religious occasions throughout the Moslem world; a closely related modern variety, Modern Standard Arabic, is used as a secular lingua franca among Arabs and is deployed generally in formal situations and in written discourse. Classical Arabic and Modern Standard Arabic both differ hugely from contemporary spoken varieties of 'demotic' Arabic. A DLC of an Arabic speaking Moslem may include Classical Koranic Arabic, Modern Standard Arabic and any of the vernacular varieties such as Iraqi Arabic, Moroccan Arabic or Algerian Arabic (see also Chapter 2). Other religious languages include Sanskrit in Hindu and Buddhist communities and Old Church Slavonic in Eastern Orthodox Christian communities of Slav heritage. Latin had the same role in the Roman Catholic Church until the time of the Second Vatican Council, but its role since then has been much attenuated. Such languages represent a spiritual heritage and may exert considerable influence on the identity of the user, even though real knowledge of such languages may be restricted to particular categories of persons and their communicative use may be limited.

It would be interesting to look for variations in DLCs that correlate with, for instance, age-group, mode of exposure (naturalistic versus formal), type and length of schooling. An example of an age-group correlation can be seen in respect of the DLC of the Russian-speaking community in Israel. The younger generation in this community has good skills (including oral skills) in Hebrew but often very poor or virtually non-existent writing skills in Russian. The older members of the same community with the same DLC display a converse picture:

they have very good writing skills in Russian, but often encounter problems with oral performance in Hebrew. A similar phenomenon of young Russian-speakers in Finland losing or failing to acquire writing skills in their native Russian while acquiring a full range of competencies in Finnish has been reported by Protassova (2004). In fact, this is a widespread pattern among migrant communities in 'submersive' multilingual situations, and seems to represent a danger for the survival of languages in which literacy skills are not supported (cf. Singleton & Ryan 2009 and see also Chapter 6).

Co-terms

Finally, it is important here to clarify differences and continuities among the terms *Dominant Language Constellation* (our own term), *dominance configuration,* as deployed by Fishman (1966) and *language constellation* in de Swaan's (2001) usage. In Fishman's understanding the word *dominance* refers to dominant languages, while in our term the word *dominant* refers to constellations. As we have explained, a DLC in our approach is a set of languages, functioning as an unit, which is the central, leading vehicle among all the languages known to the individual or present in the environment.

Let us now turn to the word *constellation* and examine its usage in de Swaan's *galactic model* (2001:4–6, 97). De Swan uses the word *constellation* in reference to several languages and also the word *galaxy* – in reference to the wider group of languages. De Swaan notes (2001:4) that the scheme of all world languages displays a strongly ordered, hierarchical pattern and to show this hierarchy he employs the metaphor of galaxy, where the 'peripheral languages grouped around the central language may be compared to moons circling a planet' (2001:4) and the position of 'supercentral' languages, those higher in the hierarchy, 'resembles that of so many suns surrounded by their planets, the central languages, which, in turn, are encircled by their respective satellites, the peripheral languages' (2001:5). This model is treated in more detail in Chapter 7, here we only wish to indicate the differences between the use of the term 'constellation' in De Swaan's model and in the concept of Dominant Language Constellation. For de Swaan, a language constellation refers to the totality of languages of the world or to the totality of languages that co-exist in a specific geographical area. Examples are the Chinese language constellation covering mainland China and Taiwan and including, among very many others, Putonghua (standardized Mandarin), Han and Zhuang, and the Indian constellation, including, according to de Swaan (2001:61–63), some eight hundred languages from the Dravidian and Indo-Aryan language families de Swaan's concept does include the notion of languages functioning together as a unit for an individual or a community.

In sum, our own concept of Dominant Language Constellation is applied to an ensemble of languages which in functional terms are closely connected, and which are treated as a constellation on the basis of the criterion that, operating together, they are vehicular for particular individuals or particular groups of people. On the other hand, our usage of *constellation* continues to make use of the image of the languages in the mind or in society being stars or planets which are further away from or closer to each other and are assembled in patterned configurations. For us the metaphor of constellation betokens a unit, an entity comprised of several elements (languages), which, as an emerging entity is more than its parts.

Concluding summary

In this chapter we have defined and illustrated the notion of *Dominant Language Constellation* (*DLC*) and discussed the role of such constellations of dominant languages in the new world dispensation. We have claimed that in modern times it is frequently a constellation of languages rather than a single language that meets the fundamental needs of language-driven cognition, communication and identification for individuals and communities. We have underlined that DLC is a concept that is specific to multilingualism, being inapplicable to a monolingual individuals or societies.

We have noted that, in our definition, DLC is related to, but is distinct from the concept and term *language repertoire*. We traced the origins of the language repertoire concept in research on monolingual situations, observing that its relevance to monolingualism is undiminished by its application to multilingual situations and that it represents a wider category than *DLC*; while having a descriptive usefulness in respect of multilingualism it is not, unlike the DLC concept, specifically or uniquely associated with multilingualism.

We have also sketched some significant DLCs of the contemporary world and explored their functioning and influence within societies. We have also explored the relationship of the DLC concept to the Fishman's concept of *dominance configuration* and De Swaan's concept of *constellation of languages*.

The DLC approach clearly needs refinement and further development. However, simply recognizing DLC as a point of departure for the investigation of multilingual populations already offers advantages. Such an optique allows us to see the concrete actualities behind the general theoretical understanding of the modern processes of globalization and localization. As a unit of investigation,

Dominant Language Constellation acts as a prism presenting the opportunity to consider the multiplicity of factors underlying an influencing multilingualism, thus pointing the way to a wider-ranging but at the same time a more detailed and systematic research approach.

CHAPTER 5

Multilinguality and personal development

Introductory

In this chapter we turn our attention to the individual aspect of multilingualism. We attempt to provide a broad-ranging treatment of the concept of multilinguality, going on to compare and contrast this conception of multilinguality with other conceptions of individual multilingualism to be found in the literature. We discuss some emerging tendencies regarding perspectives on individual multilingualism and also offer a thumbnail sketch of some widely cited models of multilingual acquisition and processing.

Individual multilingualism and societal factors

Individual multilingualism is to a great extent defined and conditioned by particular societal circumstances. Therefore, paradoxically but understandably, it is impossible to speak about individual multilingualism without referring to identity in close relation with societal issues (cf. Riley 2010: 376).

Ethnicity and nationality, intimately associated with an individual's origins, are in Europe the most frequent factors connecting language and identity. But in other parts of the world things may be different. Brann (1981: 3), discussing the context of Africa, specifically Nigeria, cautions against assuming too much regarding the above connection:

> The identity between language and ethnicity must ... not be taken for granted – however dear to the school of Humboldt and the European Romantics. There are many cases where ethnic groups live in symbiosis and are either bilingual, or ... one has adopted the language of its host, whilst retaining its ethnic identity. In Europe the example of the Normans in France and England comes to mind; in Africa the equally war-like FulBe have – in Nigeria – adopted Hausa as their second, but often as their only language. This is to say, that there is no one-to-one relationship between language and ethnicity, and that there is a constant shift of language use and language identity through migration, much enhanced by the current rural-urban movement in Africa, not dissimilar to that of Europe during

> the Industrial Revolution of 19th and of the post-Industrial revolution of the 20th
> centuries.
> (Brann 1981: 3)

Fishman reminds us of the need to examine "[h]ow and when the link between language and ethnicity comes about, its saliency and potency" (Fishman 1999: 3). He writes (*ibid.*):

> Although language has rarely been equated with the totality of ethnicity, it has in certain historical, regional and disciplinary contexts, been accorded priority within that totality. The last third of the twentieth century – often referred to as a time of "ethnic revival" – has often been witness to a renewed stress on language in various mobilizations of ethnicity throughout the world.

It is noteworthy that not only traditional groupings, but also 'horizontal' interest-related groups (Friedman 1999), be they local, national or global, may be connected via particular languages – groupings bringing together, for example, feminists, stamp collectors, ball-room dancers, electronic chess players, pizza-lovers, faith-healers, etc. etc.

Thus, a blogger on an Esperanto BBC webpage defended his choice to learn this artificial language as follows. The argument of his family and friends was that by speaking Esperanto he would be stuck with people he had nothing in common with. He responded with his personal characterization the people who make the choice for Esperanto: "[t]here is a particular type of person who wants to learn Esperanto. Usually people who are outgoing, interested in international affairs, social justice and travel."[1]

Terminology and concepts referring to individual aspects of multilingualism

As was stated in Chapter 1, we are here treating a *bilingual* as a particular case of a *multilingual*. The straightforward expression *individual multilingualism* is frequently used, both by experts in the field of multilingualism and by researchers who focus on other fields of knowledge, to denote the multilingual state of a person as opposed to the multilingualism of a community or a society. Individual multilingualism received a boost in attention when it rightly came to be seen as a relevant element in whole process of problematizing issues of identity.

---

1. <http://www.bbc.co.uk/languages/yoursay/language_and_identity/global_english/esperanto__easy_and_the_least_risks.shtml> (accessed December 1, 2011).

The term *linguistic identity* is paradoxical, as profiling an individual in these terms typically defines him/her as belonging to an entire community or entire communities, since it refers to the identification of an individual with a language (or languages) and the community of users of the language(s) in question. To a not inconsiderable extent the term's usage often has political connotations or significance. Often it is used as a 'shorthand' version of *ethnolinguistic identity*, which shows more explicitly the connection between language, identity and social-environmental norms. According to Tabouret-Keller (1998:315), "[t]he language spoken by somebody and his or her identity as a speaker of this language are inseparable". He claims (1998:317) that "[t]he link between language and identity is often so strong that a single feature of language use suffices to identify someone's membership in a given group". He goes on to comment (*ibid.*) as follows:

> … individual identity and social identity are mediated by language: Language features are the link which binds individual and social identities together. Language offers both the means of creating this link and that of expressing it. Such features imply the whole range of language use, from phonetic features to lexical units, syntactic structures, and personal names.

As an example Tabouret-Keller cites the case of a girl with a German name in France, who has to explain every time a new acquaintance asks her name that her mother was German. He also quotes in this connection (*ibid.*) a biblical illustration:

> On the battle-field after their victory over the people of Ephraïm, the Gileads applied a language-identity test to sort out friend and foe: All of the soldiers were asked to pronounce the word *shibboleth*; those who pronounced the first consonant as [ʃ] were friends, those who pronounced it [s] were enemies and therefore killed at once (Judges: XII.6). Hence a single phonemic feature may be sufficient to include or exclude somebody from any social group.

Linguistic identity, whether one wishes it or not, inevitably signals societal belonging and points to group commonalities rather than strictly individual characteristics. How then is one to distinguish the uniquely personal dimensions of identity which relate to the language one speaks but also to the other aspects of one's life?

Aronin & Ó Laoire (2004) have proposed the notion of *multilinguality*.[2] While a large component of the sense of *multilingualism*, like that of *bilingualism*, refers to situation or community, multilinguality refers more to the inner constructs of the individual language user. As opposed to the concept of *individual*

---

2. Bilinguality, in accordance with the view expressed earlier is a sub-case (maybe somewhat limited) of multilinguality. See Hamers & Blanc (1989, 2000) on bilinguality.

multilingualism, multilinguality goes well beyond being language-related, and in contrast to *linguistic identity* it is not limited to political or ethnic identification with any particular language group(s). Rather, multilinguality is seen as intertwined with many, if not all the aspects and resources of an individual.

Multilinguality

So what is multilinguality? Multilinguality is that which characterizes the individual multilingual, and it is noteworthy in this context that for any person language constitutes a major shaping influence and one of the most significant defining attributes. Aronin & Ó Laoire (2004: 17–18) have defined multilinguality as "... a personal characteristic that can be described as an individual *store of languages* at any level of proficiency including partial competence – incomplete fluency as well as metalinguistic awareness, learning strategies, opinions and preferences and passive or active knowledge of languages, language use and language learning/acquisition".

The languages of a multilingual – whether comprehensively mastered, or on the way to being acquired – function in interaction with each other, particular languages frequently having very specific roles. In the case of a sequential multilingual, his/her mother tongue will normally come into play, for example, in emotional, intimate situations and will typically be used for counting; studies, work, or travels may require the use of a different language; yet another may be used to communicate with wider family or the older generation. The precise configuration will vary from individual to individual, and the functions of a multilingual's languages may be re-assigned under the force of changing situations – growing confidence and ease in the use of a particular language, less frequent use of another language, intensive study of yet another, and so on.

Multilinguality, on this view, has to do with individual aspects of multilingualism in their entirety – taking a broad, holistic view of the multilingual individual. On the one hand, this perspective takes account of the social milieu as an important influence; on the other, it recognizes the importance of the cumulative affects on a person of emotional, psychological and linguistic aspects. In multilinguality the identity of a multilingual is seen *as a whole*, integrating sub-identities such as national identity, cultural identity, or gender identity, as well, of course as language profile.

The following definition of multilinguality emphasizes the connection between multilinguality and self:

> ... multilinguality is a facet of a self, activated and expressed through language
> and language-related phenomena, which influences the social and private life of
> an individual. Multilinguality is expressed through actions, perceptions, attitudes
> and abilities.   (Aronin & Ó Laoire 2005)

We see multilinguality as reflecting origins and ethnic belonging, political affiliations and environmental influences, reference groups, and individual development level and cognitive abilities. It is also defined as reflecting and embracing
emotions, attitudes, preferences, anxieties, and personality type. Multilinguality
is in addition deployed as a notion which is connected to such dimensions as idiosyncratic traits, embedded assumptions and individual abilities or disabilities,
personal response to the ambient culture(s) and self-image as a language-learner
and language-user. Multilinguality is comprised of linguistic and cognitive behaviour and its outcomes; it is connected to, *inter alia*, career choices, social stratification, the languages and milieu surrounding the individual, and upbringing. There
is interplay between multilinguality and affective states and attitudinal orientations, as well as social, familial and career activities and lifestyles. Social, educational, and psychological influences constantly modify personal multilingualities.
Thus, our suggestion is that multilinguality is brought into being by an interplay
of social and personal factors and that it displays itself through the entire range
of the physical, cognitive, cultural and social qualities and characteristics of an
individual (Aronin & Ó Laoire 2001).

Multilinguality is, on such a view, very personal; it includes idiosyncrasies
and peculiarities of communicators, legacies of historical events and family history, embedded assumptions, and individual learning disabilities and gifts. In this
perspective, each individual possesses his/her own multilinguality, which evolves
from all the above and from many other factors. It follows that language learning
and use in a multilingual person involves the interaction of a wide and continually changing spectrum of influences, including those arising from the mix of languages themselves – acquired at various stages and in various circumstances.

Characteristics of users of a multiplicity of languages

Research in multilingualism shows the bilingual to be not merely the sum of
two monolinguals (Grosjean 1985, 1992, 2010; Cook 1992, 1993, 2003a, 2010;
Ringbom 1987, 2007; Herdina & Jessner 2000b, 2002; Cenoz 2000; Kecskés & Papp
2000) Similarly, the user of more than two languages emerges from recent studies not as the sum of multiple monolinguals but rather as possessing very special
characteristics not found in monolinguals or indeed in bilinguals. Multilinguals

possess "a configuration of linguistic competences that is distinct from that of bilinguals and monolinguals competence" (Cenoz & Genesee 1998: 19). Cook (2001) on his website makes the following statement in respect of multilinguals (in which bilinguals are here subsumed):

> … a person who speaks multiple languages has a stereoscopic vision of the world from two or more perspectives, enabling them to be more flexible in their thinking, learn reading more easily. Multilinguals, therefore, are not restricted to a single world-view, but also have a better understanding that other outlooks are possible. Indeed, this has always been seen as one of the main educational advantages of language teaching.

There is a considerable consensus among researchers (cf. Jessner 2006; Hufeisen 2005; Kemp 2007; Aronin & Hufeisen 2009c; Cenoz, Hufeisen & Jessner 2001; Cenoz, Hufeisen & Jessner 2008) that users of more than two languages are especially favoured, that relative to bilinguals and monolinguals, they:

1. have larger overall linguistic repertoires and can participate in a wider range of language situations;
2. may possess cognitive advantages relating to a configuration of linguistic competences which is distinct from that observed in bilinguals and monolinguals;
3. may develop new language learning skills;
4. tend to use more learning strategies and to use such strategies more frequently, adding their own strategies to those suggested by their teachers;
5. seem to have enhanced metalinguistic awareness;
6. tend to be adept at the art of balancing their communicative requirements with their language resources, making appropriate use of appropriate languages;
7. appear to acquire greater sensitivity to socio-pragmatic aspects of communication, navigating confidently through complex environments;
8. are more responsive to both linguistic and non-linguistic factors in communicative situations;
9. have a greater array of identities, which are characterized by fluidity.

The data continuing to accumulate from research on tri- and more-linguals suggest that the effects of the experience of such individuals go well beyond the linguistic domain, affecting all the facets of a personality. Recently, there have been quite a number of studies devoted to the emotional aspect of languages (Dewaele 2004; Dewaele 2010a; Panayiotou 2004; Pavlenko 2005, 2006; Schmid 2004; Wieszbicka 1999).Originating from a comparison between emotion words and phrases across languages, these studies have spilled over into an examination of emotions and states accompanying and modifying language study and use. The questions under investigation in such studies are: How do multilinguals feel about their languages and how do they use them to communicate emotions in their languages. Do they choose specific languages from their repertoire to communicate specific emotions or do they have a favourite language in which to communicate emotions? How are emotion words and concepts represented in the bi- and multilingual lexicons? How are emotions involved in second and further language acquisition? Does language attrition relate to emotional states? Are some languages closer to a multilingual's heart then others? In which of a multilingual's languages do emotionally loaded phrases like 'I love you' and taboo and swear words have more impact – for the speaker and the listener.

The above having been said, it must certainly be conceded that a great deal more research is required before we can have real confidence in generalizations concerning qualitative differences between bilinguals and those whose functionality extends beyond two languages.

Models of multilingualism

The identity of the contemporary language user in relation to the languages he/she is involved with, his/her multilinguality in its multiple manifestations, is posited to be the 'X factor' that in the long run accounts for the speed, ease or difficulty and the outcome of second and subsequent language acquisition.

Models of multilingualism were developed on the basis of the realization that users of more than two languages seem to be different in many respects from bilinguals. They attempt to satisfy the need to understand the nature of third- and multiple language acquisition. Some of the models created to explain bilingualism are pertinent to multilingualism too but they typically fail to attend to the specifics of multilingualism. The number of multilingual models is still very limited. Most of the existing multilingualism models refer to the process of multiple language acquisition (Herdina & Jessner 2002; Hufeisen 1998, 2005; Green 1986, 1993; de Bot 1992, 2004). One model (Aronin & Ó Laoire 2004) referred to above in relation to the concept of multilinguality is more general and attempts to account for the whole identity of the multilingual, including the cognitive, societal, personal aspects.

Levelt's influence

A number of multilingual models have taken as their starting point Levelt's (1989) work on monolingual language processing, among them those of de Bot (1992) & Clyne (2003). Levelt's model (cf. also Jescheniak & Levelt 1994; for discussion see Singleton 1999: 106–109) represents language production as proceeding via modular steps, starting with the conceptualizer – which frames pre-verbal messages out of speech intentions, moving to the formulator – which is responsible for grammatical encoding, for accessing material from the lexicon and for the production of a phonetic plan, and terminating in the articulator – which then realizes the utterances in question.

De Bot (1992) attempts to apply Levelt's model beyond the monolingual domain. His discussion proceeds within Green's (1986) proposals regarding the activation and control of bilingual processing (see below), according to which bilinguals' languages are never switched off, whether or not selected for use, but remain available at different levels of activation (cf. Grosjean 1997). He introduces into the Levelt schema a language node monitoring and channelling information about the state of activation of languages at the individual's disposal and keeping under review the relationship between state of activation and selectedness for use/non-use. De Bot also addresses (de Bot & Schreuder 1993) the question of whether the conceptualizer can be language-independent in the light of the fact that "[l]anguages differ in the way in which they lexicalize the components of a given conceptual structure" (de Bot & Schreuder 1993: 194). More recently, De Bot has raised increasing numbers of questions concerning the possibility of modelling the psycholinguistics of multilinguality at present state of knowledge (see e.g. de Bot 2004) and has also begun to cast doubt on the very notion of the separateness or indeed separability of language systems (de Bot 2010; de Bot, Lowie & Verspoor 2007).

Clyne too refers to Levelt in his endeavour to integrate the sociolinguistic and the processing aspects of multilingualism (2003: 210–214). He focuses on what he calls *transversion* and on the *convergence* of language knowledge in multilingualism across languages. *Transversion* in Clyne's usage is applied to switches to another language that consist of material other than fixed expressions or compound nouns – a real 'crossing over' to the other language rather than merely an alternation between the languages. The term *convergence* in Clyne's work signifies the process by which one language comes to resemble another in various ways through transference. Clyne notes that multilinguals activate or de-activate their respective languages to different levels at different times in different circumstances. He also suggests that on some occasions they are careful to mark differentiation between their languages while on others they are more relaxed about various kinds of transference. The factors he sees as operative in these different situations include both psycholinguistic and sociolinguistic dimensions. He claims, moreover, that similar phenomena may occur in a monolingual context, for example as style shifts. His concluding remarks on this issue acknowledge that existing processing models, including Levelt's in particular, may shed some light on such matters but are also challenged by them. Specifically, his view is that any implication in existing models of a very neat and straightforward separation between languages in the mind would seem to be called into question by the data of multilingualism.

Activation/inhibition

As noted above Green (1986, 1993) takes the view, on the basis of his research into code-switching and his work on bilingual aphasics, that users of more than one language do not have any kind of 'on-off' switch for the languages at their disposal but that both or all their languages, at least beyond a certain level of proficiency and recency of use, remain constantly activated in parallel, although to different levels depending on circumstances. That is to say, in a given situation a specific language will be selected for active use, and will engage the mechanisms of speech processing. Any other language or other languages which are functional and operational in the multilingual's repertoire will, on this view, not be 'turned off' even though they have not been chosen for communication purposes, but will in some sense 'shadow' the selected language at a lower degree of activation.

In a subsequent development of his perspective, Green (1998) introduces the notion of inhibitory control (IC), embodying the principle that there are multiple levels of control in multilingual processing. A goal of the IC model is to account for the multilingual's ability to perform a required task in the required language. In this approach the suggestion is that before production of speech is implemented, a conceptual representation of the task in hand is generated – a language task schema, which inhibits potential competitors for production at the lemma level, making use in this connection of their language tags, which identify them as not fitted for the language task in question. This model predicts that switching between languages will take time "(1) because it involves a change in language schema for a given task, and (2) because any change of language involves overcoming the inhibition of the previous language tags" (Green 1998:73).

Thus, according to Green's model the multilingual's use of one of his/her languages involves inhibitory control over the non-target language. On this view, any competing language scheme must be inhibited in the selection of a target language, so that switching between languages will require extra cognitive capacity. Green suggests that the inhibitory mechanism underlying lexico-semantic control is a general cognitive mechanism and not specific to language processing. To be noted is that the introduction of the concept of inhibitory control is concerned with operations which lower the levels of activation of the inhibited language; it does not in any sense rehabilitate the previously discarded 'on-off' switch idea.

Language mode

Staying with the notion of levels of activation, we now turn to Grosjean's proposals regarding 'language mode', which he originally applied specifically to bilinguals, but whose application clearly extends to the processing of more than two languages. *Mode* in this context is taken to denote the "state of activation of the bilingual's languages and language processing mechanisms at a certain point in time" (Grosjean 2001:2). Grosjean (2010:39–50) talks about the kinds of questions the bilingual needs to ask him/herself in this connection: which language to use and whether or not the other language should be brought in at all. He gives (2010:40–41) the following example from his own life to illustrate the notion of monolingual language mode:

> When my wife speaks to her aunt, for example, she chooses French as the base language and de-activates her English because she knows that her aunt would not understand her if she brought English into their conversation. She is therefore in a monolingual language mode.

He contrasts this (p. 41) with a situation where a bilingual is talking to another bilingual sharing the same languages and feels comfortable bringing the other language into the interaction with the interlocutor in question. In such an instance Grosjean would talk about bilingual language mode.

Obviously, it is relatively straightforward to apply the mode perspective to other varieties of multilingualism, and Grosjean (2010:43–44) has no hesitation in doing so. A trilingual, for instance, depending on his/her interlocutor's relationship with his/her languages, may, he says, operate in monolingual mode, bilingual mode or even trilingual mode. Thus, with someone who knows the same three languages a particular trilingual does, and with whom he/she feels comfortable bringing in the other languages, he/she would tend to operate in a trilingual language mode; similarly with people who use four or more languages in everyday life. There is always a dominant language in his scheme.

Factors involved in multilingual acquisition

Hufeisen (1998, 2005, 2010; Hufeisen & Marx 2007) proposes that new factors come into play as the learning of new languages progresses and unfolds, and that these have an impact on the language learning process.

The Factor Model is influential in relation to understanding the process of multiple language acquisition. It emphasizes the distinction between learning an L2 and an L3. Whereas the learner of an L2 is n absolute novice in regard to

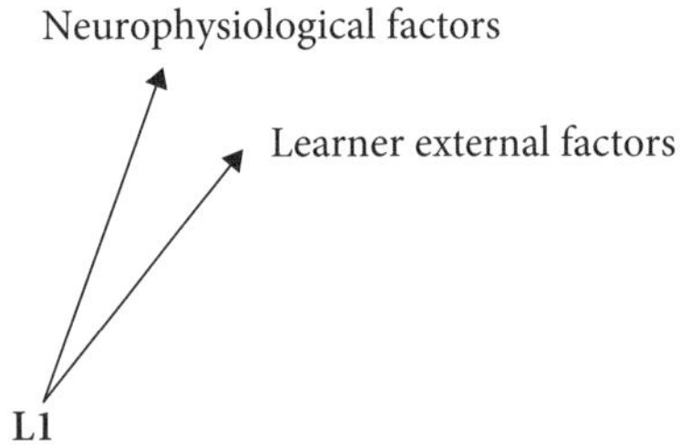

Figure 1. Learning the first language

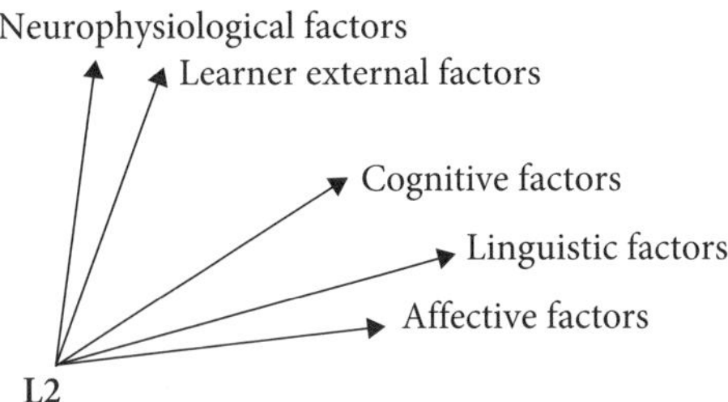

Figure 2. Learning an L2

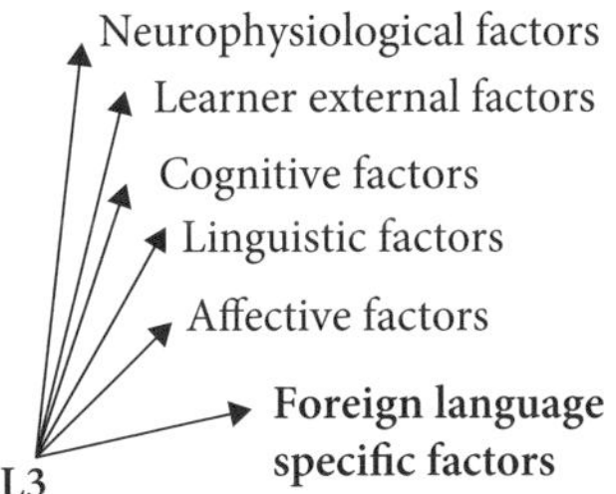

Figure 3. Learning an L3 (based on Hufeisen 2010)

additional language learning, in the case of an L3 acquirer, he/she has already had the experience of learning a first additional language, the L2 (cf. Figures 1 and 2). Figure 3 illustrates the acquisition of an L3 (or L4, L5 … Ln). The Linguistic Factor is here represented as 'upgraded', expanding to add L2 knowledge and skills to L1 knowledge and skills, but the principal addition in this figure is that of the Foreign Language Specific Factor. This factor is seen as subsuming individual foreign language learning experience, ability to compare features of L2 and L3, and ability to engage in L2-L3 transfer (and vice versa) and to make L2-L3 interlingual connections (again and vice versa). Thus the L2 learner and the L3 learner are not the same. Unlike the L2 learner, the L3 learner has a breadth of experience from his/her engagement with the L2 that can be called up and re-activated in the context of encounters with further languages. Unlike the novice L2 language learner, the L3 learner has consciously or unconsciously developed certain approaches to language learning and specific language learning strategies. These Foreign Language Specific factors are perceived in the model as highly important in getting to grips with an L3. The L2 in a way functions as a bridge to learning the L3. With each new language learnt, as well as with the passage of time, the previously established elements can be seen as undergoing change; for example, abilities may improve or disimprove with age or effort; motivation may be observed to grow or diminish under the impact of different experiences at different periods of life. All of this is taken to testify to the complex and dynamic nature of multilingualism, but Hufeisen's Factor Model also embraces stability in one respect – in its claim that learning further languages beyond the L3 is not essentially different from learning the L3, since only one new factor is involved in acquiring further additional languages: the Foreign Language Specific Factor.

According to this perspective the fundamental determinants at the outset of language acquisition are the human language faculty and the nature of environmental input. Hufeisen refers in her subsequent discussion to the acquisition of the first foreign language – in cases where an additional language is acquired non-simultaneously with the first language. In such instances, she says, further factors come into play, learner-internal factors as well as external environmental factors. She makes mention in this connection of affective factors, such as motivation, anxiety and attitudes, and cognitive factors, such as language awareness and learning awareness. She cites (2005:37) the case of an English-speaking learner who stated that learning her first foreign language helped her to accept that in other languages things can be different from the way they are in her mother tongue, and that when beginning her second foreign language she no longer had to overcome this challenge.

Hufeisen goes on to claim that the learning of further additional languages differs qualitatively from learning the first foreign language. She points to individual learner factors such as life and learning experiences, but also to the entry into the picture of specific experiences relating to learning foreign languages and to the application of learning and communication strategies. She argues that the deployment of foreign language-specific factors in subsequent language learning differentiates such subsequent language learning from what preceded it. She quotes in this connection (2005:38) a brief but revealing comment from a learner with German as his first language who already had foreign language learning experience: 'Wenn ich 'ne neue Sprache anfange, weiss ich schon was auf mich zukommt' ('When I begin a new language I know what I'm in for' – *our translation*).

The dynamic model of multilingualism

A highly influential model of multilingualism is Herdina & Jessner's (2002) approach inspired by dynamic systems theory. This model is in tune with holism of Cook's notion of multicompetence (discussed in Chapter 2) and of Grosjean's language mode conception (see above). Herdina & Jessner go further, however, in their emphasis on the dynamic nature of multilingualism, applying "dynamic systems theory (DST), also known as chaos theory or complexity theory, to the study of multilingual development, whose changing nature calls for a new thinking metaphor" (Jessner 2008:25). Their discussion makes reference to a parallel evolution of psycholinguistic thinking, making mention of DST insights regarding interactions of subsystems in complex systems and of emergentist models of language acquisition.

Jessner sums up the dynamic model of multilingualism (DMM) account as follows:

> According to DMM, the development of a multilingual system changes over time, and is non-linear, reversible – resulting in language attrition or loss – and complex. It is also highly variable since it depends on social, psycholinguistic and individual factors, apart from the different forms of contexts in which language takes place... The model ... provides a scientific means of predicting multilingual development on the basis of factors found to be involved...   (Jessner 2008:25)

Central to the DMM perspective is the assumption of the openness and interdependence rather than autonomy or modularity of psycholinguistic systems. Stability in this context is seen as related to language maintenance in interaction with language choice as determined by the multilingual's perception of communicative needs in a given place at a given time. Multilingual proficiency is defined as the dynamic interplay between various psycholinguistic systems, cross-linguistic interactions and what Jessner calls the M(ultilingualism)-factor. The M-factor refers to the emergent property deriving from those qualities that distinguish multilinguals from monolinguals – including, for example, particular degrees and modes of metalinguistic and metacognitive awareness.

An ecological perspective

Aronin & Ó Laoire (2004) adopt an ecological perspective on multilinguality (see above) which goes beyond an equation between multilinguality and individual multilingualism. For them, whereas individual multilingualism is definable in terms of the processes and results of acquiring more than two languages, multilinguality is concerned with the entire profile of the user of multiple languages for communicative purposes in relation to the social and sociolinguistic environment as well those aspects of the situation which are physical, physiological, psychological and psycholinguistic.

They comment (2004:18–19) as follows:

> Each individual possesses his/her own multilinguality, which depends on a set or sets of languages ..., levels of mastery of each language, etc. ... Multilinguality ... includes cognitive and linguistic abilities, potential to gain knowledge, self-image as a language learner and language-learner preferences, and the tangible impact of the cultural context.

They follow Jessner in seeing multilinguality in terms of modifications occurring and interacting simultaneously through the mix of language systems acquired at various stages, and suggest (p. 20) that these "constitute a kind of ecosystem or biosystem". They go on to claim (p. 25) that offering an interpretation of the notion of multilinguality in terms of an ecological unity "paves the way for new explorations in multilingual and third language acquisition contexts". These might be investigations into the nature of multilinguality and might consider the fitting of the new understanding into the practice of teaching and tertiary learning languages.

Third language acquisition and tertiary didactics

Tertiary didactics (Hufeisen & Neuner 2004) takes an approach which explicitly differentiates between L2 and L3 acquisition. Recognizing the specific nature and needs of the L3 and L3+ learners, the foundations of tertiary didactics are built on a respect for learners' multilinguality and on the axiom that "[w]hen several languages are learned, the teacher does not begin 'at zero' in each case, but rather the existing language possession is continually extended by each new language" (Neuner 2004: 16).

Migrants represent, in this context, a category of language learners with multiple subcategories. Walker (2006), for example, in her study of multilingual migrants who use various minority languages in addition to English in Aotearoa (New Zealand), emphasizes "…the complex interconnections between cognitive, sociolinguistic and social-psychological dimensions associated with language learning" (Walker 2006: 1). Walker concludes that investigations of already bilingual migrants as language learners who are engaged in the process of renegotiating their identity need to be recognized as carrying implications for language learning pedagogy. From this perspective additional language learning and teaching methods and their outcome relate to particular learner characteristics, in other words, specific individual differences – including, in particular, numbers of languages already known.

Individual differences in multilinguals

Factors leading to individual differences

The topic of individual differences in second language acquisition has been dealt with by a range of disciplines, among them cognitive psychology and applied linguistics (cf. Segalowitz 1997). The focal points in individual differences include age, often considered in the context of debate around the Critical Period Hypothesis (see e.g. Muñoz & Singleton 2011; Singleton & Ryan 2004), learners' cognitive abilities (see e.g. Ackerman 1988, 1989), and motivation (see e.g. Gardner 2006; Dörnyei & Ushioda 2009).

Ellis (1994) directs attention to three large classes of variables that may be implicated in determining individual differences in second language acquisition: learner differences, learner strategies and performance outcomes. In his 1997 book he deals with learner characteristics seen as psychological dimensions as opposed to social dimensions (which include conditions of learning). Lightbown & Spada (2006) include among learner differences intelligence, aptitude, learning styles, personality, motivation and attitudes, identity and ethnic group affiliation, learner beliefs, and age factors. To be noted is that writers on this topic consistently make mention of the difficulties and challenges faced by researchers seeking to explore the relationship between individual learner characteristics and second language learning.

De Houwer (2009) in addressing bilingual first language acquisition, indicates that a variety of factors are likely to have an impact on differences in multilingual development, including the beliefs and attitudes children encounter in parents, caretakers and the environment generally, and especially diversity in the amount of input received in each language and specific input properties such as individual speech styles or 'local influences' (p. 175).

Research on individual differences in mono- and bilinguals are by no means undermined by more recent excursions into individual differences among users of more than two languages. Such language users display a similarly wide range of individual variation – in regard to the languages at their command, their proficiency levels in each of their languages, the environments and configurations in which their language skills are deployed, and consequently their life trajectories (cf. Todeva & Cenoz 2009; Lamarre & Dagenais 2004; Hui-chi Lee 2004; Adegbija 2004; Pattanayak 1990; Kachru, Kachru & Sridhar 2008; Turell 2001; Pavlenko 2008).

Complexity and diversity with reference to multilingual individuals

Researchers looking at diversity and complexity with respect to multilingual individuals increasingly make use of the perspectives and methods of complexity thinking (cf. Aronin & Hufeisen 2009b; Aronin & Singleton 2008b). Indeed, complexity thinkers Bossomaier & Green (1998:9) might have been referring specifically to the manifoldness of multilingual individuals and the diversity of their

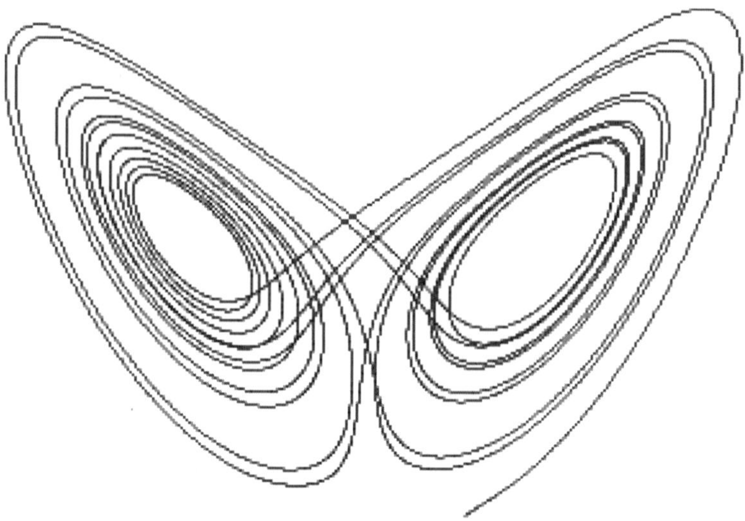

Figure 4. Graphic model of Lorenz's Butterfly[3]

situations (physical, geographical and societal) when they wrote: "[c]omplexity is exciting because, while the components may be trivial, their interaction often generates wild and unpredictable behavior" (Bossomaier & Green 1998:9).

A single feature of the language exposure experience – such as, among myriad other possibilities, the fortuitous presence in the environment of a relative speaking a specific language, or a chance encounter with a film that sparks or enhances interest in a particular language – may result in significant diversions from a given expected outcome. A comparison may be made with the 'butterfly effect' modelled by Lorenz – that is, noticeable changes occasioned by the infinitesimally tiny effect of a butterfly landing. The extreme sensitivity to initial conditions of chaotic systems means that the very slightest change in those conditions can produce radically different results (see Figure 4).

This is actually an everyday observation made by teachers and parents, who see widely varying outcomes of language teaching among pupils of the same age, the same culture and the same social class, starting at the same time at the same school in the same class.

Different outcomes would most probably have ensued had Ronjat (1913 – cf. Chapter 2) not met the person who advised him to apply the *une personne-une langue* ('one person-one language') strategy – the French linguist Grammont – or would most certainly have ensued if he had married a woman with not German as her mother tongue but Udmurt. Would he in this latter circumstance have reared

---

3.   The figure is taken from <http://www.zeuscat.com/andrew/chaos/lorenz.html>.

Louis as bilingual in both languages despite the fact that one of them would not have been a language of wider communication? Or what might have changed had Leopold chosen a strategy other than the 'one person-one language' strategy for the upbringing of his daughter Hildegard, or if she had visited Germany earlier or later in her life? Or let us take the case of the bilingual German-Spanish development of a Peruvian child described by Zierer (1977). This child's parents decided that the child should become bilingual in German and Spanish before going to school. They came to the conclusion that the best way to do this was to start with German, the weaker language in Peru, and to delay the learning of Spanish for at least two years. To make this approach as successful as possible, they spoke German to each other and to the child, found him some German-speaking play-mates, and went so far as to ask the child's Peruvian grandmother **not** to speak to him in Spanish. How would the result have been different if the child's Peruvian grandmother had been less co-operative towards her grandchild's parents' ideas of education?

Dominant Language Constellations, individual repertoires and personal life trajectories: Emerging tendencies

Life trajectories are also subject to complexity laws, and languages, with their cru-cial role in contemporary societies can have a major influence on people's routes through life. A good illustration of how early differences can lead to larger conse-quences is offered by the particularities of the childhood experience of the much-revered founder of the sociology of language, Joshua Fishman, as related by him in an autobiographical article.

> I grew up in Philadelphia, a very WASP dominated town at the time, the elder child of Yiddish speaking immigrants from Czarist Russia. The neighborhoods in which I lived, up to the time of my leaving in 1948 for graduate work in Co-lumbia University, were all middle-class Jewish neighborhoods populated largely by Yiddish speaking parents and grandparents, on the one hand, and by their proudly and demonstratively Yiddish-ignorant children and grandchildren, on the other hand. This was a rather typical sociolinguistic setting for that time and the only distinctive aspect of it was the fact that my parents were conscious and conscientious Yiddish language activists and that their children, my younger sis-ter Rukhl and I, happily and eagerly followed in their footsteps. In all truth there were a few other 'Yiddishists' like my parents, both in Philadelphia as a whole and even in our own immediate neighborhood, and there were even also a few other young people, like my sister and I, who willingly dreamed and pursued the im-possible dream of Yiddish language maintenance among the younger generation.

> Nevertheless, this was a relatively atypical preoccupation even in the immigrant generation and doubly so among the second generation. Atypical too, the overriding seriousness with which the defense and propagation of Yiddish were pursued per se.
>
> (Fishman, in Hornberger & Pütz 2006: 29–30)

Any factor or group of factors referring to identity (education, age, environment, etc.) impacts on the distinctness of multilinguality. Todeva & Cenoz's recent (2009) collection of accounts retails the life trajectories and what we would call here multilingualities of a number of highly educated multilinguals. De Bot & Makoni (2005) explore in depth yet another dimension of the variety of multilingualities emerging from the interplay of language and identity, this time homing in on the age of the speakers. It is clear, for example, that younger migrants may change their linguistico-cultural identities and affiliations on the basis of particular kinds of experience in school and under the influence of peer-interaction in a specific language or specific languages; in older migrants such shifts are rarer but may occur under the impact of, for instance, powerful affective factors (see, for example, Muñoz & Singleton 2011).

We have already alluded (see Chapter 4) to the diversity of outcomes relating to different Dominant Language Constellations (DLCs), which may be more or less advantageous for different purposes. The economic aspect of language knowledge (Coulmas 1992; Coulmas, Backhaus & Shikama 2002) is accepted to be a factor in stratifying populations, some groups being favoured in this respect others not. It is common knowledge, for instance, that knowing English allows one to be eligible for many more jobs than are available to those with no knowledge of this language, and that, more broadly one's employment prospects are enhanced by proficiency in languages of wider communication and locally important, regional languages. A range of opportunities clearly flow from knowing the 'right language' in the right time and place. Grin (1999: 20–21) shows that linguistic attributes have a significant impact on people's earned income. Recently, a further trend is gaining momentum in some contexts, that is the growth of employment benefits accruing from having knowledge of particular minority languages, especially if such knowledge is in addition to skills in a language of wider communication. (Valuing *All* Languages in Europe' ECML 2007) <http://archive.ecml.at/mtp2/publications/Valeur-report-E.pdf>) It is also true, in other words, that command of the 'right' **constellation** of languages in the right time and place can constitute a career advantage.

We quote below a story that illustrates how an individual's interaction with specific aspects of particular languages can lead to major identity modification. The story, which appeared in *LA Times,* is from the pen of the Korean-born reporter Connie Kang. It refers to a shift which does not come easily to very many multilinguals. She here describes her and others' experiences with the English pronoun *you*:

> *You* was an ally that empowered me.
>
> It freed me from the encumbrances of my mother tongue, which is one of the world's most complicated and nuanced languages, laden with honorifics. *You* pushed me out of the confines of Confucian-steeped, hierarchal Korean language into a world of egalitarian impulses…
>
> Korean has no fewer than six speech levels – each with a unique set of verb endings to indicate the degree of formality, ranging from extremely polite to actively impolite – and many gradations in between…
>
> "*You* represents the essence of democracy," said attorney Tong S. Suhr, a community leader. "*You* liberates us from that [Korean] caste system, and it makes life so much easier."
>
> Korean-born Kay S. Duncan, director of production with Jarrow Formulas in West Hollywood, says *you* helped transform her from a shy Asian woman who preferred to sit in the back of the room to an assertive executive equal to those around her.
>
> "You can say, '*You* did this, or *you* did that,' even if you're addressing the CEO of your company," Duncan said.
>
> By contrast, Ho-min Sohn, professor of Korean linguistics at the University of Hawaii at Manoa, says he has never felt at home with this three-letter word.
>
> Sohn, who came to the U.S. in 1965 from South Korea to work on a doctorate in linguistics, managed to get his degree without once using *you* when addressing his professors. It seemed so out of place for a student to claim equality with his professor.
>
> (Posted July 28, 2006 <http://www.languagehat.com/archives/002431.php>)

We can speak of several currently observable trends referring to identity and in particular to multilinguality. Following a growth in societal awareness of and interest in multilingualism (see Chapter 2) recent decades have seen an increase in the conscious manipulation of language assets both on the part of individuals and on the part of institutions and organizations. Attention has been paid to lost language skills and potential language skills, and to ways of ways of re-vigorating or acquiring such skills and then using them to advantage. Today people are freer to move around the globe, between regions, countries and continents; generally, Many languages of the world, especially those in the public eye (perhaps being revitalized under the impetus of national or ethnic feelings), are more accessible, and learning opportunities and materials are more available; there are fewer obstacles in the way of those wishing to add a new language or language skill to their language repertoire.

Moreover, language materials now give more attention to the variety and specificity of identities and linguistic needs. For example, in recent years phrase books have been published for gay individuals wishing to travel to other countries and to pursue their life-style in many languages (Barrett 2003). The languages covered in the books vary, but they all include French, German, Spanish, Italian and either Iberian or Brazilian Portuguese; some also include Czech or Dutch (Barrett 2003:545). The publication of such books assuming very specific language needs for specific groups of population in its turn, supports and legitimates identity, including sexual identity.

Identity facets associated with different languages may be used in fusion, may be separated in time and function, or may be deployed in such a way as to complement each other. An illustration of this point comes from the case of Tèo Ñòan (32) and Tòan Phầm (31), two Vietnamese male immigrants in Los Angeles in low-waged employment. Being 'non-marriageable' within their immigrant community, they went back to Vietnam to seek wives. The author of the article relating the narratives of the two men notes that members of the Vietnamese diaspora in America exploit the potential of global migration to convert their relatively low status in the First World to relatively high status when they visit Vietnam. Converting their status across transnational fields, men render themselves 'marriageable', thus 'achieving' masculinity and valorizing their self-worth (Hung Cam Thai 2005). But what principally emerges from this story in relation to the present discussion is that living in America and working hard for low wages, and then as a consequence having more purchasing power in Vietnam than most citizens of that country, is enabled by knowledge of English.

It is worth, finally, highlighting the fact that mobility and the permeability of borders in the present era mean that that contemporary multilingual identities are often in a less than straightforward relationship with ethnicity or place of origin. We have already discussed in Chapter 4 the case of Joseph (as described by Blommaert 2009), whose linguistic repertoire does not seem strictly to flow from his origins.

Concluding summary

Individual multilingualism is a traditional area of interest not only in the field of multilingualism, but across the whole spectrum of research and practice relating to the learning and teaching of additional languages. We have noted in this chapter that individual multilingualism is, on the one hand, very closely interconnected with and dependant on societal multilingualism and, on the other hand, a very special aspect of multilingualism, and that recent decades have brought new developments and thinking in respect of individual multilingual acquisition and use. We have pointed out that multilingual identity is very often in a less than straightforward relationship with ethnicity or place of origin.

We have made use here of the concept of *multilinguality*, which in our conception emphasizes the relationship between multilingualism and the unique, manifold and dynamic traits of personality. Multilinguality, on this definition, is a condition, a means and a measure of personal development, be it in cognitive, emotional, or career terms.

We have also referred to the fact that the personal life trajectories are more than ever bound up with the languages one knows or experiences at all kinds of levels. Awareness of this fact pervades popular culture in many societies and is a component of global ways of seeing the world. Moreover, we have suggested that there is nowadays increased conscious manipulation of language assets, both those that are available and those that are potentially acquirable or re-acquirable. We have also briefly explored identity in the perspective of multilinguality, making mention of ways in which there may be an interplay between multilinguality and such processes in the individual as internationalizing his/her life-style or valorizing his/her self-worth.

CHAPTER 6

Language development in multilingual conditions

Language development under bilingual and multilingual conditions

In this chapter we explore language development under bilingual and multilingual conditions. A number of the issues dealt with here are also touched on in other chapters – notably Chapters 1, 2, 5 and 8. We begin our exploration of multiple language acquisition by considering the kinds of situations where a child grows up with more than one language at his/her disposal; after this we take a brief look at the issue of the Critical Period Hypothesis in the context of sequential multilinguality; we then focus on particularities of the process of acquiring two or more languages; we go on to explore the extent to which the languages at a bi-/multilingual's disposal are integrated or separate; and finally we evaluate the advantages and disadvantages of bi-/multilinguality.

The contexts of multilingual language development

Given the facts – explored in earlier chapters – about the extent of multilingualism in the world, it is obvious that a very high proportion of children are inevitably exposed to more than one language from their earliest years. One obvious example of the kind of situation that can occur, given the ease with which people move from country to country these days, is where a person from language background x becomes the partner of a person from language background y. If such a couple has children, these may be surrounded by both language x and language y from the very beginning of their lives (assuming that both partners wish to continue using their respective languages). This situation is further complicated if the partners in question happen to be living in a country where the dominant language is z. In this kind of instance the children may grow up with competence in languages x, y and z. The family of the applied linguist Philip Riley exemplifies this latter kind of situation. His children always interacted with their mother in Swedish (a Swedish-speaking Finn); they always spoke English with their father, (an Englishman); and throughout their childhood they always communicated with their neighbourhood friends in French (since they were living in Nancy, in France at the time). The result is that as adults they are now trilingual.

In multilingual countries such instances are especially common. Of course, as Clyne (1997) points out, one has to distinguish between 'official' and 'de facto' multilingualism.

> For instance, Switzerland is an officially multilingual nation … but there, multilingualism is based on a territorial principle. While public documents for the entire nation are in French, German and Italian, most people grow up monolingually in a canton which typically has one official language. (Clyne 1997: 301)

It is worth noting that this description of Switzerland is somewhat oversimplified. For example, it leaves out of account the fact that in the 'German' cantons virtually everyone grows up bilingual – i.e. with a command of both Standard German and some variety of Swiss German (*Schwyzertüütsch*), which is as different from Standard German as Dutch is. Clyne's 'de facto' multilingual societies are those where "the same languages are generally used by the same people" but where "the various languages have differing functions" (Clyne 1997: 302). He cites (*ibid.*) the case of Paraguay, where "[a]lmost the entire population … employs Guaraní as the vernacular … and Spanish as the language of the more formal or official domains". He also refers (*ibid.*) to Luxembourg, where French and German more or less complement each other in different official domains, and Letzebuergesch is the language of everyday interaction (although he notes that in recent times Letzebuergesch has come to have the potential also to be used in official situations).

A further case mentioned by Clyne (*ibid.*) is that of Singapore, where Standard English, Mandarin, Standard Malay and Tamil are used for official purposes, where Singapore English is used in medium-level communication, and where Hokkien, Cantonese, varieties of Malay, or an Indian language other than Tamil are used in everyday domains. In a discussion of Singapore's multilingualism Kong (1996) cites the humorous Singaporese song *Mustapha*, which, reflecting the intermingling of languages and cultures in Singapore, draws – in the space of a single verse – on a variety of local languages (English, Mandarin, Malay and Tamil) as well as a foreign language (French):

> *Cherie je t'aime, cherie je t'adore* (French)
> My darling I love you a lot more than you know (English)
>
> *Cherie je t'aime, cherie je t'adore* (French)
> My darling I love you a lot more than you know (English)
>
> Oh Mustapha, Oh Mustapha
> *Yen Kathalan* (Tamil) my Mr Mustapha (English)

> *Sayang, saying* (Malay) *na chew sher wo ai ni* (Mandarin)
> Will you, will you fall in love with me (English)

Clearly, the occasions for exposure to and acquisition of multiple languages from early childhood in environments such as these are very numerous. Within different multilingual families different practices may obtain in regard to the distribution of language use. Probably the most widely cited principle in connection with the bilingual rearing is that of 'one person, one language' (Ronjat 1913 – see above, Chapter 2) – where each parent consistently interacts with the children in his/her L1. Another possibility is based on a distinction between the language of the home and the language of the outside community; thus, both parents may interact with the children in the 'home' language, while they interact with their friends and perhaps with each other in the 'outside' language (cf. e.g. Baker 1988).

Other possibilities also exist. Thus, in many multilingual households family members switch and mix languages seemingly without regard for any kind of consistent strategy (see e.g. Goodz 1994; Ng & He 2004). It is unclear what the precise effects of such switching and mixing may be, but Goodz (1994) claims that confusion between languages in such circumstances may be minimized by the fact that prelinguistic infants distinguish between languages on the basis of the prosody of each language – i.e. intonation, stress, and rhythm. He suggests that infants hear each language as a different melody and that different languages may be as distinct for young children as different songs. We return to the issue of separation/intergration of languages later in this chapter and in Chapter 8.

Children can also be brought to a state of multilinguality through formal education – thus, sequentially. How successful formal instruction is in this enterprise will depend on a range of factors – societal attitudes, the amount of exposure to additional language(s) involved, the appropriateness of the pedagogy and materials deployed, the competence and motivation of the teachers, and so on (cf. Singleton & Ryan 2004: Chapter 6). In the Republic of Ireland, for example, the exposure of children to instruction in Irish from age four is not generally seen as a success in bringing about a bilingual situation partly because of unfavourable elements in areas such as the above (cf. e.g. Singleton 2007b; Singleton & Ryan 2004: Chapter 6). The criteria one applies when designating a person or bilingual or multilingual are, of course, also relevant here (see above, Chapter 1). More successful, it seems, are the efforts made to effect a 'reverse language shift' in the Basque Country (see e.g. Cenoz 1998), where Spanish and Basque are both official languages, with Spanish markedly dominant. Thanks to an array of educational provisions promoting Basque, there has been a remarkable increase in Basque speakers in recent years, to the extent that around 40% of children between 5 and 14 years of age are now bilingual in Basque and Spanish. Moreover, English is also now available to school pupils in the Basque country from kindergarten onwards, although the result of this dimension of early education in the Basque country remains to be fully evaluated.

Simultaneous and sequential multilingual development and outcomes

The dividing line between *simultaneous* multilingual development – where two or more languages are acquired from infancy – and *successive* or *sequential* multilingual development – where additional languages are added when the first is already to some extent established – has sometimes been set at a particular age. Thus, for example, Paradis (2008) defines simultaneity in terms of exposure to the languages in question from birth or very early infancy, and sequentiality in terms of onset after age 3. Baker (2006: 97), on the other hand, takes the line that "[t]here are no exact boundaries between simultaneous and sequential bilingualism".

An issue that frequently arises in relation to sequential multilinguality is whether the age at which exposure to a given language begins is a (or indeed *the*) determinant of the level of ultimate attainment in the language in question. One widely cited perspective in this area has its origins in the Critical Period Hypothesis (see e.g. Hyltenstam & Abrahamsson 2000; for a contrary view see Muñoz & Singleton 2011; Singleton & Leśniewska in press; Singleton & Muñoz 2011), which postulates that there is a biologically programmed critical period for language acquisition, which closes abruptly at a particular maturational point (set at different ages by different researchers). Researchers favouring some version or other of the Critical Period Hypothesis claimed that unless exposure to a given language begins before the offset point of the critical period, proficiency in that language will never be identical to that manifested by those whose exposure began at birth. A variant of this claim is that different areas of language (phonology, syntax, lexicon, etc.) have different critical ages associated with them (see e.g. Singleton 2005).

The claim that sequential multilinguals who begin to be exposed to one or more of their languages subsequent to some purported critical age are incapable of becoming native-like in the late-begun language(s) has been called into question by studies which show late multilinguals performing at native-speaker levels (see e.g. Birdsong 1992, 2003; Birdsong & Molis 2001; Bongaerts 2003; Kinsella 2009; Muñoz & Singleton 2007; Reichle 2010a, 2010b). A typical recent example, dealing with phonology, the area often thought to be the most vulnerable to age effects, is a study by Jedynak (2009), which found that nine out of thirty-five post-pubertal learners of an additional language performed to native-speaker levels in terms of pronunciation of their target language, and that length of learning rather than age of onset seems to be the dominant factor relative to level of attainment. Hyltenstam and Abrahamsson (e.g. 2000:155) respond to this kind of evidence by pointing out that there is no recorded case of a post-pubertal beginner in an additional language behaving in every single detail like a native speaker, but they also acknowledge that very early beginners tend to differ too at the level of fine linguistic detail from monoglot native speakers. In the light of the above, it may very well be that the maturational issue is a good deal less important than the simple fact of possessing knowledge of another language/other languages and the generally recognized highly pervasive influence of such knowledge (cf., e.g., Cook 1995; Flege 1999; Jarvis & Pavlenko 2008). We return to the issue of cross-linguistic influence in Chapter 8.

The process of multilingual acquisition

It is clear that acquiring two or more languages is not simply a multiplication of monolingual acquisition. To adapt Grosjean's celebrated phrase (see e.g. Grosjean 1989), the multilingual is not two or more monolinguals in one person. A number of issues arise in relation to multilingual acquisition which simply have no relevance in respect of monolingual acquisition. These include the following: Is multiple language acquisition slower than monolingual acquisition? Do a multilingual's languages develop in a broadly balanced way? Are there particular elements of a specific language/specific languages that develop more rapidly or more slowly than elements in another language/other languages at the multilingual's disposal? These issues are addressed in what follows in this section. There is then the further question of the relationship in the mind between the various languages acquired by a multilingual. We address this last question in the next section.

With regard to the rate of multilingual development, the popular view is that this must obviously be slower than monolingual development because there is twice, three times, four times, etc. more for the child to acquire. According to Kecskes & Papp (2000:104), development, simultaneous or sequential, will be especially slow if the multilingual's languages and associated cultures are distant from each other:

> Multilingual development is usually longer and more difficult for language learners if their languages and cultures are distant. ... New concepts must be developed, and the existing ones have to be modified significantly to accommodate the new language and culture. This is usually not the case if the ... languages are typologically close and there is not much distance between the cultures either.

Some empirical studies also seem to support the notion of slower development for multilinguals. For example, Bialystok (1988) and Doyle, Champagne and Segalowitz (1978) found lexical development to be slower in bilinguals than in monolinguals. Other researchers note, however, that the simultaneous bilingual child's first words have been observed to appear around the same time as the monolingual's – around 12 months (see e.g. Patterson & Zurer-Pearson 2004) – and a number of studies have failed to turn up any significant difference between monolinguals and bilinguals in this connection (see e.g. Goodz 1994; Umbel, Zurer-Pearson, Fernandez & Oller 1992; cf. De Houwer 2009).

As far as morphosyntactic development is concerned, the balance of evidence seems to be that simultaneous bilingual children acquire morphosyntax at broadly the same rate as monolingual children – at least with respect to their dominant language (see e.g. De Houwer 2005; Nicoladis & Genesee 1997). On the other hand, parents of multilingual children sometimes report perceptions which indicate slight delays with respect to certain morphosyntactic features (see e.g. Sorace & Ladd 2004). Some researchers, on the other hand, have suggested that bilingual children may actually be able to decode and acquire certain aspects of grammar more rapidly than monolinguals (see e.g. Meisel 1990).

Concerning phonology, the picture is a mixed one. Some studies show, for example, that the capacity to differentiate one language from another is not delayed in pre-verbal infants in a bilingual environment as compared with infants in a monolingual environment (see e.g. Bosch & Sebastián-Gallés 1997), and that no delay is evident either in respect of segmenting words from continuous speech (see e.g. Polka & Sundara 2003). On the other hand, the well-attested phenomenon of infants' perceiving contrasts between only those sounds that are phonemic in the ambient language from a particular point onwards seems to occur slightly later in children in bilingual environments (see e.g. Bosch & Sebastián-Gallés 2003; Werker 2003). In the productive sphere also there are contradictory findings, with some researchers reporting no differences between monolinguals and bilinguals in such areas as the development of voicing contrasts, while others report lags in the latter case (see e.g. Johnson & Wilson 2002).

According to Zurer-Pearson (2002), such variations in empirical findings can often be explained in terms of the (in)adequacy of the research designs and the testing instruments used in some studies. She suggests that if instruments and research designs appropriate to bilingual situations were used, differences between bilinguals and monolinguals in terms of language progress would effectively disappear:

> Our studies of infants showed *no* statistical difference between monolingual and bilingual groups when the comparison groups were adequately matched and when appropriate controls for a monolingual bias in measurement were imposed.
>
> (Zurer-Pearson 2002: 310)

On the question of whether multilingual acquisition is slower that monolingual acquisition, then, a fair amount of controversy reigns. Not so with respect to the issue of whether multilingual acquisition proceeds in a balanced manner. The consensus here is that balanced multilinguality is extremely rare, and that, depending on circumstances, one language or another at a multilingual's disposal will be in advance of the other(s) for a particular period – at least in certain of its aspects – and that another may, as it were, take over the lead at another point. Parents of multilingual children are routinely advised to expect such shifts (see e.g. Papdaki-D'Onofrio 2003: 36). For example, when a multilingual child enters school he/she may not wish to appear different from the majority of their peers, who may be monolingual and may go through a phase of wishing to use only the language of their school-friends. Or a multilingual child may visit, or receive a visit from, relatives who speak only one of his/her languages, in which case the language in question may flourish at the expense of the others.

As Baker (2006: 104) notes, this phenomenon of shifting balance was documented in a very detailed way a long time ago in Leopold's (1939–1949) classic study of his daughter Hildegard's progress as an English-German bilingual. Hildegard resided in the United States, where her mother spoke English to her and her father German. When Hildegard visited Germany, her German became the stronger of her two languages. When she returned to the United States and went back to school, her English gained the upper hand. Another much-cited study is Fantini's (1985) tracing of the shifting fortunes of English, Italian and Spanish in the development of his trilingual subject, Mario. Mario's family was based in the United States. His parents were Spanish-Italian bilinguals. They frequently spoke to each other in Italian, but always addressed him in Spanish. Consequently, his productive capacity in Italian was limited. He was also, of course, exposed to English from an early age. On arrival at kindergarten he was Spanish-dominant, but subsequently his English caught up, so that by the age of ten his Spanish and English seemed in general terms to be at the same level.

Turning now to particularities of multilingual balance: the question here is, as stated earlier, whether there are identifiable elements of a specific language/specific languages that develop more rapidly or more slowly than corresponding elements in another language/other languages at the multilingual's disposal. Genesee (2000: 334) cites Slobin's (1973) suggestion that there is a set of universal

operating principles which are brought to bear on the problem of language acquisition, and also an array of language-specific strategies which are involved in the
acquisition of particular aspects of a given native language. Slobin further suggests that the order of development of different linguistic features depends on the
child's stage of cognitive and perceptual development, and also on the characteristics of the languages to be learned. If we consider in this context the simultaneous
multilingual child, any differences between the developmental specifics of his/her
languages are clearly not determined by cognitive-perceptive stage of development – which is constant across the languages in question – but may be affected
by the respective particularities of these languages.

This seems to be borne out by studies such as those conducted by Schelleter,
Sinka and Garman (see e.g. Schelleter, Sinka & Garman 1997; Sinka & Schelleter
1998; Sinka, Garman & Schelleter 2000). The studies in question looked at two
children acquiring, respectively, Latvian and German (both highly inflected languages) alongside English (not a very inflected language). They provided evidence
of the development of functional categories in Latvian and German from the earliest stages, but not in English, from which the researchers conclude that the nature
of Latvian and German input is rich enough to trigger functional category development, whereas the English input is not. Similar results emerge from an investigation of two simultaneous Japanese/English bilinguals by Mishina-Mori (2002),
which shows negative marking developing earlier in Japanese than in English.

Separation or integration?

The strong implication of these last findings is that the languages acquired by a
simultaneous multilingual develop separately. However, the question of whether
this in fact the case from the very earliest stages of acquisition is a controversial
one. Moreover, the whole issue of the degree to which the languages known to
an individual are separate or connected is a very important one also with respect
to sequential multilingual development and to additional language learning and
processing generally. We deal later, in Chapter 8, with the broader issue of the
integration/separation of languages in multilingual storage and processing operation. Here we address specifically the validity of a particular standpoint relating to
the early development of languages in simultaneous multilinguality.

A very influential perspective on this matter was that the simultaneous multilingual began with a single language system and that his/her languages separated only at a later stage (e.g. Volterra & Taeschner 1978; see discussion in Clark
2009:342ff.). This hypothesis posits that simultaneous multilinguals begin with
a single language system, a single fused linguistic representation, and that it is

around age 3 that they begin to differentiate their languages (see e.g. Pettito et al. 2001:455). According to this view, the child at an early stage is not in possession of translation-equivalents across languages, but rather he/she has a single lexical store, with one word from one or other of his/her languages for any given meaning. On this basis, the evidence cited in favour of the above view tended to be that of language mixing – exemplified by the following French/English instances (cited by Macrory 2006:163):

> *dans le <u>bucket</u>* ['in the bucket']
> *je peux <u>hear</u> un avion* ['I can hear an aeroplane']
> *the dinner is <u>déjà</u> cooked* ['the dinner is already cooked']

The claim was that such utterances arose because the child at an early stage was not in possession of translation-equivalents across languages, that he/she had a single lexical store, with one word from one or other of his/her languages for any given meaning. Other studies seemed to support this notion. For instance, Redlinger & Park's (1980) discovery of high mixing rates among early bilinguals was inferred by them to point to an incapacity to differentiate between their languages.

It is undeniable that language mixing goes on in the language use of young multilinguals, and that much of this mixing stems from the fact that a child may know an expression in one language for which he/she has no equivalent in other languages. Nicoladis & Secco (2000), for example, report that around 90% of such mixing they observed in very young bilinguals was explicable in terms of lexical gaps in one language or the other. That is to say, when the children lacked the word they needed in one language, but had it at their disposal in their other language, they simply drew on what they knew to supplement what they did not know. This practice may continue throughout childhood and indeed into adulthood. In an M.Phil. project on Chinese-English development, Zhang (2006) demonstrates this with respect to sibling-sibling interaction between two Chinese-English bilingual children, where, for example, the Chinese expressions *kao-ya* ('roast duck') and *fu lu* ('pickle made from soya beans') were used in English matrix utterances because the English translation-equivalents were unknown (and in the latter case non-existent).

This is a very natural strategy for the multilingual child to adopt. It of itself says nothing about the question of the separation or integration of a young multilingual's languages. Quay (1995) questions the evidence against the notion that the multilingual's lexicon is systematically distributed across languages; and she disputes the claim that there is a stage at which the multilingual has just one item in one or other language for a particular meaning. In her own case study she traced the lexical development of an infant acquiring Spanish and English from birth to the age of 1;10 via daily diary records and weekly video recordings in the two language contexts. What emerged from her study was that translation equivalents that make possible language choice were available from the beginning of speech. In a further study Deuchar & Quay (2000) show that differentiation between the young bilingual's two language systems is discernible also in phonology and morphosyntax.

Bilingual children, in other words, mostly keep their languages apart when using them and are adept – even at a very early age (see e.g. Genesee, Nicoladis & Paradis 1995; Nicoladis 1998) – in deciding which language to speak to whom. It appears, moreover, that on occasions where languages are mixed, the mixing in question may evidence an awareness – again from an early age – of the language competencies of interlocutors (see e.g. Lanza 1997). In De Houwer's words:

> Like monolingual children, bilingual children pay a lot of attention to the input they receive. They soon notice that this input differs depending on who is talking and in what situation someone is talking. Just like monolingual children, bilingual children attempt to talk like the people around them. Because of the bilingual situation, however, the bilingual child has more options than the monolingual one … [A]t a very young age bilingual children are skilled conversationalists who easily switch languages.   (De Houwer 1995:248)

De Houwer's point is demonstrated in findings reported by Barnes (2006) regarding language mixing in a child growing up in the Basque Country acquiring English, Spanish and Basque. One finding is that when using English with her English-speaking mother at around age 2, the subject, Jenny, uses more Spanish than Basque in her switches. One possible explanation of this offered by Barnes is psychotypological in nature.

> Although English and Spanish are not closely related, they are both Indo-European languages whilst Basque is not. For this reason we might expect to see more influence from Spanish in Jenny's English than from Basque. (Barnes 2006:221)

Another (not incompatible) explanation that Barnes suggests relates to the point concerning sensitivity to the interlocutor.

> Jenny has not heard her mother speaking Spanish (though she may realize that her mother understands it in family contexts). However, she does know that her mother is a fluent speaker of Spanish, having seen her use it with the child minder and others, so she may perceive her mother as a bilingual … This might explain why Jenny uses more Spanish than Basque mixes with her mother …   (*ibid.*)

Both explanations proposed by Barnes clearly imply that Jenny separates the languages at her disposal.

The advantages/disadvantages of multilinguality

As we noted in Chapter 2, early treatments of multilinguality tended to come to the conclusion that multilinguals were disadvantaged because of competition between the languages. Jakobovits (1970), for example, talks about a 'balance effect', and claims that Macnamara's (1966) research review provides persuasive support for its reality in a negative sense. Macnamara looked at 77 studies of situations where an additional language had a prominent place on the primary school curriculum; Jakobovits summarizes his findings thus:

> The majority of these studies confirmed the balance effect indicating that on the whole children who were required to learn, use, or be educated in two languages had a weaker grasp of either language than monolingual children.
>
> (Jakobovits 1970: 57)

The results of Macnamara's own study of the effects of a heavy emphasis on the Irish language in Irish primary schools were in keeping with this general trend, appearing to indicate that English-speaking Irish pupils "do not achieve the same standard in written English as British children who have not learned a second language' (estimated difference in standard, 17 months of English age)" and that they do not achieve either "the same standard in written Irish as native-speakers of Irish (estimated difference, 16 months of Irish age)" (Macnamara 1966: 35).

One should note immediately that Macnamara's interpretation of his results were subsequently queried (see e.g. Cummins 1977), and that other studies have supported a more positive view of early bilinguality. Jakobovits refers in this connection to Peal & Lambert's (1962) study, which "shows that French-Canadian children in one bilingual setting in Montreal who have developed a good grasp of English are superior in both verbal and non-verbal intelligence to their French-speaking monolingual peers" (Jakobovits 1970: 58). One can also cite in this context Swain & Lapkin's (1982) review of research based on a number of French immersion schemes for Canadian Anglophones, including both late and early immersion programmes, which yielded no evidence of any long-term negative effects on first language development. Indeed the evidence that emerged suggested that such programmes can result in improved language development generally, especially in respect of metalinguistic awareness (Swain & Lapkin 1982: 36f.).

Moreover, as Hamers & Blanc (2000: 89) point out, advantages for bilinguals have been found in relation to a whole range of further abilities. Research shows that bilinguals are more likely than monolinguals to have understood the denotatum of an expression is distinct from the expression itself (see e.g., Bialystok 1987; Ben Zeev 1977; Ianco-Worrall 1972), and that they manifest higher degrees of semantic and grammatical awareness (see e.g. Bialystok 2001, 2002). Further cognitive advantages have been found for bilinguals in areas beyond the linguistic domain such as Piagetian conservation tasks and visual-spatial abilities (see e.g. Diaz & Klinger 1991) and in the capacity to solve problems based on conflict and attention (such as sorting cards by colour and then re-sorting by shape) (Bialystok 1999).

A recent research review by Bialystok (2009) indicates a very wide extent of cognitive advantage for bilinguals – at least for those who use both languages regularly to a high level of proficiency. As some of the above-cited studies show, and as more recent work has also demonstrated, bilingual children seem to develop the ability to solve problems that require the resolution of conflicting or misleading cues earlier and more efficiently than monolinguals (e.g. Bialystok & Martin 2004; Carlson & Meltzoff 2008). Nor are such advantages in executive processing confined to bilingual children; they have also been shown for young adults (Bialystok 2006) and middle-aged and older adults (Bialystok, Craik, Klein & Viswanathan 2004). With reference to later life Bialystok notes that bilingual individuals appear to be protected against the onset of dementia by the 'cognitive reserve' deriving from the extended stimulation afforded by bilingual functioning (Bialystok, Craik & Freedman 2007).

With regard to the cognitive impact of 'beyond bilingualism' multilingualism, the investigation of this interface is only just beginning, but a recent research report commissioned by the European Commission (2009) on multilingualism (defined as including the 'beyond bilingualism' variety) comes to the following conclusion:

> Multilingualism appears to help people realise and expand their creative potential. In addition, thinking, learning, problem solving and communicating, all of which are transversal knowledge-steeped skills used in our daily lives, show signs of enhancement through multilingualism.   (European Commission 2009: 23)

One should not ignore either the social dimension of the advantages of bilingualism in terms of the wider possibilities it offers for communication in the family and in the community, on an international scale and at inter-community levels. Li Wei (2000: 23) connects these to the enhancement of mutual understanding and the amelioration of relationships. Baker (1993) talks about bilinguals' *communicative sensitivity*, referring to the proposition that bilinguals are "more attuned to the communicative needs of those with whom they talk" and have "two or more worlds of experience" (Li Wei 2000: 23). Clearly, such dimensions of bilingualism have implications for general enjoyment of the social dimension of life and also for employability.

A further contribution to this discussion of the benefits of multilinguality is a recent article by Furlong (2009) who explores the way in which knowledge of a number of languages may foster creativity. She takes as her starting point the findings by Bialystok on the cognitive effects of bilingualism – which, as she rightly says, point to something which is "perceptual, not limited to the use of language" (*ibid.*: 365). She cites in this connection Vygotsky's viewpont that "the psychological processes of perception in the creation of art and in the creation of a word are identical" (*ibid.*). She goes on to advance the following argument: "given high level plurilinguals" increased perceptual awareness of words, they are likely to gain new insights, create new analogies and experience creative moments in any domain where perception is at work" (*ibid.*).

How then is one to reconcile the seemingly diametrically opposed perspectives regarding the effects of multilinguality? Cummins (1984: 101) draws attention to the prejudice against bilinguality which existed in the first half of the twentieth century. It was during this time that many of the studies with negative results were carried out (*ibid.*: 103). He also emphasizes the methodological deficiencies of the majority of the early studies, noting that the "[f]ailure to control for factors such as SES [socioeconomic status], urban-rural differences and language of testing render [*sic*] most of the findings uninterpretable." In addition, he refers to Lambert's (1975) point that the early studies mostly focused on sequential bilinguality in immigrant or minority children whose first language was effectively being replaced by the language of the majority population. This point remains valid for more recent studies showing negative effects for early sequential bilinguality, almost all of which "have been conducted in Western cultures with children of minority groups schooled in the majority language" (Hamers & Blanc 2000: 93). The multilinguality of this kind of situation Lambert calls 'subtractive' in contrast to the 'additive' sequential multilinguality achieved by children whose first language is prestigious and not threatened with replacement by additional languages. Cummins (1984: 107) notes that most studies showing advantages associated with bilinguality have been carried out in 'additive' situations.

The distinction between additive and subtractive situations is often made metaphorically in terms of 'immersion', 'language bath' versus 'submersion', 'language drowning', 'sink-or-swim' (see e.g. Baker 2006: 216ff.; Swain 1981; Skutnabb-Kangas 1981: 138ff.), and is well illustrated by differences between French immersion programmes in Canada and what are called 'immersion' but are in fact 'submersion' programmes in the United States:

> The Canadian French immersion programs include instruction in, and about, the first language. Once mother tongue instruction is introduced, it is provided on a continuing basis throughout schooling. Few minority language students [in the United States] enjoy this privilege in public school systems. Yet, given the overwhelming use of the majority language in school and the wider environment,

> speakers of a minority language constantly face the possibility of the second (i.e.
> majority) language replacing the first …
>
> Furthermore, in the French immersion programs, all children who enter the program at the primary level do so with the same level of target language skills – none. This is in contrast to the situation – which in the United States is often referred to as 'immersion' – where children who are to learn the target language are mixed together with other children who are native speakers of the target language … Additionally, their teachers may not understand the children's first language, which, it has been suggested, may lead to the teaching of a pre-scribed curriculum which relates little to the existing interests or knowledge of the children …
>
> (Swain 1981: 18f.)

As has been noted, 'subtractive' situations are posited as leading to the impoverishment, ultimately the suppression of the L1. It has also been argued by some that the 'subtractive' situation is not particularly effective at promoting L2 proficiency either. Cummins (e.g. 1984, 1991) offers a particular – and controversial – perspective in this connection on Cognitive-Academic Language Proficiency (CALP) – roughly those dimensions which involve decontextualized and cognitively demanding uses of language, which he distinguishes from Basic Interpersonal Communicative Skills (BICS). For Cummins (CALP) is not to be conceived of as language-specific but as a common base underlying performance in any of the learner's languages. According to this standpoint, CALP in subsequently acquired languages is essentially a function of first language CALP – at least in the initial stages of the acquisition of additional languages. Moreover, CALP must be established to a certain threshold point if cognitive deficits are to be avoided, and a proficiency threshold must also be attained in the additional language(s) if cognitive advantages are to ensue.

Evidence for these claims, known as the interdependence hypothesis, comes from a study by Cummins, Swain, Nakajima, Handscombe, Green & Tran (1984) of Japanese and Vietnamese immigrant students in Toronto, whose scores on academic measures of English correlated positively with their scores on academic measures of, respectively, Japanese and Vietnamese. Other findings consistent with the interdependence view are those of Rosier and Farella (1976) on the Rock Point programme. Navajo students at Rock Point in the United States, who had previously been schooled through English alone, and whose performance in English was below normal grade level, were subsequently provided with a bilingual programme which introduced literacy through Navajo. Levels of performance on English tests improved markedly, and, as students proceeded through the grades, moved progressively closer to national norms (cf. also e.g. Abu-Rabia 2001; Duncan & De Avila 1979; Hakuta & Diaz 1984; Lemmon & Goggin 1989; Secada 1991; Verhoeven 2006).

Interesting findings along not dissimilar lines emerge from Thomas & Collier's (1997) research with language minority students in the United States, which found that bilingual programmes for such students were the only school programmes to assist them to fully reach the 50th percentile (scoring above 50% of the other test takers) in both their native language and English in all subject areas and to maintain that level of high achievement. The greater the number of years of primary language, grade-level schooling a student had received, the higher his/her English achievement was shown to be.

Cummins frames his interdependence hypothesis in terms of additional languages depending on the first language. However, there is also evidence of proficiency in an additional language having an impact on L1 proficiency. Hamers & Blanc (2000) cite a Swedish educational report which gives an account of Swedish children learning English as a second language and which notes that

> elementary-school children who already had a high competence in their mother tongue and who started to learn a foreign language at an early age would improve their competence in their mother tongue more than peers who did not have exposure to a foreign language.   (Hamers & Blanc 2000:98)

One can also find evidence of such bi-directionality in Swain & Lapkin's above mentioned (1982) finding that where immersion students differ from non-immersion students in terms of general language development they typically outperform the latter "in such areas as punctuation, spelling, vocabulary and usage" (p. 37). The point is that in the case of Canadian-type immersion programmes, whilst literacy skills are not necessarily established in the first language prior to the introduction of the second language, they are gradually introduced, and in any case the first language has been established to a very high level so that "most immersion children come to school with the prerequisites to literacy that Wells' (1979) study has indicated to be important" (Swain's 1981:27).

There are undoubtedly many difficulties with the interdependence perspective. For one thing, is not clear *precisely* what is to be included under the heading of CALP. Cummins himself (e.g. 1983) shies away from a hard and fast distinction between CALP and BICS, representing them rather as on a continuum of context-embeddedness, with the former being located at the less context-embedded end of the scale. However, this leaves a considerable amount of vagueness surrounding the concept. Another problem is that the hypothesis addresses only cases where languages are acquired sequentially and is silent on the question of the simultaneous acquisition of two or more languages. A third is that it leaves largely out of account influences which are not language-related on cognitive-academic development and indeed on language development itself. On the other hand, the interdependence hypothesis does seem to provide the beginnings of a plausible explanation, at least in very broad terms, for the differing outcomes of immersion and submersion. It also offers a different angle on the discussion of the topic of developmental competition between languages by suggesting that knowledge of one language can actually support and improve knowledge of another language.

It should be kept in mind that the interdependence hypothesis relates only to certain aspects of language proficiency. However unsatisfactory the definition of CALP may be, this definition can probably be taken to exclude such dimensions as phonetics/phonology, everyday lexis, and the morphosyntax of routine oral communication, which are generally seen to be in the BICS category. The interdependence hypothesis states that in these kinds of areas young learners of additional languages are not dependent on the establishment of a common base via the first language, which is why they may do better than older learners in these domains. However, the corollary of this position is that in such areas, even if a common CALP base is established, it is not operative in a supportive role in respect of the additional language(s). In respect of BICS, therefore, the hypothesis has nothing to say about the proposition there is developmental competition between languages.

A further point worth noting is that, as far as the acquisition of additional languages by immigrants is concerned, it is likely that the vast majority of immigrant children do not receive the kind of support for their first language that Cummins posits as necessary for the common base to be put in place. This implies that their acquisition of additional languages is typically 'subtractive' and replacive. For example, English-only programmes for Spanish-speaking minorities in the United States, which are labelled as 'immersion education' in fact lead to a situation where the children in question become essentially Anglophone in the academic context, whilst the prevalence of English, their second language, in the media and in most public domains means that opportunities for the fostering of cognitive-academic skills in the first language outside the classroom are also severely limited (cf. e.g. Johnson & Swain 1997: 12). The implication of this, according to Cummins's hypothesis, is that the interaction between the first and subsequent languages is not positive and mutually supportive. The common base is, on this view, not established and there is no bulwark against competitivity between languages – with the result that most immigrant children end up with their L2 dominant and their L1 weakened (cf. Bialystok 1997: 123; Jia & Aaronson 1999).

Concluding summary

In this chapter we have looked at multilingual development. We have explored the wide variety of circumstances which can lead to a person having two or more languages at his/her disposal, noting that both home and community patterns of language use (of various kinds) and formal language instruction may play a role in this process. We have briefly looked at the age factor issue in the context of sequential multilinguality and have then gone on to examine the process of multilingual acquisition.

We have seen that on the issue of whether multilingual acquisition is slower that monolingual acquisition different researchers and studies come to different conclusions. With regard to the question of whether multilingual acquisition proceeds in a balanced manner, it is generally agreed that the state of development of a particular language relative to other languages in a multilingual's repertoire will depend on the extent to which the child has had occasion to be exposed to and to interact in the language in question relative to his/her other languages. With respect to developmental specifics of the various languages being acquired by a multilingual we have discerned a growing consensus that these may be affected by the respective particularities of these languages. We have then considered the matter of the degree of integration of the languages acquired by a multilingual, and have drawn from the available evidence the conclusion that, while in multilinguals there is interplay among their languages, there is also separation – and that this includes the very early stages of simultaneous multilinguality.

Finally, we have turned our attention to the advantages and disadvantages of multilinguality and have pointed to research findings which suggest that, provided that a multilingual child's languages all receive appropriate support, including support in the cognitive-academic dimension, real linguistic and cognitive benefits can accrue from multilinguality – in addition, that is, to the benefit of being able to operate through more than one language.

CHAPTER 7

Classifications of multilinguals, multilingual contexts and languages in multilingual environments

Introductory

In this chapter our aim is to present the reader with a selected range of classifications deployed in the study of multilingualism studies – some widely used, others new. The classifications take as their point of departure Edwards's (1994) tripartite division of the main elements in multilingualism into *speaker*, *settings* and *language*. In what follows we use a slightly different nomenclature: *user*, *environment* and *language*. Our terminology seems to us to be more comprehensive: *user* covers not only speakers but also signers and writers, and *environment* captures a wider range of phenomena than *setting* – which is in line with the fact that since 1994 when Edwards's book was published the purview and perspectives of multilingualism studies have been broadened considerably.

Our ordering of the typologies and classifications of multilingualism, our 'classification of classifications', sheds some clarificatory light, we hope, on the ways in which multilingualism has been approached. It might also be helpful in providing a starting point for further advances in typologizing in this domain. In addition we present here some elements of critique of the typologies under scrutiny to give some general impression of the ways in which they have been received in the research community.

One further preliminary point to be noted that the typologies and classifications related strictly to bilingualism are here distinguished from those related to 'beyond two' multilingualism (trilingualism, quadilingualism, etc.). This distinction is in keeping with our view that, although bilingual and 'beyond two' multilingual phenomena have much in common, and although 'beyond two' multilingualism studies have to a large extent grown out of bilingualism studies, there exist important features of 'beyond two' multilingualism, mainly related to complexity issues, that warrant separate consideration.

Why typologies?

Despite the fact that a single term is used to denote multilingual individuals and groups, we know that multilinguals differ in all kinds of ways. The same holds true of the countries and regions we call 'multilingual', which also present many differences. In fact, one can go so far as to there is no absolutely cut-and-dried distinction between individuals and communities which are labelled 'multilingual' and those which are not; rather the picture is complex and fuzzy, special for each specific situation. We can take in this context the example of Brussels, capital of Belgium, an officially bilingual region with French and Dutch as official languages. This city's linguistic situation would be more accurately characterized in terms of community bilingualism, with the recognition that many individuals living in Brussels do not use both French and Dutch in their everyday lives but rather operate in one or other of these languages. In other instances, bilingual or multilingual individuals live out their lives in formally monolingual countries. Such is the situation in Austria, for example, where large numbers of Poles fleeing from Martial Law Poland were welcomed and given citizenship in the 1980s, and where they and their children now function on a daily basis in both German and Polish.

Given the great diversity of sociolinguistic situations and patterns associated with the use of two or more languages, it is only natural that attempts should have been made, throughout history indeed, to organize what we think we know about multilingual individuals, groupings, regions and language use in order to be able to deal with the scale and complexity of multilingualism. Out of such endeavours emerges a spectrum of classifications and typologies. Edwards, in his book on multilingualism (Edwards 1994: 137–145) very passionately makes the case for the need for a focus on typology, arguing (p. 138) that even a simple checklist of important variables can make a useful contribution in this connection. Edwards acknowledges the problems pointed to by some critics of typological exercises, such as that a typology may embody prevailing assumptions, may have limited analytical utility, and may imply permanence or stasis. Nevertheless, he strongly defends the notion that classifications and descriptions have real utility, noting that "[c]ross-context comparisons might well be facilitated, for example, if attention was given to the same variables in all settings", and referring for support for his point of view to the names of notable sociolinguists such as Haugen, Stewart and Ferguson who "*have* felt it meaningful to employ a typological approach" (*ibid.*).

The relevant definition of typology in the *Oxford English Dictionary* (2011) runs as follows:

> The study of classes with common characteristics; classification, esp. of human products, behaviour, characteristics, etc., according to type; the comparative analysis of structural or other characteristics; a classification or analysis of this kind.
>
> <http://www.oed.com/view/Entry/208394?redirectedFrom=typology#eid>
> (accessed August 2, 2011)

Just like other disciplines and sciences, the study of multilingualism clearly needs to typologize, needs to arrive at some kind of systematic listing and organization of the processes and entities it is attempting to elucidate (cf. Aronin & Hufeisen 2009b: 113). Classifications and typologies would seem to be especially important in the investigation of multilingualism studies for two reasons: first, as the study of multilingualism, which is a relatively new field, develops and grows it will certainly need its own theoretical apparatus; second, the vast complexity of multilingualism demands classifications and typologies if we are even to begin to make sense of it.

In the rest of this chapter we outline and discuss some of the typologies and classifications which we see as having a bearing on multilingualism. Reflecting the historical evolution of the academic study of multilingualism we begin by looking at typological issues relating to multilingualism in the context of its relationship with bilingualism. We then go on to more recently proposed classifications specific to multilingualism in the narrow sense of phenomena involving more than two languages.

Bilingualism and bilinguals

Hamers & Blanc (1989: 1), commenting on various theoretical frameworks, felt it necessary to limit the scope of their typological discussion in the context of bilingualism to classificatory schemas deriving from theoretical reasoning and having a predictive character:

> Typologies of bilingualism are mentioned only when they are based on theoretical grounds and have therefore a predictive character: we consider a typology useful only in so far as a new classification of phenomena permits a better understanding of the psychological, sociological and linguistic processes and their interplay when languages are in contact.

We will follow the same principle of selectivity in relation to typologies and classifications. An approach which tightly focuses typological proposals in this manner would seem to have much to recommend it.

The first typologies (and most of the currently used ones) were typologies of bilinguals and bilingualism, which implicitly or explicitly laid claim to subsuming multilinguals and multilingualism in the 'beyond bilingualism' sense. Unsurprisingly, none of these classifications proved universally useful. Some, however, have stood the test of time and usage. One such is the typology of bilinguals suggested by Weinreich (1953), which subcategorizes bilinguals into *co-ordinate bilinguals,* whose linguistic systems are posited to be entirely separate; *compound bilinguals,* whose two systems are posited to draw on common mental representations at the level of meaning; and *subordinative bilinguals,* whose weaker language system is posited to lack semantics and to be parasitic on the stronger system in this domain.

Li Wei (2000: 6–7) has compiled a list classifications of bilinguals comprising 36 items. One quite rarely used category figuring in this list is that of *covert bilingual* – "someone who conceals his or her knowledge due to attitudinal disposition" (Li Wei 2000: 6); another is *diagonal bilingual* – "someone who is bilingual in a non-standard language or a dialect and an unrelated standard language" (*ibid.*). Also featuring in the list (*ibid.*) are *natural bilinguals* – those who have not undergone any specific training and *ascendant bilinguals,* "whose ability to function in a second language is developing due to increased use". *Passive bilinguals* or *receptive bilinguals* are defined in the list as those who understand a second language in either its spoken or written form, but do not necessarily speak or write it, while *productive bilinguals* are defined as those who not only understand but also speak and possibly write in two or more languages (p. 7).

When an individual's mastery of both languages is roughly equivalent it is common practice to speak of *balanced bilingualism* and, whereas in cases in which greater proficiency in one or other of the languages is evident, this is typically signalled by the use of the notion of *dominance* in respect of the stronger language. Differences relating to the age of onset of the second language are expressed by means of differential use of the terms *early bilingual* and *late bilingual.* Another division is that between *subtractive bilingual* (or *bilingualism*) and *additive bilingual* (*bilingualism*). The former is defined as someone whose second language is acquired at the cost of full proficiency in his/her first language, and the latter as a person whose two languages are acquired in a complementary and enriching fashion – i.e., without mutual damage. This distinction between additive and subtractive bilingualism clearly relates to a distinction between the range of possibilities supplied by particular environments to children acquiring second languages (cf. Jia & Aaronson 1999, 2003). A related distinction is that between *elite bilingualism* and *folk bilingualism* (De Mejia 2002). The oft-cited characterization of *elite bilingualism* is that by Paulston as "the privilege of middle-class, well-educated members of most societies" (Paulston 1975 cited by Harding &

Riley 1986:24). A variation of this dichotomy sets in opposition the notions of *elective bilingualism* and *circumstantial bilingualism* (Valdés & Figueroa 1994). The former is described as characteristic of "individuals who choose to become bilingual and who seek out either formal classes or contexts in which they can acquire a foreign language … and who continue to spend the greater part of their time in a society in which their first language is the majority or societal language" (Valdés & Figueroa 1994:12). The latter, like *folk bilingualism*, is related to the conditions of ethnic groups under which they 'involuntarily' have to acquire the second language, becoming bilingual simply in order to survive (Valdés & Figueroa 1994; De Mejia 2002).

It has to be said that the above dichotomies stand in some need of qualification. Thus, for example, the meaning of *involuntary* is also rather stretched in case of immigrants who are genuinely eager to learn the language of their host country, and would appear to apply more readily to the case of middle-class children learning a foreign language at school without any real inclination to do so. Where in the above classifications, to take a further example, would we place the bilingualism of functionaries in countries such as the Scandinavian countries, where it is absolutely necessary to demonstrate knowledge of an additional language in order to qualify for entry into the civil service, and where promotion may relate to degrees of proficiency in such an additional language?

Dichotomous typologies are widely used both in bilingualism and multilingualism studies because dichotomies represent clear and easily accessible ways of classifying, of 'situating' the phenomena in question. They also have their more challenging dimension. Particular dichotomies or sets of dichotomies are applicable only to specific situations; but they do not provide an overarching definitional system. Moreover, as the number of dichotomies grows, the dichotomies themselves have to be classified. We are learning also, as studies in this area progress, that bi- and multilingual phenomena are hugely complex, and that, while using dichotomies may offer a rough-and-ready starting point, a truly scientific account requires far more delicate and nuanced characterizations of the realities with which we are dealing. Finally it is quite clear that the dichotomous perspective does not work so well and sometimes does not work at all when we apply it to the acquisition and use of three or more languages.

Classifications and typologies

Classifications that are applicable to situations involving more than two languages clearly need to take into consideration the multiplicity of languages and need perhaps to focus more particularly on the complex and overlapping interaction, interdependence and interrelationship of what we call here ***user***, ***environment*** and ***language***. Edwards (1994) makes use of broadly the same concepts in his deployment of the terms *speaker, setting,* and *language*. We discuss our slight emendation of his terminology in the introduction to this chapter.

User, the first of the above constituents, is simply applied to individuals who use, study, or acquire languages. The umbrella word ***environment*** in this connection denotes the time and place where the languages are used: community, school, family; business, courts, tourism, education, and other formal and informal domains. Frequently encountered near-synonyms of this term are *situation, setting,* and *context. Environment* is usefully comprehensive in including in its coverage not only the current political and historical circumstances, but also attitudes, knowledge, expectations, assumptions, and educational possibilities. The meaning of the third constituent, ***language***, seems clear; noteworthy is the fact that it very often has reference to multiple languages in simultaneous use.

Of course, however, many of the concepts used in bilingualism studies can be used more broadly. For example, the notion of different degrees of typological closeness (e.g., Italian/Spanish versus Chinese/Spanish) is obviously relevant not just to bilingual situations but to all situations where more than one language is involved. Another widely used distinction inherited from bilingual studies is that between the descriptors *successive* and *simultaneous/sequential*. We can note in this context that more variation, diversity and resultant complexity is associated with 'beyond bilingualism' use than where just two languages are in the picture. This is graphically illustrated by Cenoz's (2000) widely cited Table 1.

Table 1. Second language acquisition vs. multiple language acquisition (after Cenoz 2000: 40)

Second language acquisition	Multiple language acquisition
1. L1→ L2	1. L1 → L2 → L3
2. Lx + Ly	2. L1 → Lx/Ly
	3. Lx/Ly → L3
	4. Lx/Ly/Lz
	5. L1 → L2 → L3 → L4
	6. L1 → Lx/Ly → L4
	7. L1 → L2 → Lx/Ly
	8. L1 → Lx/Ly/Lz
	9. Lx/Ly → L3 → L4
	10. Lx/Ly → Lz/Lz1
	11. Lx/Ly/Lz → L4
	12. Lx/Ly/Lz/Lz1

With just two languages involved in the acquisition process we need to consider only two possible acquisition orders: the second language can be acquired either after L1 (L1 → L2) or at the same time as the L1 (Lx + Ly). In the case of third language acquisition there are already at least four possible acquisition orders. The three languages can be acquired consecutively (L1 → L2 → L3) or with a simultaneous component: the simultaneous acquisition of two languages (Lx/Ly) could take place after the L1 has been acquired (L1 → Lx/Ly,) or before the L3 is acquired (Lx/Ly → L3). Or there could be simultaneous contact with all three languages (Lx/Ly/Lz) This diversity may be further increased where the acquisition process is interrupted by the process of acquiring an additional language and then restarted again (L1 → L2 → L3 → L2).

The extreme complexity associated with multiple language use has led to the classification or typology of trilinguals, quadrilinguals and so on being approached from a variety of angles. It is worth bearing in mind also that the above-mentioned division into environment, users and language is not always entirely straightforward, the borderlines between these categories being often less than watertight. Very often when considering such matters it is useful to be able to have in mind specific cases of exemplars relating to given sociolinguistic circumstances and educational needs.

Hamers & Blanc (1989: 155) in their chapter dedicated specifically to multilingualism insightfully comment on the transition of analysis lens from bilingualism to multiple language knowledge and use as follows.

> … we move from a micrological to a macrological level of analysis and to disciplines which are concerned with sociostructural factors, like sociology, sociolinguistics and the sociology of language. Because these disciplines deal with a multiplicity of factors and multidimensional phenomena, it is difficult to control all these factors. As a result, theories are thin on the ground and what pass for models are often mere typologies and taxonomies which are more descriptive then predictive […] But social and cultural phenomena have also a psychological reality, and the intergroup and interpersonal levels are only the two poles of a social-interaction continuum. This chapter therefore also considers intergroup relations from the point of view of the individual as member of a group and calls upon disciplines like the social psychology of language and the ethnography of speaking. One problem is how to integrate these different levels of analysis into a unified interdisciplinary framework.

Along these lines, typologies relating to multiple language knowledge and use thus aspire to integrate different levels and to be interdisciplinary but also to be harmoniously unified into one framework.

Classifications of users

Perhaps the most obvious way of classifying users of multiple language is according to the number of languages at their disposal. Good examples of research are some of the studies carried out by Dewaele. In one such study (Dewaele 2007), his 106 adult participants were broken up (according to their initial status before encountering the additional language) into monolinguals (L1), bilinguals (L2), trilinguals (L3), and quadrilinguals (L4), and an attempt was made to relate this classification to the identification of possible differences in levels of communicative anxiety (CA) and foreign language anxiety (FLA) when speaking with friends, speaking with strangers and speaking in public. It was found, for example, that knowledge of more than two languages was linked to lower levels of FLA in the L2. Dewaele also found that a "significant effect [in terms of anxiety levels] of number of languages known to the participant … did emerge in the L2 when speaking to friends" and that "the difference between the bilinguals and the quadrilinguals is significant but not between the trilinguals and quadrilinguals" (Dewaele 2007: 403).

It is worth noting that studies which explicitly distinguish between bilinguals, trilinguals and more-linguals are rather the exception than the rule. De Bot (2004: 22), Jessner (2006) and Franceschini (2009) have pointed to the fact that, in Jessner's words,

> [t]he growing interest in TLA [third language acquisition] and its cognitive and linguistic effects has … given rise to doubts about all the experiments which have been carried out with 'bilingual' subjects who, in fact, might have been in contact with other languages, but had never been asked about their prior linguistic knowledge.
> (Jessner 2006: 15)

Another kind of classification is according to particularities of experience of language acquisition and language use. Thus, Hoffmann (2001a: 18–19), examining cases of early multiple language acquisition subdivided the children involved according to the origins of their multiple language using abilities. Hoffmann's data (2001a: 19) reveal:

1. Trilingual children who are brought up with two home languages which are different from the one spoken in the wider community;
2. Children who grow up in a bilingual community and whose home language (either that of one or both parents) is different from the community languages;
3. Third language learners, i.e. bilinguals who acquire a third language in the school context;

4. Bilinguals who have become trilingual through immigration; and
5. Members of trilingual communities.

Hoffmann acknowledges that there are many multiple language users who may be placed in more than one category and that in some cases categories overlap; she also notes that speakers may move in and out of particular categories in the course of their lives. That is to say, the typology she offers is to be seen as flexible, allowing for the fitting of cases to the mobility and the dynamic nature of multilingualism. In this typology Hoffmann classifies trilinguals taking into account both the circumstances under which and the social context in which her participants became users of three languages. As we can see, the categories deal with both 'trilingual' and 'bilingual plus' children.

She further notes that "[o]ne could also establish other typologies reflecting, as criteria, features related to acquisition such as age, acquisition process (simultaneous, successive or a combination of them), acquisition context (home, community, classroom, school), language competence and skills attained, among others" (Hoffmann 2001a: 19).

Classifications of environments

One approach to the classification of environments has been to focus on the family situation. Thus Barron-Hauwaert (2004) researched bilingual and then trilingual families from different parts of the world, going on to discuss the One-Parent-One-Language (OPOL) strategy in bringing up a bilingual/trilingual child. She summarises her research in the following terms:

> The world of trilingual family is similar, yet different to the bilingual family. The languages cannot be equal and *have more of a link to a particular place and time,* such as school or activities.   (2004: 156 – our italics)

In other words, she identifies place and time as important considerations in thinking about trilingual families.

Barron-Hauwaert (*ibid.*) has the following to say about her trilingual families:

> There are many different varieties of trilingual families, from those living in third language country, to parents using a third language together. [...] Probably in the future we will see more trilingual children due to mobility of the international working communities.

Her second remark implies a view that trilingual families are the product of environment, and that the globalization processes which are changing the environment and the language dispensation will bring about more trilingualism. The fact that language practices in the family are anchored in place and time, and are very intimately connected to environment could not perhaps be so clearly discerned when only bilingualism was under consideration; with more focus now on multiple language acquisition and use, this aspect of multilingualism is becoming more obvious.

Six types of multilingual acquisition scenarios are listed by Romaine (1989 and 2nd edn. 1995: 183ff.). This typology refers primarily to bilingualism, but the author clearly takes the acquisition and use of more than two languages into consideration; for example, she states that the outcome of Type 4 scenario is a trilingual child and later notes that "multilingual communities are in the majority, so many children grow up in cases where individual and societal multilingualism coincide" (Romaine 1995: 186). We have summarized the types of early childhood bilingualism and the categories proposed by Romaine (1995: 183–185) in Table 2.

Despite its bilingual bias, and its failure to problematize the concept of 'native language' (cf. discussion above, Chapter 3), this is clearly a very helpful typology, although it has to be noted that the different types frequently overlap in real life. An extended typology taking more account of situations involving more than two languages would be a desideratum for the future.

A more recent typology of trilingual families suggested by Braun & Cline (2010) takes into consideration the complexity of contemporary multilingualism. Thus, for example, predominantly monolingual environments are recognized as including bilingual and multilingual families, which have a variety of linguistic possibilities and therefore patterns of use in respect of all the languages they have been exposed to. Three types of trilingual families are singled out by Braun & Cline:

1. Type I trilingual families are those in which the parents each speak a different native language and neither of the parents speaks the community language as a native language. The parents in the families of this type do not share a common native language.
2. Type II families are those where each parent speaks two native languages but the parents do not share a common native language. One of the parents in such families may or may nor speak a community language as his/her native language.
3. Families where one or both parents are trilingual are referred to as Type III families.

Table 2. Types of early childhood bilingualism according to Suzanne Romaine (1989/1995)

	Name of the type	Parents	Community	Strategy
Type 1	'One Parent – One Language'	Have different native languages with each having some degree of competence in the other's language.	The language of one of the parents in the dominant language in the community.	The parents each speak their own language to the child from birth.
Type 2	'Non-dominant Home Language' / 'One Language – One Environment'	Have different native languages.	The language of one of the parents is the dominant language of the community.	Both parents speak the non-dominant language to the child, who is fully exposed to the dominant language only when outside the home, and in particular in nursery school.
Type 3	'Non-dominant Home Language without Community Support'	Share the same native language.	The dominant language is not that of the parents.	The parents speak their own language to the child.
Type 4	'Double Non-dominant Home Language without Community Support'	The parents have different native languages.	The dominant language is different from either of the parents' languages.	The parents each speak their own language to the child from birth.
Type 5	'Non-native Parents'	Share the same native language.	The dominant language is the same as that of the parents.	One of the parents always addresses the child in a language which is not his/her native language.
Type 6	'Mixed Languages'	The parents are bilingual.	Sectors of community may also be bilingual.	Parents code-switch and mix languages.

The authors of the typology applied it to an analysis of parents' choice of language strategies with their children and obtained telling findings testifying to the differences between the three types of trilingual families. For example, their "data show that the OPOL method was generally successfully implemented by Type I parents, but not so often in families where one or both parents spoke two or three NLs" (Braun & Cline 2010: 120). Still, the authors themselves point to difficulties they encountered in exactly classifying the trilingual families in their study in the UK and Germany ("Some of these families were difficult to define in terms of their linguistic background" – p. 117). The difficulties in question arose from the fact that, unlike many bilinguals, who may make relatively frequent switches between their languages, their trilinguals seemed to tend towards rather exclusively opting for each of their languages in accordance with very specific circumstances (Barron-Hauwaert 2003) – depending on interlocutors, location, etc. While acknowledging the problems that **any** classification of multilingual (as well as monolingual) competencies will run into, we see Braun and Cline's typology as a step ahead insofar as it recognizes and focuses on the complexity and variety of trilingual families and the environments they inhabit. This typology enters more deeply into the realities of language patterns and practices, especially as reflected in the current global linguistic situation. This is very much a 'beyond bilingualism' typology, since it attempts to deal with a multiplicity of factors and, more importantly, **the interaction between these factors**, and is thus consistent with the complexity approach, which is so suitable for exploring the multilingualism of the present age.

Classifications in education

Another strand of multilingual classification worthy of consideration in today's global society is that of education. Genesee remarks in this connection that "[m]ultilingualism and multilingual education challenge rigid binary classifications and even complex ones such as Mackey's typology of various forms of trilingual education that yielded 250 alternatives" (Genesee 2009: x). Most typologies in this context have their origins in typologies for bilingual education, although the better ones allow for the inclusion of trilingualism and beyond. We briefly mention some of these educational typologies in what follows.

Mackey's (1970) typology considers the dimensions of home language, school curriculum, community and national languages and the status of the languages. He discusses different possibilities in relation to the above four dimensions. This results in the identification of at least 250 different types of bilingual education. On the one hand, the comprehensiveness of this typology is its strong point, but, on the other, this makes it rather difficult to use in practice. For example, in Mackey's second category, concerning the patterns of language use in the school curriculums, the curriculum and the language of instruction is represented as varying according to several parameters:

1. The medium of instruction may be one language, two languages, or more.
2. The pattern of language development may be one of maintenance of two languages, or transition from one medium of instruction to another.
3. The distribution of the languages in the curriculum will vary with regard to both time and the subjects taught through the language and also with regard to the optimal use of each language in serving students as they seek personal development.

Baker's evaluation of the typology proposed by Mackey is as follows:

> This extensive typology, while important to linguists and theorists, does not seem to have helped empirical research to formulate hypotheses, nor does it appear to be a natural way of reflecting the key issues of bilingual education. Concerns raised by parents and politicians, academics and administrators are often to be found in the distinctions between transitional and enrichment, folk and elitist, and submersion and immersion bilingual education. Research has provided some important evidence on each of these concerns.   (Baker 1988: 48)

Baker himself developed one of the most widely used typologies of bilingual education. He distinguishes ten types of bilingual education and places much emphasis on *aims* – societal and educational and also in terms of language outcomes. Baker's typology takes into account whether a child comes from a language minority population or a language majority population, includes consideration of the languages of the classroom, and also reflects the distinction between additive and subtractive bilingualism. His divisions relating to monolingual, 'weak' and 'strong' forms of education for bilinguals are summed up in Tables 3 to 5 (Baker 2006: 215–216).

Table 3. Monolingual forms of education for bilinguals

Type of programme	Typical type of child	Language of the classroom	Societal and educational aim	Aim in language outcome
MAINSTREAMING/ SUBMERSION (structured immersion)	Language minority	Majority language	Assimilation/ Subtractive	Mono-lingualism
MAINSTREAMING/ SUBMERSION with withdrawal classes / sheltered English / content-based ESL	Language minority	Majority language with 'pull-out' L2 lessons	Assimilation/ Subtractive	Mono-lingualism
SEGREGATIONIST	Language minority	Minority language (forced, no choice)	Apartheid	Mono-lingualism

Table 4. Weak forms of bilingual education for bilinguals

Type of programme	Typical type of child	Language of the classroom	Societal and educational aim	Aim in language outcome
TRANSITIONAL	Language minority	Moves from minority to majority language	Assimilation/ Subtractive	Relative monolingualism
MAINSTREAM with foreign language teaching	Language majority	Majority language with L2/FL lessons	Limited enrichment	Limited bilingualism
SEPARATIST	Language minority	Minority language (out of choice)	Detachment/ Autonomy	Limited bilingualism

Table 5. Strong forms of bilingual education for bilinguals

Type of programme	Typical type of child	Language of the classroom	Societal and educational aim	Aim in language outcome
IMMERSION	Language majority	Bilingual with initial emphasis on L2	Pluralism & enrichment. Additive	Bilingualism & biliteracy
MAINTENANCE/ HERITAGE LANGUAGE	Language minority	Bilingual with emphasis on L1	Maintenance, pluralism and enrichment. Additive	Bilingualism & biliteracy
TWO WAY/DUAL LANGUAGE	Mixed language. Minority and majority	Minority and majority	Maintenance, pluralism and enrichment. Additive	Bilingualism & biliteracy
MAINSTREAM BILINGUAL	Language majority	Two majority languages. Pluralism	Maintenance, biliteracy and enrichment. Additive	Bilingualism

Typologies are constantly being refined and added to. For example, in 1997 Garcia proposed 14 types of forms of bilingual education (1997: 410) and in 2008 she added two new models of bilingualism to the additive-subtractive types: recursive and dynamic bilingualism. Recursive bilingualism is relevant in instances where the bilingual language practices of a community have undergone suppression and involves a reconstitution of this tradition of bilingualism with new functions. Dynamic bilingualism is understood as the complex ways in which bilinguals in which really use their languages: in all possible modalities, using all kinds of language practices – developing 'to adapt to the ridges and craters of communication" (Garcia 2009: 5; see also Garcia forthcoming). Ytsma (2001), for his part, proposed a tripartite typology of trilingual education consisting of 46 types of trilingual education at primary school level. His typology is applied to trilingual, bilingual and monolingual areas and is based on linguistic context, linguistic distance between three languages involved and the organizational design of the teaching of the languages at school.

Cenoz (2009) comments that the problem with typologies is that they have to be comprehensive and at the same time as simple as possible – not an easy task given the diversity of bilingual education and the specific characteristics of sociolinguistic contexts where bilingual schools are located.

In contradistinction to the large number of typologies of bilingual education, there have been very few attempts to create typologies of education involving more than two languages. This may have to do with due to the multidimensionality of such education: linguistic, educational and sociolinguistic. These dimensions have proved crucial for categorizing bilingual education and will clearly be vital for characterizing education where more than two languages figure. In line with Baker (2007), Cenoz (2009: 26) insists on distinguishing between the above two cases on the grounds that where more than two languages are involved this is very likely to reflect differences in terms of pupils' home languages. She suggests that the diversity and complexity associated with the latter instance calls for the use of modelling based on continua rather than dichotomous or trichotomous analyses of the relevant features. She argues (2009: 33–39) that her proposed continua be applied to as a tool to aid in the discernment of different degrees of multilingualism, her claim being (p. 39) that this approach "can accommodate some of the most typical cases of multilingual education that cannot easily find a place under taxonomies".

Typologies of multilingual societies

Wider environments than family and education are communities and societies. Typologies of multilingual societies may seem to be easily constructed on the first sight, but in fact have turned out to be very problematic. To start with, the notion of community applies to an extensive range of arrangements and groups, including political, territorial, religious and virtual dimensions. A major reason for the difficulty in constructing a viable, workable typology of multilingual communities is the very large number of factors to be taken into consideration simultaneously. Das Gupta notes:

> Patterns of language division in multilingual societies vary widely. In order to comprehend a specific pattern, it is important to consider, among other things, the number of language groups, their relative size, the degree of relatedness and distinction among them, variations in the standard languages and dialects, the differential literary traditions of the languages, the relation of language division to other social divisions, and the importance attributed to the language factor by the speech communities concerned.   (Das Gupta 1970: 14–15)

One very well-known attempt to devise a typology of multilingual communities was that of Kloss (1966). Kloss was aware that usually there are varying degrees of correlation or a lack of correlation between the multilingualism of a community and number of languages individuals of this community use. He speaks of three types of communities – monolingual, bi-trilingual and multilingual (i.e., beyond trilingual) – in each of which he distinguishes four types of citizenry – monolingual, diglossic, bilingual and tri- or multilingual (beyond trilingual). Kloss refers to a number of factors: whether bilingualism is personal (voluntary) or impersonal (decreed, imposed); the legal status of languages and the attitude of the population towards language shift; which segments of populations use languages and to what degree of mastery (full or coordinate bilingualism or marginal knowledge); the origin (indigenous, colonial) and prestige of languages involved and their linguistic distance from each other.

While this attempt to construct a typology of multilingual countries is laudable, the limitations of the typology restrict its usefulness. Schiffmann (1996: 34–35) points to a number of problems. Kloss's typology fails to distinguish between passive and active command of a language variety, between a register and repertoire, and between diglossia and other forms of bilingualism. Schiffmann notes,

> [It] does not distinguish whether a community is multilingual as a result of language policy or despite it. That is, is multilingualism an outcome of the policy, or does it develop or persist contrary to or independently of the policy?
>   (Schiffmann 1996: 34)

Another reflection offered in this connection by Spolsky (2009: 183) refers to "widespread variation in the sociolinguistic ecology of most social groupings, and the even greater variation in most nations, growing all the time as a result of globalization and migration". It is patently the case that we need to recognize the fuzziness and multiple scales of what we call linguistic community, or community in general. Thus, for instance, when we contemplate the notion of a multilingual society, we have to take into account both communities within particular geographical confines and scattered or worldwide diasporas?

Typologies of languages

The typologies of languages discussed here are essentially social in nature. Our interest in ordering languages, be it in the whole world, a country or a smaller community of language users, in this framework is inseparably linked to issues of social status, power and social affordances. This kind of perspective was commonly adopted in the 18th and 19th centuries and is manifested Humboldt's (1836) essay on the heterogeneity of language and its influence on human intellectual development. The idea is that not only do languages differ from each other as regards their outer form, but also that the character and structure of a language express their users' inner life and knowledge, and that therefore it is likely that languages differ from one another in the same way and to the same degree as those who use them. It may be noted that Humboldt's attitude was in line with the general popular attitude of the time according to which some languages are better endowed for more serious functions like science and poetry, while others are not. Assessments based on such a perspective could perhaps be said to be language valuations rather than typologies or codifications, but they can nevertheless be identified as the predecessors of typologies the current era.

It seems that the attempts to order languages in one way or the other were undertaken earlier than classifications of multilingual speakers and the multilingual policies. 19th century linguistics yielded significant works by, among many others, Grimm (1785–1863), Humboldt (1762–1835 – see above), and Schleicher (1821–1868). It is to such linguists, especially the last-named, that we owe the whole notion of the systematization of languages into language families, which has continued to be referred to in multilingualism research focused on cross-linguistic influence (cf. e.g. Ó Laoire & Singleton 2009). As indicated earlier, we shall not discuss here the purely linguistic dimension of typologies of languages, whether according to genealogical or to structural features. On the question of inequality between languages, the current consensus (cf. Mesthrie et al. 2009) is that all languages are capable of expressing the entirety of that which a culture or community needs to communicate, or in the case of any deficit, have the potential to develop whatever is necessary to meet the relevant communicative requirements of its users.

Our focus here will be rather on sociolinguistic differences closely connected with social processes taking place in the modern world. In this domain inequalities are discernible. As Mesthrie et al. (2009: 34ff.) rightly argue, whereas it seems to be true that all languages are equal in linguistic terms, it is obvious that they are not all equal at a social or sociolinguistic level. Clearly, different languages have conspicuously different power and status. We can immediately cite in this context the phenomenon of *diglossia* discussed earlier (in Chapter 2). In polities or communities where this phenomenon is in force, whether as classically defined à la Ferguson (1959) or more broadly (see Fishman's, 1967, development of the notion), the relevant typology distinguishes a 'High' variety (in terms of social profile and deployment) from a 'Low' variety (in precisely the same terms).

The typology of languages proposed by Stewart was probably the first typology to deal with the sociolinguistics of multilingualism, a topic which had interested him from the early 1960s. Here we give his later revised version of his typology, as published in 1968. His typology attempts to specify language types in a multilingual society not on a global scale but "at the national level" (Stewart 1968:533). The focus of his typology is on social factors, on the premise that languages differ not only in their linguistic systems but also "in their histories, their relationships to other linguistic systems, the extent to which they have acquired codified norms of usage, and in the manner of their transmission from generation to generation" (Stewart 1968:533). According to Stewart such characteristics may have an effect on the role which a particular linguistic system assumes in the linguistic makeup of a multilingual polity. He notes further that linguistic systems are characterized by different configurations of attributes which cause them to be differently categorized in terms of social value within a given country. Stewart talks about such categories in terms of *language types*. For the practical purposes of his typology, specifically intended for describing national multilingualism, Stewart proposed an analysis of seven general types of languages on the basis of the presence or absence of four attributes. These four attributes are: (1) Standardization – acceptance of a formal set of codified norms; (2) Autonomy – uniqueness and independence of the language; (3) Historicity – development over time in association with some national or ethnic tradition; (4) Vitality – use of the language by a community of native speakers.

Table 6. After Stewart (1968:537)

Attributes				Type
Standardization	Autonomy	Historicity	Vitality	
+	+	+	+	Standard
+	+	+	–	Classical
+	+	–	–	Artificial
–	+	+	+	Vernacular
–	–	+	+	Dialect
–	–	–	+	Creole
–	–	–	–	Pidgin

Table 6, then, yields seven main language types which are notated sociolinguistically: S (standard: a standardized vernacular – e.g. standard French, C (classical: a standard which has died out as a native language – e.g. the Arabic of the Koran), A (artificial – e.g. Esperanto), V (vernacular: an unstandardized native language of a speech community – e.g. Bayerisch), D (dialect: to cover situations in which a particular dialect enjoys special status – e.g. Cockney), K (creole – e.g. Haitian Creole and finally, P (pidgin – e.g. Neomelanesian of Papua New Guinea). (For a critical discussion on pidgins and creoles, see De Graff 2005.)

In addition Stewart (1968:540–541) codified ten important functions of language into:

1. official language, used at the national level
    – symbol 'o'
2. provincial language, official only in given regions
    – symbol 'p'
3. language of wider communication (other than an 'o' or 'p' variety)
    – symbol 'w'
4. language of wider international communication (other than an 'o' or 'p' variety)
    – symbol 'i'
5. capital language, communicatively dominant in the area of the national capital (other than an 'o' or 'p' variety)
    – symbol 'c'
6. group language, used for communication within a specific speech community
    – symbol 'g'
7. educational language used for educational purposes, at primary or secondary level (other than an 'o' or 'p' variety)
    – symbol 'e'
8. school subject, language widely taught as a school subject (other than an 'o' or 'p' variety)
    – symbol 's'
9. literary, language used primarily for literary or scholarly purposes
    – symbol 'l'
10. religious, language used for religious purposes
    – symbol 'r'.

Of the foregoing Stewart writes (1968:542): "[it] should be clear that this classification rates linguistic systems according to degree of use only, and cannot be taken by itself as an index of relative social importance." On the other hand, it is noticeable that all four of his major attributes are connected with society and that the seven language types generated do relate to perceived social status – Standard being at the top of this scale and Pidgin at the bottom.

Stewart also categorized degree of use in respect of language varieties operative within national communities. He devised a rating system consisting of six classes, each class denoting a degree of use in terms of the percentage of relevant users (Stewart 1968: 542):

Class	Percentage
Class I	75% +
Class II	50% +
Class III	25% +
Class IV	10% +
Class V	5% +
Class VI	Below 5%

Thus, the sociolinguistic notation suggested by Stewart can describe the specific situation and give a sociolinguistic profile of a country. For example, the sociolinguistic profile of Dutch Antilles in the Leeward Island Group is defined as:

Class I	English	D
Class IV	Dutch	So
Papiamentu	Kg	

(Stewart 1968: 544)

Obviously, no typology is going to provide a universal tool for each and every situation in a complex multilingual reality. The best one can perhaps hope for in any given context is an instrument which offers a consistent and research-informed modus operandi for analysing the context in question and which may tangentially offer insights in relation to others.

In recent times, with the advent of globalization bringing increases in mobility, ethnic movements, preoccupation with identity, the challenge of ordering languages of the world has again become a matter of urgent interest. As a consequence, in multilingualism studies research effort has once more turned in the direction of minority languages, regional languages and lesser-used – especially endangered – languages, as well as international languages and languages of wider communication. Questions on topics such as the foregoing are increasingly under debate with reference to their interaction with ethnic minority issues, with language policies and politics, and with local and global economic processes.

Among recent multilingual typologies we find global classifications of languages which strive to order the totality of languages of the world, while others concentrate on a specific category of languages – such as, for example, pluricentric languages, minority languages, lesser-used languages, and endangered languages. Yet, other typologies describe language arrangements in a country or a polity – where specific sets of languages may be disposed in opposition to each other, in juxtaposition with each other or in some other kind of relation to each other. Another strategy is to home in on one single language and to classify its various roles as allotted by contemporary social condition. Cook's treatment of English in this manner (see below) is an example of this last type of approach.

For Extra the point of departure in ordering languages derives from the proliferation and divergence of language roles in the contemporary world. For example, he proposes the outline of a hierarchy of languages for Europe as follows (Extra under review):

– English as a lingua franca for transnational communication;
– National or 'official state' languages of European countries;
– Regional minority languages across Europe;
– Immigrant minority languages across Europe.

De Swaan (2001), for his part, proposes in his Galactic Model a hierarchy of languages for the entire world, which has been neatly recycled in tabular form by Cook (2008) (see below, Figure 1).

For De Swaan "the global language system comprises the many thousands of language groups on earth in a single, strongly ordered pattern" (de Swaan 2001: 176). The basic layer of the hierarchy, according to De Swaan, embraces the thousands of *peripheral* languages which are used by less than 10% of humankind but comprise 98% of all the world languages. Examples include Wolof[1] spoken in

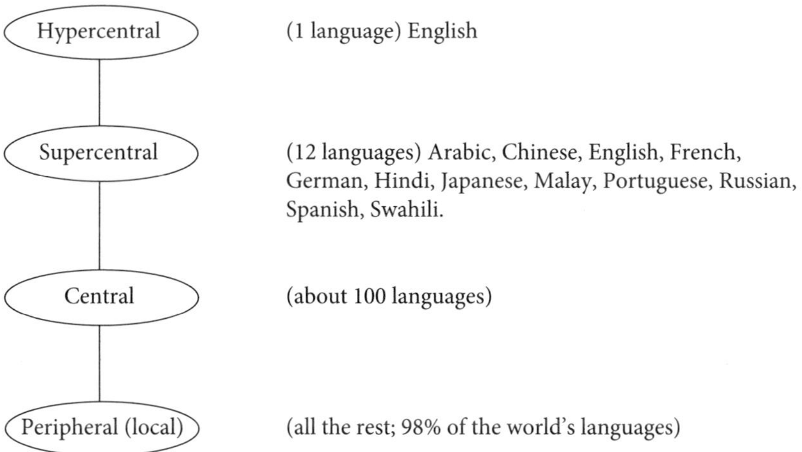

Figure 1. The hierarchy of languages (Cook 2008; Cook forthcoming a, adapted from de Swaan 2001)

---

1.   N.B. Wolof is certainly not peripheral in the local context.

Tanzania and Senegal in Africa, Chakesang, Deori, Khezha and Lahauli in India, and Occitan and Corsican in France. De Swaan likens these peripheral languages to moons circling a planet (de Swaan 2001:4). The 'planetary position', the next layer of the hierarchy, is assigned to about 100 *central* languages, usually the 'national' or official languages of states or provinces, used in politics, in the lawcourts, in education, in textbooks, and in the print and broadcast media. Examples are Bengali, Italian and Dutch. Only twelve *supercentral* languages are recognized: Arabic, Chinese, English, French, German, Hindi, Japanese, Malay, Portuguese, Russian, Spanish, Swahili.[2] These are compared to 'suns' in the Galactic Model, and, with the exception of Swahili, they each have more than one hundred million speakers. Of *supercentral* languages de Swaan (2001:5) has the following to say:

> If the mother-tongue speakers of a central language acquire another language, it is usually one that is more widely spread and higher up in the hierarchy. At this next level a number of central languages are connected through their multilingual speakers to one very large language groups that occupies a 'supercentral' position within the system. It serves purposes of long-distance and international communication. Quite often this is a language that was once imposed by a colonial power and after independence continued to be used in politics, administration, law, big business, technology and higher education.

The single language labelled *hypercentral* is English. The supercentral languages, are represented as connected to the central languages, and the latter, in their turn, are represented as surrounded by the peripheral languages. Each layer of the hierarchy is seen as linked to the higher and lower levels via multilingual speakers.

All of the sociolinguistic classifications of languages that have evolved in recent times acknowledge that languages and groups of languages are unequal in sociolinguistic terms and reflect such inequality in typologies that are explicitly or implicitly hierarchical. Languages positioned higher up in proposed hierarchies are typically characterized by extensive territorial reach, high numbers of speakers, centrality in the world order, more formal and more public domains of use, and literature. The lower levels of hierarchies are populated by languages which are less widespread, have fewer speakers, may have limited amounts of literate and literary usage associated with them, many of them tending rather towards the oral medium, and may manifest fewer semantic-pragmatic functions and signs of recent/current linguistic development than languages higher up the scale.

---

2.   Swahili is a major Bantu language of East Africa. Its estimated fifty million speakers render it the most widely spoken language in Africa. Its name is a matter of some debate: its name in the language itself is *Kiswahili*, and many (though by no means all) Africanists prefer this term.

Languages situated lower in the hierarchies are unanimously noted as being greater in number. They are often seen as being poorly endowed in terms of numbers of native speakers, but occasionally (as, for example, in the case of many of the languages of India) their native-speaker numbers are extremely buoyant. They also, as a rule, attract fewer L2 learners. All the typologies place English at the top of the hierarchy, even if it is not universally singled out as uniquely occupying a very particular position.

Graddol (1997: 12) notes that "[t]he taper of the pyramid reflects the fact that fewer language varieties occupy this position: greatest linguistic diversity is found at the base amongst vernacular languages". Not all speakers will be fluent in language varieties at the higher levels. The normal pattern of acquisition will begin with those languages at the base. Many of the world's population never require the use of varieties at the uppermost layer because they never find themselves in the communicative position which requires such language. For example, an Indian from the state of Kerala whose mother tongue is a tribal language may also speak Tulu (2 million speakers) and the state language Malayalam (33 million), or the neighbouring state language of Kannada (44 million). If they know any Hindi or English it is likely to be their fourth or fifth language. However, more and more people in the world will learn languages in the uppermost layer as a result of improved education and changing patterns of communication in the world.

Although a simple pyramid figure captures something of the hierarchical relationship between language varieties, it perhaps suggests too neat a pattern of language use. For the majority of the world's population, a particular language will exist at more than one level (for example, serve as a public language as well as a language in the family)…

A different approach is taken by Clyne (1992b) in his focus on the languages that Kloss (1978 II: 66–67) calls *pluricentric languages*. These are described as languages with several interacting centres, each providing a national variety with at least some of its own (codified) norms. Chinese, Korean, English, French, German Swedish, Dutch and Spanish are considered to be pluricentric. English has centres and standard versions in the United Kingdom and in the United States of America as well as in Australia, Canada and South Africa. The German language has one centre in Germany and another in Austria, yet another in Switzerland. As for French, apart from France it has centres in Canada, Switzerland and Belgium. Distinguishing pluricentric languages from those which are not pluricentic is a kind of typology in itself. In addition, Clyne is of the view that a typology of pluricentric languages themselves can make a theoretical contribution. At the practical level further studies may be expected to offer insights regarding possible ways for achieving conditions for symmetric pluricentricity. Clyne (1992b: 4) refers in this context to Ammon's (1989) proposal:

a quantitative model of codification taking into account the existence of model speakers (and spoken model texts), model writers (written model texts), codex of spelling (orthographic dictionaries, explicit rules), defining dictionaries, codex of pronunciation, codex of morphology and syntax, and codex of style. This facilitates a scale from full endonormativity to full exonormativity (models and codex entirely from outside). The scale enables Ammon to differentiate between 'full centres', 'nearly full centres', 'semi-centres', and 'rudimentary centres of a language'.

Edwards's typology of minority languages is the fruit of long endeavour in this area (Edwards 1991, 1992). It seeks "to create a comprehensive scaffolding" (Edwards 1992: 144). It is founded on the three basic categories of variable: speaker, language and setting. Working with these, Edwards (1994) arrived at an account of minority language situations involving 33 variables. Considering each of the numbered cells one might note especially:

- urban–rural distinctions and their role in language maintenance and decline;
- the matter of within-group or without-group marriage;
- the nature and degree of dialectal variation and fragmentation;
- the issue of language attitudes and beliefs, etc. and the possibility of their contributing to the prediction of shift/maintenance outcomes.

Such a framework would be especially useful in conjunction with individual case-studies, although Edwards urges caution:

> …these questions are not, themselves, anywhere near specific enough to comprise a completed and applicable typology, they are merely suggestions of the sort of items which could be grouped together by cell … [T]he reader is reminded that this is to be taken only as an approximation, in the expectation that further work will result in changes and refinements. No scheme will capture every nuance of every situation.
>
> (Edwards 1994: 145)

Edwards's cited examples of minority language situations include the Nguni group (Xhosa, Zulu, etc.) and the Sotho family (Tswana, Sotho), with a total of some 15 million speakers, in South Africa, where English and Afrikaans were at the time of his study the country's official languages. He also refers to French in Canada, and to Celtic language speakers in France and Britain. Drawing in his discussion on the works of White (1991) on geographical aspects of minority language situations, and those of Haugen (1972) on ecological issues, he proposes (1994: 138) three basic distinctions for his typology of minority language situations.

1. *unique, non-unique* and *local-only* – encompassing minority languages which are unique to a specific state, those which are non-unique but which are still minorities in all contexts in which they occur, and those which are minorities in one setting but are majority varieties elsewhere;
2. *adjoining* or *non-adjoining* – dealing with the types of connections between groups speakers of the same minority language in different states;
3. *cohesive* and *non-cohesive* – addressing the degree of spatial cohesion existing among speakers within a given state.

To be noted is that Edwards (2010) disapproves of the use of "unnecessary neologisms and sundry hair-splitting exercises" with respect to discussion as to when a revival of a language is not a revival but a restoration, a rebirth, a renaissance, a revitalization, etc. and suggests a **tentative** classification, a "simple" and "very crude outline" (p. 50) of revival scenarios. (In our terms this is a partial classification, not a classification for ALL languages.)

a. a language with few speakers, where no written or taped records exist;
b. the same, except that some written and taped materials exists;
c. the same, except that written and taped material exists;
d. a language with some native speakers remaining, but where none are monolingual;
e. the same, but where some at least are monolingual;
f. the same but where monolingualism and *normal family transmission* of the original language occur;
g. the same, but where substantial numbers of speakers are monolingual, where there is language transmission, and where the original variety retains important domains (especially outside the home and family).

As a *coda* to this discussion of Edwards's work we offer our view that, although his (1994, 2010) classifications may sometimes lack the kind of specificity that researchers crave, in general terms these classifications provide a valuable contribution in at least sketching the broad outline of salient differences between language situations. His resistance to the notion of entering into minute detail chimes with our own observations about the complexity of multilingualism. According to our approach, mere 'number-crunching' does not meet the case; what is required is a perspective on multilingual phenomena which is genuinely and consistently informed by complexity thinking.

One factor that clearly needs to be kept in the picture is economic reality. Ammon (1995) suggests a rather straightforward way of estimating the economic strength of a language by simply ranking the economies of the countries, where

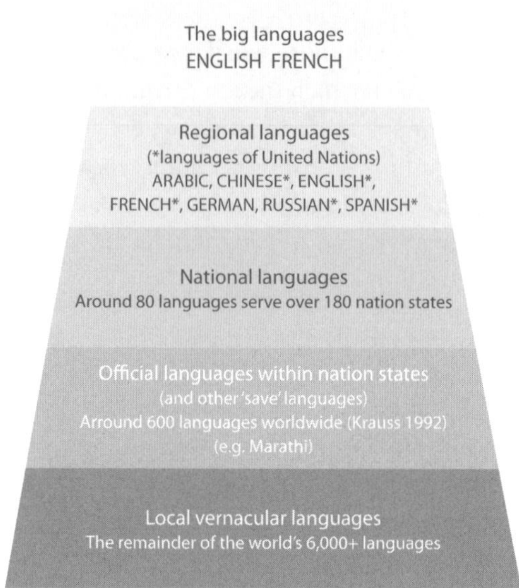

Figure 2. International order of languages (Graddol 1997: 13)[3]

native speakers of given languages are domiciled. The table presenting the international order of languages for the late 1980s on this basis is given in Graddol (1997).

Another 'economics-based' approach is to take into account all the countries in which a language is spoken and to assign to the language in question the appropriate *pro rata* proportion of Gross Domestic Product of each country in question. On this basis, the model calculates for each language the "Gross Language Product" (GLP) – "the total value of transactions conducted in a given language" (Oflazer 2003). Below is an example of a language classification arrived at in this manner.

Table 7. Estimates of Gross Language Product (GLP) of major languages in $billion (engco model) (Graddol 1997: 29)

1.	English	4,815	8.	Arabic	408
2.	Japanese	4,240	9.	Russian	363
3.	German	2,455	10.	Hindi/Urdu	114
4.	Spanish	1,789	11.	Italian	111
5.	French	1,557	12.	Malay	79
6.	Chinese	985	13.	Bengali	32
7.	Portuguese	611			

3. <http://www.britishcouncil.org/learning-elt-future.pdf>.

When Graddol set himself the task of understanding the role of English and of other languages that are used alongside it (1997:12), he placed economic matters centre-stage. Although the primary focus of Graddol's ongoing investigation has been the future of the English language (Graddol 1997, 2006), and although he has not claimed to provide an explicit classification or hierarchy of languages, his discussion of the economic dimension of languages allows us to come to grips with the hegemony of some languages over others. He comes to the conclusion that languages are hierarchically ordered in accordance with their level of economic power.

Graddol (1997:12) states that "languages are not equal in political or social status, particularly in multilingual contexts". He goes on to suggest that "[l]anguages in multilingual areas are often hierarchically ordered in status" and that "[t]o the extent that such relationships are institutionalized, the hierarchy can be though of as applying to countries as much as to the repertoire of individual speakers". Graddol presents graphic schemas showing language hierarchies at the levels of country (India), politico-economic zone (the European Union) and the world (see Figures 3 and 4).

Graddol notes, however, that calculating a language's economic strength is, in fact, a far from straightforward matter. He writes (1997:29):

> … international trade is often a complex, cross-border business: goods are taken from one country, refined or given added value by a second, sold to a third, repackaged, resold and so on. Such multilateral trade brings with it greater reliance on lingua francas.

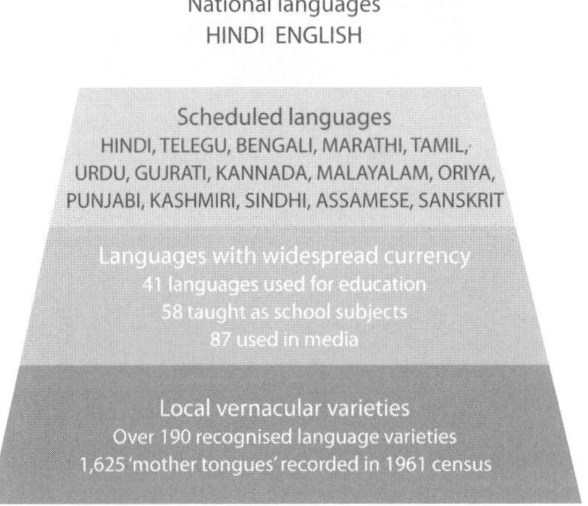

Figure 3. A language hierarchy for India (Graddol 1997:12)

Figure 4. A language hierarchy for the European Union (Graddol 1997: 13)

Concluding summary

Classifications and typologies of multilingualism are complex because multilingualism is complex by definition. Each of the classifications on offer may elucidate some facet or facets of the phenomenon but cannot hope to embrace the entire panoply of multilingualism – not, at least as things stand in our current state of research, and perhaps never.

Classifications focusing on bilinguals and bilingual societies sometimes constitute the precursors of typologies of multilingualism involving multiplicities of languages. Some of the approaches and insights of bilingual classifications can be applied more widely for specific purposes to situations where more than two languages are involved.

While dichotomizing, trichotomizing, etc. have a role to play in the establishment of multilingual typologies, there is a need to conceptualize multilingualism in other ways too – taking account of its continuities and complexities. Also to be borne in mind is the purpose to which a typology is intended to be put; a given typology may be extremely useful in one context of use but less so in others.

Unsatisfactory though our current endeavours to classify and typologize the multifaceted and complex nature of multilingual reality may be, they offer some first benchmarks, and they shed invaluable guiding light with reference to the difficulties and challenges that future research will need to address.

CHAPTER 8

A multilingual monolith?

Introductory

In this chapter we explore the question of whether knowledge of two or more languages constitutes a monolith in terms of acquisition and processing or is better conceived of in terms of separable entities. In Chapter 6 we dealt with this issue as it relates narrowly to the development of two and more languages in infants. The present chapter revisits the question in a broader context, surveying a wide range of relevant evidence. It recognizes that, in multilinguality in all its manifestations, the multilingual's language knowledge needs to be seen in terms of dynamic interconnection and interplay, and is in this sense 'holistic'. It argues, on the other hand, that the competencies associated with different languages known to the multilingual are at some level and in some sense differentiable and differentiated.

Languages together

There is, of course, plenty of evidence – from a wide range of research domains that all the language resources at a multilingual's disposal dynamically interact (cf. Herdina & Jessner 2002), and such evidence clearly indicates a high degree of cross-linguistic connectivity. One obvious indication of such interaction is the way in which languages known to an individual 'interfere' with each other.

Nor is awareness of such 'interference' at all recent. One can cite in this connection Postgate's (1922: 48ff.) recounting of some tales of caution dating from the First World War.

> … on one occasion the mild [French] expression *demander une explication* ['to ask for an explanation'] gave dire offence to the Government of the United States because it looked like 'to demand an explanation', while the English translation of the Allied Note answering Germany's first offer of peace in January 1917, renders *prétendu* as 'pretended' where it clearly means, as generally, 'alleged'.

In the same place Postgate tells the story of an English bishop 'who concluded an address to French troops with the prayer 'Que Dieu vous blesse' ['May God wound you']. Vildomec's (1963) treatment of cross-linguistic influence in a multilingual context also makes much of its 'interfering' dimension: "if two languages a subject has mastered are similar … they may 'co-operate' in interfering with other tongues" (1963: 212).

One interesting dimension of cross-linguistic interplay is the case of the blending of forms from one language with those from another. Some of the findings emerging from the Trinity College Dublin Modern Languages Research Project, for example, clearly demonstrate this process. These findings relate to coinages which exist in the form given in neither the L1 nor in any additional language, but which are the fruits of cross-lexical 'consultation'. The following are cases in point – English-speaking subjects' attempts at French expressions, drawn from word-association and translation data.

> *lionesse*
> (word-association test stimulus *lion* ['lion'], cf. English *lioness*)
> *harnesses*
> (expression to be translated 'seat belts', cf. English *harness*)
>
> (Singleton 1996: 248)

Hammarberg (2009: 140ff.) provides some similar examples. Sometimes the attempts of his native English-speaking subject, Sarah Williams (SW below), at word construction in her L3 Swedish drew on English, as the following instances illustrate:

SW's form	Target	English gloss
briba	*muta*	*bribe*
viska	*visp*	*whisk*
pluggan	*kontakten*	*(electric) plug*

Even more frequently SW tapped her German (L2) resources:

SW's form	Target	English gloss	German gloss
alejne	*ensam*	*alone*	*allein*
ågen	*ögen*	*eyes*	*Augen*
langvilt	*tråkig*	*boring*	*langweilig*
förglickt	*jämfört*	*compared*	*verglichen*
osten	*påsk*	*Easter*	*Ostern*
tatsak	*faktum*	*fact*	*Tatsache*

So far we have been looking at instances of 'negative transfer' but much recent research looking at cross-linguistic influence goes beyond an 'interfering' perspective. One research direction starts from the idea that perceptions of the 'distance' or degree of relatedness between the languages known or being learned by individuals, have an impact on the extent to which language users attempt to transfer between them. This notion is very much associated with Kellerman's work (e.g. 1977, 1979, 1983), but was already under way before Kellerman's intervention (e.g. Sjöholm 1976) and has continued to be explored since (e.g. Ringbom 1987; Singleton 1987, in press; Singleton & Little 1984/2005; Ó Laoire & Singleton 2009). In common with some other recent explorations of cross-linguistic influence, such studies focus on facilitatory as well as interfering aspects of cross-linguistic interaction (cf. Ringbom 2007). Another interesting research direction – also often with a facilitatory focus – deals with multilingual transfer in the sense of the transfer of experience, processes and strategies across additional language learning situations (see e.g. Gabryś-Barker 2009).

Such evidence clearly argues for extremely high levels of interaction between the languages in question. It has indeed induced some researchers to write in very strongly integrative terms about the relationships among the multingual's languages. For example, Safont Jordà has the following to say:

> This interdependence characterising third language learning leads us to consider learners' first second and third languages as a whole linguistic system, which they command simultaneously. In fact, it seems more logical to consider languages known by a multilingual speaker as a whole unit than to view them as separate entities that develop in isolation.   (Safont Jordà 2005: 13–14)

Just how far we should take such integrationist arguments is a matter of debate. Safont Jordà's view has much in common with Cook's multicompetence approach, which we certainly find persuasive. Our perspective, however, on the idea, apparently implied in her argumentation, that the multilingual mind is characterized by a fully unitary linguistic system is, as will become clear in what follows, rather different.

Separatist arguments

A powerful argument against the total unitariness of language knowledge in multilinguals derives from the fact of formal differences among languages. Faced with the challenge of coming to grips with the formal shape of an unfamiliar word, a person will refer to the formal structure of more familiar items and then analogize (see Bybee 1988; Stemberger & MacWhinney 1988). To take an example from English, someone encountering *ripeness* for the first time will refer to the structure of such words as *lightness* and *sadness*. Since the languages known to such an individual may have highly divergent morphological phonological systems (e.g. /nəs/ does not figure as a morpheme or a syllable in Chinese), it is highly likely that the search on which such analogizing depends runs through the lexicon of each language separately.

Even more persuasive evidence of separation comes from the phenomenon of the selective recovery of languages lost following brain damage and from that of aphasia affecting only one of a multilingual's languages (see, e.g., Fabbro 1999: Chapters 12–16). Whitaker, for example, (1978: 27) discusses the case of an English classics scholar who recovered Greek, Latin, French and English (his L1) in that order, while Grosjean refers (1982: 260) to that of a native speaker of Swiss German who recovered first French and subsequently Standard High German, but who never recovered his native variety. This kind of phenomenon also extends to bi- and multidialectalism. Fabbro (2002: 204) reports the case of an Italian native speaker of Veronese (a variant of Venetian), who exclusively used Veronese in all her daily activities, except for a few words of Italian two or three times a year, but who, following a brain insult, expressed herself exclusively in Italian. Her condition subsequently improved to the point where she understood Veronese, but she continued to speak only standard Italian.

With respect to aphasia, Paradis & Goldblum (1989) report the case of a trilingual subject who was a native speaker of Gujarati, an Indo-European language spoken in central India, which was the language he mainly used with his family. However, the person in question lived in Madagascar, and so he had additionally acquired Malagasy, Madagascar's official language. At age six he had also learned French at school, and he used this language on a daily basis in his professional activities. Following a neurosurgical operation, he evidenced disorders typifying Broca's aphasia in Gujarati but no deficits in his other languages. Two years after the operation he had fully recovered Gujarati but had difficulties with Malagasy in terms of verbal fluency and syntactic comprehension. Four years after the operation no disorder was detected in either language.

Another kind of language loss also points to separation. Languages may be lost not only as a result of brain damage but also as a result of neglect in favour of another language. Where, for example, a child migrating to a particular community has an L1 which is different from that of the majority of members of the host community, where his/her home language receives little or no support from the community in question and where his/her parents make little or no effort to support it either, the language in question may attrite to the point of virtual disappearance. A number of case-studies of such L1 attrition are reported by Kouritzin (1999). One such case (Kouritzin 1999: 75–96) is that of Lara, who had had migrated with her family from Finland to Canada at age two, and had subsequently lived for four years in a small town within a tight-knit Finnish community. Lara was thus until the age of six a Finnish speaker with very little English. From age six onwards, however, having moved to a large city, and under the influence of her parents' decision that the time had come to integrate with English-speaking Canada, her development in Finnish came to a halt and English progressively took over. Lara reports that the last time she tried (and failed) to converse in Finnish had been when she was eighteen years old. Her current perception is that she has lost her L1. Here, then, we have an instance of a family taking a decision to favour one language and effectively to abandon another, with the result that the latter language was lost. This clearly implies choice, which in turn implies separation.

Finally in this connection, we can refer to the fact that in their everyday functioning multilinguals are attentive in their use or non-use of particular languages to the competencies of their interlocutors. Of course there are many cases of multilingual societies where there is a promiscuous intermingling of languages. We cited earlier in this connection the instance of Singapore. To be noted, however, is that in societies like Singapore, the intermingled languages in question are accessible to the community at large. Multilinguals' sensitivity in the deployment of their languages to their interlocutors' range of linguistic knowledge clearly relates to the necessity of being understood by the interlocutors in question. Such selectivity obviously implies that the multilingual is able to differentiate between his/her languages. In some multilingual communities, selectivity is, in fact, socially promoted. For example, in Afghanistan, where most people "speak at least one of the official languages …, but a number of other languages are in common use", one particular language, Duri, "is the language of government, commerce and culture" (Mackenzie 2005:434). It goes without saying that the specific range of functions allotted to specific languages both require and reinforce separation.

It is interesting to explore in this context Li Wei's (2011) discussion of the notion of *translanguaging*, which he characterizes as is both going between different linguistic structures and systems and going beyond them and as including the full range of linguistic performances of multilingual language users. He sees the act of translanguaging as transformative, creating a social space for the multilingual by bringing together different dimensions of, *inter alia*, experience, attitudes and cognitive capacity into one coordinated and meaningful performance. Li Wei is patently not talking about language confusion here, or about an absence of language differentiation. On the contrary, the focus is on opting *between* language resources, on the *co-ordination* of such resources and on multilinguals' constant decision-making as to what strategic moves they should make to achieve specific communicative effects in social interaction.

One can note that language separation often has quite extreme effects. Where the expectation is that language x is being spoken but where, in fact, language y is being used, comprehension may be blocked, even where both languages are known to the individual in question, as the example below (from the psychologist Elisabet Service) shows.

> My sister, while studying in France was once addressed on the street in Finnish. Only after several attempts by the speaker did she understand her own native language, the point being that she was expecting French. I have had a very similar experience trying to make Finnish out of something that was easy enough to understand when I realized it was English.
>
> (Service: personal communication to David Singleton)

Instances of code-switching are not counter-evidence to the notion of language separation. They can certainly be seen as (see de Bot & Schreuder 1993) as evidence in favour of the notion that a multilingual's various languages are continuously activated, though each to a different level (cf. Green 1986, 1993; Paradis 1981), and thus for the possibility that in some circumstances words from the language other than the one in use may "slip in" (de Bot & Schreuder 1993:212), but this does not undermine the essential separability of a multilingual's languages. One might add that the manner in which code-switching proceeds appears to be sensitive to the particularities of the languages involved. For example, Myers-Scotton (2003) notes that code-switching between Arabic and English exhibits a very high proportion of embedded English inflectional phrases (i.e. phrases including a tensed verb) where Arabic is the matrix language. Myers-Scotton argues that the reason for this untypically large number of embedded language 'islands' is the essential incongruity between the Arabic frame and the nature of English verbs. Such sensitivity to cross-linguistic incongruities constitutes further evidence of the separation of languages in the mind. We return to the question of code-switching below.

Striking a balance

There is much reference in the current literature to Cook's (e.g, 1992, 2003a) notion of 'holistic multicompetence', which posits a very high degree of integration of language competence across languages. Dijkstra is also (e.g. 2003) often cited as an advocate of the position that the mental lexicon is fully integrated and 'fundamentally nonselective', no matter how many languages are involved. Cook's initial (1991) definition of multicompetence was "the compound state of mind with two grammars" (p. 112). One of his goals in proposing this concept was to change the view of people making use of additional languages. His perspective was that such individuals should not be seen as failed native speakers of the additional languages in question but rather as multicompetent users – knowing and using additional languages at any level (cf. Cook 2002). Multicompetence has been used as something of a watchword by researchers who wish to emphasize the close relationship between the various branches of language knowledge and cultural knowledge stored and deployed when functioning occurs in more than one language and culture. For example, Kanno (2003: 7), writing about the negotiation of bilingual/bicultural identity, has the following to say.

> I take the 'multicompetence' (Cook 1992, 1999) view of bilingualism and biculturalism: that is, to think of a bilingual person's linguistic and cultural repertoire as a whole, rather than separating out each language and culture as if 'the bilingual is (or should be) two monolinguals in one person' (Grosjean 1992: 52).

Cook (1992) cites a range of evidence in support of his multicompetence model. He refers, for example, to the finding (cf. Caramazza & Brones 1979) that when a bilingual subject in a psycholinguistic experiment is asked to react in some way to a word in one of his/her languages – by, for instance, deciding whether or not it is a real word – the time taken to react is related to the frequency of any cognate that the word may have in the other of his/her languages. Thus, reaction to a relatively infrequent word in English such as *extend* will be speeded up if the subject is a French-English bilingual, given that the French cognate of *extend* – *étendre* – is relatively frequent. Cook also notes the fact – demonstrated by experiment (cf. Cristoffanini, Kirsner & Milech 1986) and also by common experience – that translation between languages is faster when the items to be translated resemble each other in formal terms. Translating German *Arm* into English *arm* is thus quicker than translating German *Bein* into English *leg*. Another piece of evidence cited by Cook is that when a bilingual processes a word-form which is identical across his/her two languages but where the meanings of the form in the respective languages are unrelated (e.g. *coin* – English "piece of money", French "corner") he/she accesses its meanings in both languages rather than just the meaning specific to the language being used (cf. Beauvillain & Grainger 1987). Such evidence as is referred to above is argued by Cook to indicate constant interaction in bilingual language processing between the internalized knowledge bases relating to each of the two languages in question.

Cook and his colleagues (Cook, Bassetti, Kasai, Sasaki & Takahashi 2006; see also Kesckés & Papp 2000; Pavlenko 2010) also seem to come close to advocating the idea of a common conceptual base in multilinguals. They report in this connection on a study investigating whether Japanese speakers' categorisation of objects and substances as shape or material was influenced by their acquisition of English, the hypothesis being that for simple objects the number of shape-based categorisations (which English tends to favour) would increase with more experience of English in relation to material-based categorisations (favoured by Japanese). This hypothesis was confirmed by the results of the study, which was taken to have implications in respect of the effects of acquiring a second language on categorisation have implications and in consequence for a merging of conceptual representation.

As for the perspective of Dijkstra and his colleagues (e.g. Dijkstra 2003), this focuses very specifically on the lexical domain and rests on findings from a range of experimental studies (including his own) indicating that, when a particular word form is activated, formally similar words known to the individual in question are activated also, whatever the language affiliation of the words in question (at least in respect of languages which are genuinely active in the individual's mind). On this view "the bilingual brain cannot avoid language conflict, because words from the target and nontarget languages become automatically activated" (van Heuven, Schriefers, Dijkstra & Hagoort 2008:2706). A not dissimilar kind of interpretation can be applied to the language-specific processing cost paid by bilinguals in the syntactic domain (Hernandez, Bates & Avila 1994). One notes that parallel activation and language conflict do not of themselves argue for unitariness; in our view, quite the contrary.

While their rhetoric appears sometimes to come close to claiming cross-linguistic unitariness, both Cook and Dijkstra in the end retreat from such a conclusion. Cook concludes (2003:7f.) that while "total separation is impossible since both languages are in the same mind", it is also the case that "total integration is impossible since L2 users can keep the languages apart," going on to suggest that "between these two extreme, and probably untenable positions of total separation and total integration, there are many different degrees and types of interconnection." The evidence of merging conceptual representation also needs to be treated carefully. We need to beware of over-interpreting evidence such as the Cook et al. (2006) results, which bespeak cross-linguistic conceptual influence increasing with exposure rather than straightforward unitariness. Cook's above-cited comments bring to mind the old linguistic truism (see Lyons 1963:37f.) about every language articulating the world uniquely in terms of its various structures and consequently in terms of its concepts and configurations of concepts. What this implies is that, in order to function intelligibly in the relevant communities, users of additional languages have to make use of conceptual systems specific to such additional languages, systems which are of their nature differentiated from those of their other languages. The reality of a degree of cross-linguistic conceptual permeability and transfer does not undermine the other reality of this essential differentiation (cf. Singleton 2003, in press).

A sidelight is thrown on this discussion by a phenomenon observed by Flege and others (Baker, Trofimovich, Mack & Flege 2002; Flege 1999; Flege & MacKay 2011; Kopečková 2011; Singleton & Kopečková in press) in the phonetic/phonological sphere. This concerns the sharing of phonetic space by different and similar L1 and L2 elements. Even among the most successful acquirers of the pronunciation of additional languages differences from the target accent may remain with regard to specific L2 sounds which closely resemble but are subtly different from corresponding L1 segments. In such cases the persistent effect of L1 phonology appears to be difficult to overcome. This phenomenon has been variously interpreted. One way of looking at it is to say that cross-linguistic resistance to assimilation is sometimes strongest when the cross-linguistic similarities are also strongest, and that this constitutes a further argument against any easy discarding of cross-linguistic boundaries in theorizing about multicompetence.

To return now to Dijkstra (2003), he for his part, acknowledges, on the basis of his own findings, that individual languages can be at different levels of activation, and proposes a model in which the items and processes associated with each of the languages known to an individual may be activated or de-activated as a set. This is especially emphasized in the context of production:

> … to speak a word in order to name a pictured object, it is mandatory that language be specified. Even in the case of highly similar cognate translations, words in two languages rarely have an identical pronunciation, so language must be known if performance is to be error-free.   (Kroll & Dijkstra 2005: 320)

Cross-linguistic interaction as blur

An extremely radical point of view is offered by 'integrational linguistics'. This school of thought was founded by Roy Harris. In a book entitled *The Language Myth* published in 1981, Harris attacks the myth which presents language as a fixed verbal code designed to permit the transfer of 'thoughts' or 'ideas' from one human mind to another on the assumption that this code is known to all members of a linguistic community. As Crystal (1981) in his review of this book points out, the weaknesses of the above vision of how language operates have already been widely critiqued within linguistics before Harris's intervention. In any case, Harris's own standpoint rapidly became associated with a claim that both within the individual and within the community the continuum of variation within the operations of language is such that it makes no sense to talk about clear demarcations, and that languages blur into each other in myriad ways (see e.g. Harris 1998).

Informed by similar thinking, Toolan rejects (2008: 4) the notion that concepts of separate languages are "objectively grounded in linguistic facts". Such a position points to an interpretation of cross-linguistic influence as simply further evidence of the general blur that purportedly besets the entire language phenomenon. De Bot, looking at this same question from the point of view of Dynamic

Systems Theory (cf. de Bot, Lowie & Verspoor 2007) and focusing specifically on multilingual processing, has also begun to question the notion of the separateness or indeed the separability of language systems.

The 'blur' conception of multilingualism might be considered to be favoured by evidence that language users confuse the languages they are using. Our earlier discussion of code-switching is of relevance here. A superficial view of code-switching might take it as favouring a sort of all-in-together perspective on language knowledge, and indeed, as we saw, in Chapter 6, language alternation has been used as an argument for the complete unitariness of the bilingual's language system in early stages – a perspective which, as we noted, has receded under the impact of further research. We also explored arguments concerning the import for language separation of code-switching, taking account of the ways in which code-switching functions at the level of linguistic detail responds to structural differences between the alternating languages, evidence again highly favouring separation at some level.

An additional point that might be made here is that recent thinking has emphasized the sociolinguistic aspect of language alternation. Thus, for example, Gafaranga (2009: 307–308) claims that "[a] significant amount of evidence, gathered in various sociolinguistic contexts and looked at from powerful theories of social interaction, show that language alternation is a conversational strategy". This view of code-switching represents it not in terms of the blurring of language boundaries but rather in terms of a high degree of language-sensitive (and language-difference-sensitive) structuring. Staying with the sociolinguistic perspective, a further approach looks at language switching in contexts where its causation seems to be a kind of imposed politeness in minority-language situations. Writing on the topic of the language realities in the Catalan-language area, for example, Vila i Morena (2008: 43) writes of the way in which sociolinguistic norms seem to reproduce themselves across generations, perpetuating patterns whereby the use of Catalan systematically gives way to Spanish but not vice versa. Vila i Morena comments as follows.

> In most cases, it is the very Catalan L1 parents who unconsciously teach their children to switch when addressing a non-Catalan speaker. Non-Catalan L1 children learn in everyday interaction that it is common for the other speakers to switch to Spanish.

It is not our intention to enter into the detail of this argument, merely to point out that between two languages as close as Spanish and Catalan there are well-defined patterns of wholesale switching – of a kind and in a direction of which Catalan activists disapprove, but around which sociolinguistic distinctions between the languages seem to be on the whole systematically maintained.

Even in cases where language alternation produces what to the casual observer might appear to be a total mish-mash, it turns out often to be possible to determine the motivations for particular switches and to find good reasons for claiming that, far from confusion, the speakers are manifesting at every stage subtle and rationale-generated strategies involving differentiation. The example below is provided by Canagarajah (2009: 14–15). It involves the instance of candidate for an academic position (L) in Sri Lanka trying to reduce the distance between himself and the bilingual senior professor interviewing him (P) by switching away from English and deploying Tamil as his matrix language.

P: So you have done a masters in sociology? What is your area of research?
L: Naan **sociology of religion** – ilai taan **interested**. entai **thesis topic** vantu 'the rise of local deities in the Jaffna peninsula.
     '*It is in* **the sociology of religion** *that I am* interested. *My* thesis topic *was* The rise of local deities in the Jaffna peninsula.'
P: Did this involve a field work?
L: oom, oru **ethnographic study**-aai taan itay ceitanaan. kittattatta **four years** – aai **field work** ceitanaan
     '*Yes, I did this as an* **ethnographic study**-*I did* **field work** *for roughly* **four years**'.
P: appa koota **qualitative research** taan ceiyiraniir?
     '*So you do mostly* **qualitative research**?'

Canagarajah's (2009: *ibid.*) commentary on the above notes that, while the senior professor, (P), is comfortable in academic English, the candidate, L, is locally trained and lacks high-level proficiency in English, but makes full use of his receptive multilingualism and of the English scholarly expressions at his disposal in coping with P's questions, and strategically draws on the English at his command to shift the interaction in his favour.

> Although L lacks the ability to form complete sentences in English, his mixing is effective. … The phrases are well formed, although in being the clichés of academia these would not have demanded much competence from the speaker. This mixing of languages is better than using Tamil only …   (p. 15)

L's approach is eventually successful.

> Although initially P continues to speak English and maintains a certain amount of distance (perhaps deliberately, as English provides him power and confirms his identity as a senior scholar), he is eventually forced to take L seriously because of his successful strategies. P finally converges to L's PE [plurilingual English] …, after which they speak as equals.   (*ibid.*)

In other words, it transpires that what might have appeared at first sight to be a chaotic throwing together of codes with neither rhyme nor reason, perhaps bespeaking an absence of boundaries between the codes concerned, is in fact a delicately patterned exploitation of two languages available to both speakers, taking account of different levels of proficiency between the speakers in one of the languages and of differences in the status and function of the two languages. The whole interaction is shot through with the different strategic objectives attached by the more junior interlocutor to his use of each of the two languages. No confusion here, then, but skilfully exploited differentiation at every turn of the way.

Evidence which might perhaps be perceived as clinching the case for a completely undifferentiated notion of multilingual language knowledge would be that deriving from instances where a language user seems unsure of the affiliation of a given lexical expression. Anecdotal evidence of this phenomenon abounds, and is not difficult to find in research contexts either. One such instance is to be found in a study dating from some years ago (Singleton 1987), involving an English-speaking learner of French, Philip, who also had formal knowledge of Latin (from secondary school) and Irish (from primary and secondary school) plus some colloquial knowledge of Spanish picked up in Spain during a period of teaching English as a foreign language in Barcelona. When endeavouring to use French, Philip made use of a large number of Frenchified Spanish lexical expressions. For example, when trying to express the meaning 'although' on one occasion he produced a Frenchified version of the Spanish term for 'although', *aunque*, which he pronounced [aˈɔke]. From Philip's own comments on his use of [aˈɔke] it became evident that, although he was aware that he had been engaging in a transfer strategy involving resources beyond his secure knowledge of French, he did not know whether he had drawn it from Spanish or Latin.

In general, however, Philip appeared to be clear about his borrowing from Spanish and to be fairly focused and self-aware about an underlying rationale in this connection. He mentioned, for instance, that he knew Spanish and French both to be descended from the same parent-language, Latin, and he reported deliberately exploiting his knowledge of Spanish expressions to fill gaps in his French. Indeed, Spanish turned out to be the privileged source of transferred expressions in his French, which indicates a very well-motivated transfer strategy, whether or not this was always conscious, since, of the languages he knew, Spanish was the resource most likely to enrich his French lexical potential in a communicatively successful manner. Thus, Philip was far from confused, marshalling and deploying his linguistic resources in a highly intelligent and discerning manner. As for not being sure whether *aunque* was Latin or Spanish, given his rather limited command of Spanish and his barely surviving knowledge of Latin, we should surely not make too much of this – especially in the light of the fact that Latin and Spanish in fact have many expressions in common.

De Angelis (2007:65f.) discusses the matter of language confusion with reference to some more recent findings. For instance, she explores the case of a French-Canadian learner of Italian with previously acquired knowledge of Spanish who, when speaking Italian, expressed the notion of 'table' using the Spanish word *mesa* instead of the Italian word *tavolo*, apparently believing *mesa* to be the appropriate Italian word. Also cited by De Angelis is the case of an English-speaking learner of Spanish with prior knowledge of Italian who was acquainted with both *dinero* (Spanish for 'money') and *soldi* (Italian for 'money') but was incapable of saying which word belonged to which language. A third instance discussed by De Angelis derives from a study carried out by Bardel & Lindqvist (2007): one of the participants admitted to mixing up their additional languages, Spanish and Italian, and confessed on uttering *ahora* to being unsure whether it was Italian or Spanish. De Angelis takes a similar line in this connection to that sketched above with respect to the proficiency factor in Philip's uncertainties regarding Spanish and Latin. She suggests that "language tags or cues may have different strength values at different stages of the acquisition process, and strengths may vary depending on changes in language proficiency over time" (De Angelis 2007:86). One notes that this is a very different kind of account from the proposition that one should dismiss the whole idea of psycholinguistic boundaries between the languages known to an individual. It is also worth remarking on the fact that in all three of the above examples the additional languages in question are Spanish and Italian, which, like Latin and Spanish, share a fair amount of lexis, so that the answer, for instance to the question of whether *criminalista* or *terrestre* or *vista* is Spanish or Italian is both! One doubts whether such confusions would have arisen if the languages in question had been Japanese and Swedish.

This last point brings us to a cross-linguistic phenomenon of particular relevance for the present discussion – namely, that of cognateness effects. De Groot, for instance, notes that "[c]ognates are translated faster, more often (fewer omissions), and more often correctly that non-cognates" (de Groot 1995:173), concluding that cognates are less segregated by language than non-cognates. Kirsner and his colleagues, looking at a similar range of evidence, go further, suggesting (1993:228) that "some fraction of the second language vocabulary is represented and stored as variants of the first language vocabulary", the size of this fraction depending on "the extent to which the two vocabularies involve reference to a shared set of roots or stems". Kirsner et al. seem here to be proposing an absence of boundaries between the L1 mental lexicon and the L2 mental lexicon for at least a portion of L2 vocabulary. It should immediately be noted that arguing for cross-language integration for a very particular set of lexical items on the basis of formal and semantic similarity is an entirely different notion from any suggestion that two lexicons are globally commingled. Furthermore, great care is required in the interpretation of Kirsner et al.'s words. The term *variant* warrants especial focus. The idea here seems to be that, e.g., Anglophone learners of French store French *table* as a 'variant' of English *table*. *Variant* appears to imply that the French version is stored with its specifically French pronunciation and also that it is tagged to be deployed whenever the active language is French. This obviously implies selectivity rather than full integration and the dismantling of all purported frontiers. In sum, Kirsner et al.'s position is far from favouring the notion of a general blurring of languages. Their version of integration is founded on the specific motivation of formal near-identity and semantic proximity, and they tacitly accept the idea that the integration is far from complete, the L2 items retaining their distinctiveness as variants.

Paradis has the following to say on the above matter:

> Cognate recognition or priming is not evidence of an extended system (one system for both languages or of a tripartite system (with a common store for cognates only). Cognates have the same effect as synonyms within the same language, not because they are represented within a common system across subsystems, but because the form of the cognate serves as a cue to the recognition of the word in the other language … It does this even when the cognate is in a language that the speaker has never heard or read before.   (Paradis 2004: 218)

He refers in this context to arriving in Bucharest and immediately being able to decipher signs in Romanian (which he had never learned) on the basis of his knowledge of relevant French cognates. A study recently republished (Singleton & Little 2005) similarly shows subjects without previous exposure to Dutch making sense of a text in Dutch on the basis of English and German cognates.

We can without difficulty extend the above considerations from the bilingual context to situations involving more than two languages. The closeness of cross-linguistic connection among cognates has unsurprisingly also been noted in relation to of multiple language acquisition and processing. Thus, for instance, Müller-Lancé (2003: 119) retails a finding that "[i]nterlingual cognates were extremely frequent as transference bases or associations (e.g. stimulus Cat. *primerament* > Fr. *premièrement* > Sp. *primeramente*)". In another study, in this case involving the introspections of users of three or more languages on their translation of a passage in an unknown language (Swedish), it was found that participants' responses to questions regarding cross-linguistic help from their other languages focused on and listed interlingual cognates (Gibson & Hufeisen 2003: 92ff.) In the above instances the evidence seems to be that the learners in question, far from conflating the cognates of the languages in question, were well aware of their respective affiliations. Even more instructive in this connection are Jessner's (2003, 2006) data, which show a high degree of awareness and monitoring around cognates and a high degree of consciousness (sometimes exaggerated) of the 'otherness' of cognates in respect of the target language.

Wesche and Paribakht (2010: 36–37) recently addressed the role played by cognates in facilitating performance in an additional language. They refer, *inter alia*, in this context to Sjöholm's (1976) comparison of the English language test performances of applicants to the English Department of a Finnish university whose L1 and L2 were either Finnish and Swedish respectively or Swedish and Finnish respectively. Both groups of students used Swedish – which is typological-ly closer than Finnish to English – as their principal source of resource expansion in English. The L1 Swedish speakers, however, obviously had a better command of Swedish, and Sjöholm interprets these students' better performance in English as due to shared cognates between Swedish and English. Perhaps more relevant to the present discussion is the fact that the L1 Finnish speakers recognized Swedish as a better basis than their L1 for cross-linguistic borrowing with respect to their attempts at producing English – presumably again at least partly on the basis of identifying higher numbers of Swedish-English than Finnish-English cognates. Once more we see evidence here of awareness, discernment and language differ-entiation around cognates.

A curious case involving cognates is that of the relationship between Korean and Japanese, which is most visible and audible in terms of the large Chinese-based lexicon imported into both languages. In other respects, although there are morphological and syntactic similarities between Japanese and Korean, a clear ge-netic relationship between the two languages has not been proven. Fouser (2001) carried out a study of two English-speaking subjects both of whom had learned Japanese and who had then gone on to learn Korean, both being resident in Korea at the time of the study. The study's aim was essentially to explore the ways in which the earlier experience of Japanese interacted with the later experience of learning Korean, and to answer the question of whether the two languages were "too close for comfort". Fouser's findings were that both learners reported drawing actively on their knowledge of Japanese in learning Korean, believing this to be helpful. One of the subjects reported brief unintentional switches to Korean when using Japanese, while the other claimed that he continued to think in Japanese. We have already discussed the question of 'leakage' from one system to another via code-switching and discounted it as a demonstration of a lack of boundar-ies between different categories of language knowledge. As for the case of one of the subjects' thinking in Japanese while using Korean, such parallel processing is widely accepted but does not signify a dissolution of the boundaries between the languages. What is clear is that whatever similarities and shared Chinese cognates the learners perceived in the two languages, there was no question of confusion between them; on the contrary:

> … both learners showed keen awareness of their language learning processes and the relationship between Korean and Japanese. This helped them to be selective in drawing on their Japanese in using Korean, which was evident in their responses …
>
> (Fouser 2001: 167)

Fouser concludes that at least for these two learners the answer to the question posed in the title of the study must be 'no'.

Especially interesting is the case of cognates which owe their existence to the entry into a language of items from another language. For example, *parking* has been borrowed from English into French with the meaning 'car park'. Such borrowing-derived cognates often change their sense in the borrowing process. They may then used in the original source language by second language learners of that language who have been exposed to the items in question in their own language. Thus a Francophone learner of English may use the term parking in English in its French sense of 'car park'. Daulton concludes (2008: 72ff.) from a study of Japanese learners of English that they systematically expand their resources in English by exploiting their familiarity with English loanwords in Japanese.

This does not necessarily betoken a confusion of languages, however. On the contrary, it indicates a high degree of language difference awareness. Nor, clearly, is the basic fact of the integration of English loanwords into Japanese – many of which are still perceived to have a 'foreign' aura – a denial of boundaries between languages. The fact that English-speakers still pronounce restaurant with a French /ã/ in the final syllable does not imply that English speakers cannot distinguish English from French. The fact that an awareness – however dim – of other origins in such cases remains, on the contrary, argues further in favour of separability.

Japanese learners are no doubt cognizant of the English-language origins of many of the English loanwords they use in Japanese, on the basis of the phonological shapes of the words in question, on the basis of their written *katakana* forms (*katakana*, a syllabic script, being reserved for Western borrowings), on the basis of having encountered their counterparts in English or on the basis of general knowledge. When they exploit their familiarity with such words in their use of English, therefore, they are not mixing or conflating languages; they are rather making very sensible use of their knowledge, or perhaps even only their suspicion, that Japanese borrowed the items in question from the language they are coming to grips with.

Mention of cross-lexical interaction between English and French brings us to a final piece of research we wish to refer to in the present context. This comprises two studies carried out in Ireland (Singleton & Ó Laoire 2006a, 2006b; Ó Laoire

& Singleton 2009) involving teenage learners of French who were native speakers of English, and who had extensive knowledge of Irish, whether as an L2 or as a second L1. The languages involved in these studies all belong to different language families, English being a Germanic language, Irish a Celtic language, and French a Romance language. However, the languages are not equidistant from each other. The Norman invasion of England in the eleventh century and of the continuing close relations between England and France during the Middle Ages brought about a flood of French borrowings into English resulting in a situation where the French and English lexicons have thousands of cognates (cf. Claiborne 1990; McArthur & Gachelin 1992; Pei 1967; Robertson 1954; Van Roey, Granger & Swallow 1988).

The Romance component of the Irish lexicon is significantly more restricted. Some loanwords from ecclesiastical Latin were borrowed by Irish following the Christianization of Ireland, but, apart from being few in number, these words became assimilated to Irish to the point where their degree of similarity to forms in contemporary Romance languages, including French, is hardly discernible. As for French influence, after the arrival of the Anglo-Normans in Ireland in the twelfth century, French had a major role among the languages of medieval Ireland together with Irish, English and Latin (cf. Picard 2003), and French influence can be seen in the fact that some hundreds of Irish lexical borrowings from French have been identified (see e.g. Risk 1969). The point, however, is that French loanwords in Irish are counted in hundreds, whereas in English they are counted in thousands.

We have seen, then, that in lexical terms the distance between English and French is considerably less than that between Irish and French. It is also obvious from the experience of generations of teachers of French working with English speakers and teachers of English working with French speakers that learners rapidly notice the cognates shared by English and French and attempt to exploit such cognates. Hence the longstanding and continuing market for dictionaries of French-English 'false friends' (see e.g. Kirk-Greene 1981; Thody & Evans 1985; Van Roey, Granger & Swallow 1988).

The hypothesis in the above studies, therefore, was that, faced with a task in French which confronted them with some of their lexical gaps in French, the participants would resort to English rather than Irish to expand their resources. Their choice of the more promising source available to them (English rather than Irish) for expressions that could be put to work in French indicates a high degree of linguistic sophistication and – since choice implies separability and separation – it again runs counter to the notion that cross-lexical interplay is simply a matter of blurred boundaries between languages.

Concluding summary

We began this chapter by noting that there is plenty of evidence that the languages at an individual's disposal connect and interact with each other. We cited in this connection some references to and examples of cross-linguistic influence. We saw that evidence of the very high degree of connectedness and interaction often discernible among a multilinguals language competencies has prompted some researchers to posit (or come extremely close to positing) complete integration of multilingual language knowledge. We went on to suggest, however, that the evidence in question, properly interpreted, runs counter to this viewpoint, pointing out that certain prominent researchers have been tempted to flirt with the notion that the multilingual language knowledge is radically unitary have in the end resisted it.

Our final discussion point was the suggestion of Harris and others that languages blur into each other. Our discussion accepts that in certain instances – in cases, for example, of low proficiency or highly cognate languages – the frontiers between languages in the mind may sometimes be permeable (cf. Singleton in press). On foot, however, of a review of some of the evidence from research which may at first sight appear to support Harris's 'blur' conception as it relates to cross-linguistic interaction, the conclusion here has been rather that at least in the instances scrutinised here what is in fact operative is a highly sophisticated set of processes based on experience-driven language awareness and which in fact takes language differences into account.

CHAPTER 9

Towards a comprehensive view of multilingualism

Classic and emerging perspectives

In the previous eight chapters we have discussed facts, insights and proposals regarding language and languages in the context of multilingualism, many of which, despite the relatively recent advent of multilingualism research, have already acquired 'classic' status. We have sketched the essentials of human language and its suggested differences from animal communication, have provided some definitions of multilingualism, have offered a range of perspectives on the scope and role of multilingualism in the contemporary world, and addressed the notions of *language repertoire* and *dominant language constellation*. We have dealt too with questions relating to the acquisition of multiple languages and surveyed various classifications of multilingual people, environments and languages. We have in addition endeavoured to explore relationship between identity and languages. A number of issues remain, however, that are currently emerging from the shadows. The more we learn and the more we understand about multilingualism, the more we become aware of so far unexplored research paths. In the last chapter of this volume we shall turn our attention to a number of such emerging approaches.

Conceptualization and re-conceptualization

The complexity and diversity of findings from recent multilingualism research encourage new efforts in the direction of the *conceptualization of multilingualism*. The conceptualization and re-conceptualization of empirical knowledge and theoretical reflection in this area have indeed become imperative needs, given the ongoing global developments discussed in Chapter 3.

As we have suggested elsewhere (Aronin & Singleton 2008a; Aronin & Hufeisen 2009b), conceptualization and re-conceptualization in this context need to encompass (a) the development of a thesaurus of multilingualism; (b) the creation and utilization of appropriate constructs; (c) the construction and deployment of models specific to multilingualism in its widest sense, as opposed to models applicable only to mono- and bilingualism; (d) the development of useful working metaphors; and (e) the raising of discussion to philosophical levels.

(a) *A thesaurus of multilingualism.* Constructing a thesaurus would be aimed not only at achieving sharper definitions of terms and concepts – and their interrelationships – in multilingualism studies but also an attempt, in the process, to facilitate theory- building in this fledgling field of research. The current very active quest for definitions in the multilingualism domain is one of the key aspects of the development of a multilingualism thesaurus. Thus, Kemp (2009) and Franceschini (2009), among many others, have attempted to clarify the notion of multilingualism; Blommaert has offered the concept of *truncated multilingualism* (Blommaert 2008, 2009); Herdina & Jessner (2002) have added new dimensions to the notion of transfer; Cenoz (2009) and Cenoz & Jessner (2009) have given us a new definition of multilingual education; and Aronin & Singleton have proposed some first definitions of the relationship between affordances and multilingualism, and more specifically of language affordances (Aronin & Singleton 2010). An increasingly salient research practice is that of attempting a clearer demarcation of the boundaries of similar or overlapping terms such as *metalinguistic awareness, linguistic awareness* and *language awareness* (cf. Jessner 2006).

A particularly engaging example of this last trend is Hammarberg's (2010) discussion of the terms *first language, second language* and *third language,* which he suggests should be replaced by, respectively, *primary language, secondary language* and *tertiary language.* Hammarberg claims that the chronological approach to the terms *L1, L2, L3, L4,* etc. is "untenable, being based on an inadequate conceptions of multilingualism" (Hammarberg 2010:91). He writes that "the problems with the expressions first, second and third language have become more apparent with the emergence of research on L3 acquisition" (Hammarberg 2010:91), and argues that the time is ripe to work towards changing these established terms in favour of the terms he proposes.

(b) *Constructs.* A number of constructs have been developed in the consideration of phenomena pertaining specifically to multilingualism and its complex nature. Among those that have been most widely adopted and have been most fruitful in the insights they have yielded are those of *interlanguage* (Selinker 1972, 1992; see also De Angelis & Selinker 2001) and *multi-competence* (Cook 1992; 1996 and cf. the discussion in Chapter 2). An example of a construct which has been more recently pressed into service is that of *Dominant Language Constellation* (DLC) discussed above in Chapter 4 (Aronin & Ó Laoire 2004; Aronin 2006; Aronin & Singleton 2008d).

(c) *Models specific to multilingualism.* Models specific to multilingualism in its broadest sense provide frameworks for coming to a clearer understanding of the particular processes and phenomena of multilingualism. Such models have received comprehensive treatment in several publications (cf. Jessner 2008; Hufeisen & Marx 2003; 2007; Hufeisen & Neuner 2004; Hufeisen 2005; Gabryś-Barker 2005) and are dealt with above in Chapter 5.

(d) *Working metaphors.* Metaphorical thinking has been acknowledged as an important means of conceptual advance in the humanities. Especially pertinent to a better understanding of the various dimensions of multilingual reality are metaphors which reach 'beyond', which expand horizons of all kinds. Metaphors relating to place, local and global, the environment, context, boundaries, are often called upon to facilitate both the conceiving and the expression of newly evolving ideational elements and configurations in multilingualism research. Examples of the richness of such metaphors are the areas of *language ecology* (see e.g. Haugen 1972; Mühlhäusler 1996; Fill & Mühlhäusler 2001; Edwards 1992; Bronfenbrenner 1993; Hornberger 2002; and Kramsch 2008) and *linguistic landscape* (see e.g. de Bot 2004; Cenoz & Gorter 2008b; Gorter 2006; Backhaus 2007).

(e) *The philosophical level of conceptualization.* Raising the treatment of multilingual phenomena to the philosophical level of conceptualization and discourse situates it within the framework of human essentialities. Such an approach has resulted in the proposal of a new academic research direction concentrating directly and specifically on multilingualism – and not dealing with it tangentially as, for example, in the case of the general area of philosophy of language, which covers the nature of language and uses of language across a very wide range. We envisage the philosophy of multilingualism as both a subfield of philosophy and a subfield of multilingualism studies – by analogy with the philosophy of science, which partakes of both philosophy and science. We see it as having the potentiality of endowing multilingualism research with higher-level, more abstract dimensions (Aronin & Singleton forthcoming). Since it features among the most recent avenues of investigation in the multilingualism domain, it will be discussed in the next section alongside other emerging research avenues.

Some emerging investigative avenues

As was noted in Chapter 2, current multilingualism research has triggered many new developments, which have set new topics before the researcher. What follows addresses the following such new foci:

1.   The philosophy of multilingualism
2.   The material culture of multilingualism
3.   Affordances in multilingualism
4.   The complexity of multilingualism.

The philosophy of multilingualism

The philosophy of multilingualism is proposed as a discipline allowing scholars to subject multilingualism in its entirety to philosophical scrutiny (Aronin & Singleton 2008c; Aronin & Singleton forthcoming). While it might seem obvious at first sight that multilingualism can draw on the long-established concepts and procedures of the philosophy of language and can simply be assimilated to the latter, this turns out not to be the case. The reason for the only subsidiary relevance of traditional philosophy of language to multilingualism is that philosophical schools and movements which have specifically focused on language have barely addressed the phenomena of multilingual individuals and societies. They certainly have had little or nothing to say about the specificities of emerging contemporary multilingualism in all its variety and pluridimensionality.

A philosophy of multilingualism would have its own particular purview and methods distinct from those of the philosophy of language as normally understood. The scope of the philosophy of multilingualism would include, for example, not only the philosophical ramifications of discussion relating to language as a human faculty, but also the philosophical implications of multicompetence as a human capacity. Its methods would go beyond those employed in the philosophy of language, and would include approaches used in the conceptualization of language-using human society and those deployed in language-related complexity thinking. It can be argued that the current intensely multilingual phase of the world linguistic dispensation requires a philosophy of multilingualism with its own subject-matter, differing from that of the philosophy of language in its customary definition. The subject matter of the philosophy of language is compared in Table 1 with that of the proposed philosophy of multilingualism.

As we can see from the above, central interests of philosophers of language traditionally have revolved around questions having to do with the nature of language and the nature of meaning (Morris 2007: 1), questions arising out of a philosophy of multilingualism would address issues relating to acquirers and users of two or more languages, to the environments of learning and using two or more languages, and to the patterns and imperatives of learning and using two or more languages.

Table 1. Examples of differences in the kinds of questions posed by the philosophy of language and a philosophy of multilingualism

Philosophy of language	Philosophy of multilingualism
What is language?	What philosophical issues might attach to the construction of a multilingual's identity?
What is it for words to have meaning?	What philosophical significance is to be sought in the similarities and differences between bilingualism and multilingualism in the sense of knowledge and use of more than two languages?
What is the nature of the meaning of words?	How might the worldview of those proficient in more than two languages be different from that of bi- and monolinguals?

A philosophy of multilingualism would appear to have the potential of embarking on at least two broad research directions:

i.   an endeavour to connect multilingualism to already established concerns of philosophy;

ii. an endeavour to bring newly emerging points of discussion in multilingualism research into the realm of philosophical examination.

Multilingualism studies, in common with all the human sciences, already make use of concepts which have been long familiar to philosophers, such as *dichotomy, inherent qualities, form/content, relativism, determinism,* and *quantity/quality.* Likewise, *cognitive notions* which fall within the purview of philosophy, such as *belief, understanding, reason, judgment, sensation, perception, intuition, guessing, learning* and *forgetting* (Lacey 2001:90) are clearly of crucial importance in multilingualism research. *Metaphysics,* which is the study of the fundamental nature of reality, being and the world, could, in its role of explicating objects of interest, turn its attention to multilingual minds, multilingual persons, multilingual universals, multilingual facts and figures. A promising locus of interaction is also conceivable with *analytic philosophy,* which is concerned with clarity and precision in argument, drawing, in this endeavour, on formal logic and the very close analysis of language. It is not impossible that an interaction of the kind proposed above might bring modifications to the very concept of 'language' in the light of the phenomena of multiplicity and multifacetedness.

The concepts of *identity* and *ethics* have clearly been a matter of philosophical debate for millennia. We find philosophers and multilingualism poring over the same problems. In the present era these discussions can draw on the sizeable body of findings specifically addressing the issues emerging from globalization studies. Ethics features in decisions regarding language policy, language planning and language education under multilingual circumstances. Such decisions may relate to the allocation of official status to languages and the consequent distribution of resources for different languages, the selection of curricular languages, as well as the division of curricular languages into those to be used as media of instruction and those to be treated as objects of study. Issues deriving from the global spread of English and connected concerns associated with the maintenance and revival of endangered indigenous and heritage languages also very obviously have important ethical dimensions.

In the context of the realization that monolingual and monocultural individuals and communities are in the minority, identity-related matters are inevitably are central to multilingualism research. We know from research that the identity of multilinguals is especially complex, dynamic and unpredictable (see for example, Lin 2007; Lytra 2007). Owing to the very nature of individual and community multilingualism, multilingualism studies inevitably engage with issues of stability and change, with issues of time and space, and with issues of complexity.

Multilingualism plays an increasingly important role in the life of humanity, complexifying vital aspects of human life. Changes of this kind demand reflection and commentary drawing on both the traditions of philosophy and the fruits of the recent empirical research into multilingualism.

With regard to the second research direction referred to above, that is, the notion of bringing newly emerging points of discussion in multilingualism research under the wing of philosophical exploration, some of the relevant research avenues are discussed in what follows.

The material culture of multilingualism

A new subject of interest in multilingualism studies, one especially close to metaphysical problematics, is the material culture of multilingualism, which deals with "linguistically defined objects" (Aronin & Ó Laoire 2007; Aronin & Ó Laoire 2012). The scientific exploration and analysis of material culture dimensions of multilingualism have previously received little or no attention. In fact, of the three principal components of multilingualism – i.e. user, language and environment – the last of these seems to be have been least researched. Traditionally research on the environment in which multilinguals find themselves has focused almost entirely on the dynamics of interrelationship with other people in a family, community or school and on explaining commonly occurring multilingual phenomena – e.g. language shift and language attrition. There has been scarcely any research on how multilinguals interact with their proximate and distant *physical and material environments*. The studies in this direction have been concerned mainly with technology and internet use, research questions rarely focusing on objects as such, and still more rarely on the materialities which always and everywhere permeate human existence from the cradle to the grave. This is very obviously a major omission given the determinant role of material culture in our existence.

A notable exception is one particular aspect of material culture, *linguistic landscape*, the study of which is proliferating (cf. Gorter 2006). Linguistic landscape research, the investigation of "the use of language in its written form in the public sphere" (Gorter 2006: 2) is believed to offer a valuable source of insights into language use and attitudes, as well as existing language hierarchies in various locations. Linguistic landscape studies shed light, for example, on minority language situations since they illuminate interrelationships between the official and indigenous or immigrant languages (see for example, Gorter, Van Mensel & Marten 2012; Coupland & Garrett 2010). Currently, technological progress presents infinite possibilities for taking pictures and interpreting ways in which languages are visually present in a particular space. There is no doubt that linguistic landscape studies have assembled a valuable factual database and have rendered accessible a very useful source of new insights. At this stage it might be suggested that linguistic landscape studies need to lay down some clear theoretical foundation, to define an aim beyond rather superficial description. In any case, linguistic landscape is but one part of a much wider reality of material culture which has been studied by ethnologists.

Material culture studies can and should expand far beyond the present research scope of the focus on linguistic landscape. Virtually the entire physical world manifests linguistically defined and linguistically marked objects and events. The scope of the study of materialities goes beyond the linguistic landscape; material culture objects are found not only in public areas but also in private homes and restricted office spaces. Material culture objects are not limited to noticeboards, advertisements and posters, but also include furniture and private possessions, cosmetics and medications, architectural complexes, buildings, and roads. Material culture also includes events and time-spaces outside the public domain. The physical environment includes not obviously tangible phenomena such as sound waves and smells, but also, for instance, organizational decisions relating to events and procedures involving ordering in time. Materialities, in fact, characterize existence as a whole, be it the existence of an individual or that of a community. A further argument for going beyond linguistic landscape is the fact that material culture studies have a solid and time-proven theoretical foundation in sociology and ethnology studies. Material culture studies fit well with preoccupations of multilingualism studies, and offers new perspectives on the phenomena of multilingualism. In its turn, research into the material culture of multilingualism will enrich and push forward theories on society, culture and global shifts (Aronin & Ó Laoire 2012).

Material culture is dynamic and covers the whole scale and all the aspects of human life; it surrounds us everywhere. Its study is essentially the study of the whole range of artefacts and objects. It also includes the exploration of landscapes, cityscapes, roadscapes, villages, localities, dwellings, private households and collective homes, public spaces and their diverse ways of organization and use. Objects found both in public spaces and in the homes – cups, umbrellas, of course, books, brochures and other printed matter, pieces of embroidery, vases, pens, but also technological artefacts – computers, cars, etc.

With respect to the material culture of multilingualism, we are interested in **objects** which are **used** in various ways, moved, bought, presented, demonstrated, borrowed. Multilinguals or monolinguals interact with linguistically defined objects in their daily life; these items connect people with their multilingual environment and way of life and are means of socialization.

How do researchers study them? Ethnographers and sociologists examine the qualities of artefacts and pay close attention to their production. The study of human interaction with material is included in the methodology. Materialities are seen as a reflection of identity, individual and group values. These include: ideas, morals, ethics and standards; rituals and events are also included in the purview of material culture studies. It is also helpful to establish the position of investigated artefacts in space and how they are located in relation to each other (for example, left, right, one on top of the other, etc.).

In reference to multilingualism the study of material culture is pertinent for several reasons. First, material culture is tangible. Objects and spaces are 'solid' they 'stabilize the experience' (Schlereth 1985b: 10). Material culture evidence, therefore, is arguably less susceptible to subjective bias than other kinds of evidence. Such evidence is in addition possessed of temporal durativity and may also broaden representativeness. It is not surprising then, that in the ethnography literature the main value of material studies is seen in their *evidential function* (Schlereth 1985b: 9). This function is especially appealing in contexts where researchers are dealing with aspects of multilingualism which may have ephemeral and elusive qualities – such as attitudes, language preferences, and various strands of language performance.

Materialities are subject to measurement. One may, for example identify, count, and register the occurrences and the modes of use of objects relevant to multilingualism, noting the degree of involvement of particular multilingualism-related objects in a specific place, or their usage within a specific time period in the life of an individual or group.

The following is an example of how the evidential function of materialities of multilingualism can be exploited and where more or less exact measurement is possible. In a pilot study of material culture by the multilingual students of the M.Ed. programme at Oranim Academic College, the students acted as both researchers and participants. Their DLC is Arabic/Hebrew/English and they already have not inconsiderable teaching experience. They look after the education of their children and confidently navigate their way through the mixture of cultures, traditions and global influences that surround them, and they build their home environment with a high degree of awareness of all its dimensions. Their research task was simply to identify and count the linguistically defined objects in their homes or any other place of their choice: school, library, car, etc. The student-researchers were surprised to discover that their homes and lives contained a multitude of linguistically defined objects, and that these were repositories of family and personal narratives for them. Another discovery they made concerned the role of languages and their associated cultures, about which they had had misconceptions before embarking on the project.

This study of the material culture of multilingualism led the student-researchers to realize the place of English language and culture as well as other languages and cultures in their lives and to make conclusions, such as the following:

> After collecting artifacts, I now realize that material culture gives a voice to language and culture. Although so much of the life we care about takes place at home, this private space surrounds us with so much culture that we are usually unaware of it. By interpreting culture through an analysis of artifacts it led to quite different kinds of information. First I now understand that the relationship of behaviour to the material world is far from passive. Artifacts are active voices which present our attitudes and behavior.
>
> Consciously or unconsciously various cultures are brought into our lives. In a sense they possess our homes. I found that although my husband and I thought we were encouraging Arab culture, it was quite the opposite. I found many artifacts from the English, Russian and Jewish cultures. It is amazing how analysis of artifacts has given me an insight into my family's attitude towards the world.
>
> (Amel Dabbab: January 2010 Fieldwork report on material culture)

Such a testimony to rethinking one's long-term assumptions about one's actual multilingual life-style and results of efforts regarding multilingual reality prompted this particular young multilingual researcher to say: "It is powerful to make statements with artifacts". The notion of 'density of artifacts' can be of practical help. The potential of mapping, comparing the density of same or similar forms in certain localities, seems promising in 'having one's finger on the pulse' of multilingualism and understanding variation across space and change in time.

For the purpose of practical research into the materialities of multilingualism, a definition of language-defined object and a typology of such objects has been proposed (Aronin & Ó Laoire 2007; Aronin & Ó Laoire 2012). The relevant material evidence here is constituted by 'language-defined objects'. A 'language-defined object' may be defined as "a meaningful wholeness of material and verbal components considered as a representation of its user or users, exclusively in relation to its linguistic environment" (Aronin & Ó Laoire 2012). These can include objects as diverse as stelae, shirts, gates, books, electrical gadgets, cosmetics containers, roads, furniture, laser displays during a concert and even tattoos on the human body. Awareness of 'language-defined' material objects can, in relation to multilingualism, contribute to enhancing delicacy of differentiation according to, for example, areal, familial, individual and situational criteria.

Aronin & Ó Laoire (2007, 2012) have proposed the consideration of three types of objects and phenomena of relevance to multilingualism.

a. Objects involving texts, sentences, written characters and/or images inscribed or carved. Included in this category are, for instance, stamps, books, and other published products, such as advertisements, and even tattoos.

b. Objects in multilingual environments. In this connection the authors argue that an object does not have to contain inscriptions in two or more languages in order to be considered multilingual, since the environment of the object also has to be taken into consideration. By way of illustration, we offer the picture below (see Figure 1) taken in Israel, Haifa, in a health club.

The picture images an interaction between multilingual reality and its material culture. It includes reference to the dynamics of multiple layers of sounds of multiple languages in speech and in music, object combinations continuously changing as determined by time and motion, and even smells. The uniform shirt of the employee has the English word 'Maintenance' on it. The employees wearing these shirts are speakers whose mother tongues include a range of languages – including Russian, Ukrainian, Moldavian and Hebrew. The interior of the club contains objects marked with Hebrew script and resounds with the phonic manifestations of a variety of languages (in addition to those mentioned, Arabic, French, Spanish, Italian, etc.). Taken in its actual environment, in its interaction with the manifold linguistic detail of that environment, the material object in question, the shirt with the English word on it, is a language-defined object richly evidencing multilingualism.

c. Objects which do not have anything written or inscribed in or on them may nevertheless also fall within the purview of the present discussion. Consider road signs and road markings. These do not always contain written text. Nonetheless, these objects require processing and action according to the conventions of the particular communities in which they are operational (including written text conventions).

Figure 1

When material culture interacts with language, it produces a vivid composite, image of human behaviours. Fishman (2001) speaking about language revitalization and maintenance emphasizes that for revitalization to happen it is vital that language should be passed from parents to children, and that this transmission should be supported in daily community life. Both family and community life are unthinkable without material objects and events, and we may assume that linguistically defined objects and community events play a significant role in this connection.

The description, interpretation and quantification of artefacts can thus be very useful as supplementary research evidence, especially where the available documentary and statistical data relative to a given topic are incomplete. Some of the particular avenues of interest proposed by Aronin & Ó Laoire (2007, 2012) include:

– **language-defined materialities and their classifications:** sound waves, stone carvings, buildings, the human body, the Internet, virtual materiality, etc.
– **multilingual material culture in the built environment and in places more generally defined:** including private households and public places such as schools, community halls and universities, cityscapes, roadscapes, etc.

- **the material culture of learning:** artefacts and places of learning and teaching, such as classroom material culture – texts and vocabulary, learning aids, etc.
- **historical changes:** changes in artefacts and objects used at various time periods as well as attitudes towards these changes.
- **attitudinal dimensions and identity dimensions:** attitudes to the facts regarding the presence or absence of multilingual language-defined materialities, in, e.g., particular places or processes; the reflection of identity in materialities.

The above list makes no claim to be exhaustive.

Another relatively new philosophical construct and an area of recent interest to multilingualism is the theory of affordances.

Affordances in multilingualism

The 'theory of affordances' – is a perspective which has its origins in the work of the perceptual psychologist James Gibson (e.g. Gibson 1977, 1979). The term *affordance,* which he coined, is defined as relating essentially to the perceived opportunities for action provided by any given entity for any given actor, affordances being seen as those "perceived and actual properties of the thing, primarily those fundamental properties that determine just how the thing could possibly be used" (Norman 2002:9). To take an example from nature, in the winter months grizzly bears in British Columbia realize the affordance of heavy snowfall in digging their burrows and having their cubs in these burrows. In summer the bears have affordances in the form of their claws and Pacific salmon, which return to spawn in the rivers of the area. Such affordances sharply increase in a particular period when the salmon virtually swarm in the rivers, and the bears can almost without an effort scoop them out of the water.

The notion of affordances has proved to be fruitful in a range of fields of knowledge. Importantly, different facets of this notion have been pursued in accordance with the needs and preoccupations of particular domains of investigation. In perceptual psychology, for example, the concept of affordances is applied to the study of adaptive environments, adaptive aids, self-motion, orientation, interactive environments aspects of aviation and technology (Warren & Owen 1982; Hutchby 2003; Gross et al. 2005). In the area of design and human-computer interaction, the emphasis has been on the perception of affordances. Examples of affordances in this domain of ergonomics are buttons for pushing, cords for pulling, knobs for turning, handles for pulling, and levers for pushing. Valenty & Good (1991) extended the application of the concept of affordance to the topics of social knowing and social interaction. Here the emphasis is on social coordination and social interaction in the acquisition of knowledge and behavioural competence and on the importance of cultural practices in organizing the shared focus of attention and in revealing and creating affordances for action and interaction. In the domain of language learning, the importance of affordances was highlighted by Segalowitz, who sees "a language … like any other physical environment, as possessing affordances" (2001: 15), by Singleton & Aronin (2007) in reference to multiple language learning, and by Van Lier (2007) with regard to action-based teaching and learning.

The term *affordance* in this whole approach is used as a common denominator for a number of things which are normally not considered to be items constituting a set. Thus, the currency of a language, the possibilities it offers, its status – all of these are affordances. Affordances pertinent to language are to be found in any human environment. They may take the form of either physical or non-physical phenomena and have an infinite variety of manifestations – including, among many others, objects and artefacts of material culture, events, people with their individual and particular capacities and skills, global and local societal trends, historical and political processes, governmental and unofficial institutions, social perceptions, social mythology, and attitudes. Linguistically defined materialities, discussed above, are physical affordances of multilingualism, the objective physical properties of environment and speakers furnishing further kinds of language affordances. Speech and language use are activities that involve physical objects and relationships – the speakers, physical entities with a variety of properties including speech apparatus; the air that carries the sound waves; the places where people speak; the proximity of interlocutors; and, of course, the physical objects the speakers manipulate during their communication behaviours.

There are also non-tangible phenomena that are in themselves significant language affordances. These would include ideologies, political situations, ethical considerations, emotions, attitudes to languages, and specific language knowledge. Metalinguistic awareness is the affordance which constitutes the locus of interaction between the objective properties of a speaker and those of a language or languages. One aspect of this is the perception of typological closeness between languages and cultures, as in the case of the Romance family of languages. Users and learners of languages such as French, Italian and Spanish who become aware of their commonalities, and whose attitudinal perspective inclines them make use of such commonalities, thereby access additional affordances. The same is true in the case of Slavic languages, where speakers of Russian can understand Ukrainian, Byelorussian or Croatian with more ease than more typologically distant languages such as Dutch or Finnish.

Aronin & Singleton (2010) in their discussion of affordances relevant for multilingualism mention general language affordances, societal language affordances and individual language affordances, the first category subsuming the other two more specific categories. With regard to general language affordances, these are characterized as those whose realization renders communication using a language or languages (and the acquisition of a language or languages) possible. Clearly, the human capacity for language itself endows humans with language affordances. The importance of such affordances was highlighted by Segalowitz, who sees "a language …, like any other physical environment, as possessing affordances" and as supporting "a particular set of constructions, … which are available for packing a message if the speaker knows how to use them" (2001: 15).

Aronin & Singleton designate as social language affordances the language affordances supplied by a given society. These may encourage or discourage the acquisition and use of a given language or languages in a community. Historical, political, cultural, and religious elements are especially pertinent for social language affordances, although the latter also include, for example, physical features such as geographical relationships and attributes (nears or far, surrounded or secluded, easily accessible or difficult to reach, etc.) relating to language communities.

Social affordances may relate, *inter alia*, to the status and role of a language in a country (e.g. official versus non-official), to the place of a language in the educational system (e.g. language of instruction versus subject of study versus proscribed), to the role of a language in the media and in publications, to the existence or not of basic or additional services in a particular language (be these e.g. medical facilities or theatre performances), and to the frequency of encounter in a given community with interaction proceeding in a given language. By way of example let us consider the current social language affordances in the Basque Autonomous Community (BAC) in Spain (Cenoz 2009), where the introduction of teaching through Basque has increased the pool of affordances available for this language as well as having altered the configuration of affordances for other languages present in this area – Spanish, in the first place, and English as a foreign language. In particular, the Basque language has acquired a legal basis, by becoming an official language (legal affordances); has been elevated to the rank of language of instruction where previously only Spanish and French had this role (educational affordances); and has been supported through the re-opening and financing of Basque-medium schools ('*ikastolak*') (practical educational and financial affordances). In addition to the extended use of Basque at primary and secondary levels of schooling, multilingual education including a prominent role for the Basque language is also at university level.

Affordances seem to be 'specialised', for a variety of possible outcomes if taken up. Reporting on the establishment of the current Basque educational system (a social-educational affordance), Cenoz points out that it "has contributed to increasing the number of Basque speakers but it has a limited influence on the language use" (Cenoz 2009: 234). This outcome to date of the enormous effort made to reverse language shift in the Basque Country may disappoint those who might have had higher expectations. But it makes perfect sense if we see the situation in the following way: affordances for an educational encounter with Basque leading to some proficiency in Basque were *offered* and were *taken up* by the people in the Basque country; with respect to actual use of Basque, however, it seems that affordances of another kind are required – affordances promoting more correct and more frequent use of Basque. These latter, according to Cenoz, would lie in the sphere of sociolinguistic context, that is to say, as we understand it, would comprise some other specific varieties of social affordances.

It is to be noted that social language affordances are of their nature dynamic, fluid and time-space specific. As some affordances in a particular space-time increase, others shrink either because of imposed policies or because of the unfolding development of situations. One example of the ebb and flow of affordances comes from the Republic of Tatarstan, a sovereign part of the Russian Federation, which lies between the Volga River and its tributary Kama, extending east to the Ural mountains. Since the 1550s, when Tatarstan was conquered by the troops of Tsar Ivan IV ('Ivan the Terrible'), the affordances for the Tatar ethnic language (of the Turkic Altai language family), have shared space with the affordances for Russian. In addition, lesser-used languages of ethno-religious minorities spread through history over the area – Chuvash and Bashkir (Turkic languages), Mari (which is a member of the Finno-Ugric language family), Udmurt (a Finno-Permic language), and Mordvin (belonging to the Finno-Volgaic branch of the Uralic language family) have also occupied some place in the sociolinguistic environment. The fact that many members of these ethnic groups are in fact Tatar-speaking, means, among other things, that the need to take up the affordances that exist for above-mentioned lesser-used languages is not so pressing, and that affordances for encountering and deploying these languages are consequently less numerous than such affordances for Tatar and for Russian in this locality.

There have also been ups and downs for the two dominant languages in Tatarstan. Four years after the Bolshevik Revolution in 1921 the Tatar language was declared obligatory in all state institutions of the Tatar Republic, but from the 1930s onwards the usage of Tatar declined. The ethnic Tatar pupils were schooled in their own language only in rural schools; elsewhere Russian took over. The affordances which remained for the Tatar language diminished further in the 1930s when the plan of building a non-nationalist communist society was adopted in the USSR and the spheres of use of national languages shrank. According to the *Encyclopaedia of National Languages of Russia* (2002: 357–358) by the end of the 1980s only 7% of ethnic Tatar children were schooled in Tatar schools; there was 0.7 copies of a Tatar book per person in 1989; radio broadcasting in Tatar accounted for three hours per week in 1990, and TV broadcasting in Tatar for about one hour per week. This scarcity of affordances has led to the Russian language increasingly being perceived as a de facto native tongue while Tatar is essentially taught as a second language.

At present both Russian and Tatar are official languages (political-social affordance). The overwhelming majority of the Tatars speaks Russian (physical-social affordance in the fact of the physical environment where mostly Russian is heard) and the Russian language is still predominant especially in commercial circles (practical-social affordance). With the recent political changes affordances available for the Tatar language have increased. Before the political shift of the late 1990s only 10.6% of Tatar children were being taught through Tatar in pre-school education, while by 2006 this figure was reported to have increased by 65% (Garipov & Solnyshkina 2006). Although Tatar is taught and also functions as a medium of instruction (e.g. in the Kazan university), some feel that there is a need for more affordances to be put in place to further improve the social role of this ethnic language, which "is still not the working language of higher and professional education" (*ibid.*: 132). It is reported that the Tatar public is insisting on the establishment of an independent Tatar ethnic university financed by the state, which signifies that there is a popular demand for more affordances for the Tatar language (*ibid.*). Affordances for Tatar play an important role on a family level too. When affordances for the Tatar language are provided within a family, they are taken up by the children, so that "[t]o a certain degree, the family language environment determines the attitude of a person to the language of his or her people" (*ibid.*: 133). Thus, the attitudes towards and the use of the language in question differ, depending to some extent on whether this particular affordance is furnished or not at familial level.

Turning now to individual language affordances, these are highly variable, since individuals differ widely in terms of their age and health, specific aptitudes, personality traits, attitudes, motivations and interests, linguistic skills, metalinguistic awareness, etc. Also, importantly, individual language affordances also differ in respect of the degree to which a person is capable of benefiting from the societal affordances supplied by the global and local environment available to him/her. There are, of course, limits to the extent to which one can actually draw a line between societal language affordances and individual language affordances, but distinguishing between societal affordances and individual affordances allows us to see ways in which societal affordances may be prerequisites for recognizing and effectuating individual affordances. Speaking metaphorically, societal affordances very often 'open the door' to the operation of individual affordances. No one would expect an infant born into a family and country where English is the ambient language to start speaking Persian, because the specific language(s) acquired by a child will be that or those of his/her familial and social environment. There is evidence testifying to the role of societal affordances in allowing individual affordances to be taken up. Elsewhere (Aronin & Singleton 2010) we have described a rare case of the wilful circumvention of existing societal language affordances. Eliezer Ben-Yehuda, the key-figure in the revival of Hebrew as a spoken language, had an ambition to change social-linguistic affordances. On the cusp of the 19th and 20th centuries in a country then called Palestine ruled by the Ottoman Empire and where Yiddish, Russian, Turkish, Arabic, German were heard on the streets, he personally ring-fenced and zealously guarded the linguistic affordances relating to Hebrew for his son, Ben-Zion, who became the first native speaker of Modern Hebrew.

Feral children, of course, are the showcase of the leading role of social affordances in the realization of the individual affordances. Feral children are children who, owing to cruelty, neglect or unfortunate circumstances, have been denied access to the language affordances of human society. Prior to rescue, such children fail to develop language. Despite every normal child's biological capacity (biological affordance) to acquire a human language, acquisition does not happen unless the child's environment provides the necessary minimum of language affordances. The reported case of a Ukrainian feral child, Oxana Malaya, the 'Ukrainian Dog-girl',[1] found in 1991, illustrates the point. Oxana (born 1983) was abandoned by her parents at the age of two and spent about six years with the dogs in a shed behind her house. When she was belatedly noticed by social workers, she was eight and had only minimal elements of human language. Beyond this her communication consisted of growling and barking like a dog. In other respects too she displayed the behaviour and skills of a dog – walking on all fours and crouching in a doglike way, sniffing at her food before she ate it, and having extremely acute senses of hearing, smell and sight. For several formative years the girl was deprived of social language affordances. Once the relevant social affordances were provided for her, she was able to effectuate her individual biological language affordances. As of 2010, at the age of 26, despite the prognosis of the specialists who believe that it is unlikely that she will ever be properly rehabilitated into 'normal'

---

1.   <http://www.1tv.ru/documentary/fi=5925>,
<http://www.youtube.com/watch?v=93HymGXC_wM>.

society, Oxana has done amazingly well. She is capable of normal human communication and even of expressing emotions and judgments towards her parents who abandoned her. Oxana's case emphasizes the role of societal affordances and the manner in which important individual affordances require to be activated via social affordances.

The deployment of the concept of affordances in multilingualism studies could be beneficial for several reasons. First, affordances have *explanatory value*. The theory of affordances can provide an additional framework for the description and explication of the attributes of multilingual communities and individuals. Affordances can contribute to the clarity of the explication of phenomena. A case in point is the classic concept of domain (Fishman 1972). Thus, concerns have been raised, for example, as to whether the domain concept is applicable to contemporary Denmark and actual patterns of language choice in multilingual settings (Haberland 2005: 227). These concerns can be resolved if we view modern situations within the framework of affordances approach. In particular, from the perspective of affordances a domain can be defined as an environment which provides a substantial number of affordances favouring a specific language or specific languages (as opposed to another or other languages) in a multilingual society (Aronin & Singleton 2010: 121–122). Such a vision is compatible with widely accepted ideas concerning complexity (see below) which include high sensitivity and dependence on initial conditions. In this perspective, there is no place, for example, for an expectation of strictly predictable outcomes. Common experience tells us that some people do not see opportunities where other people do see them, and that, even if opportunities are perceived, not everyone grasps them. Affordances offered by an environment may be neglected for various reasons. As Parker & Stacey put it in their *Hobart Paper*, "[p]eople have choices, they often react in ways that are stubbornly individual, even peculiar ..." (Parker & Stacey 1994: 23). The situation that can be observed in contemporary multilingual settings where not all individuals make use of the language opportunities associated with a particular domain, is actually only natural. We see the domain as existing at the intersection and agglomeration point for affordances relative to a particular language or particular languages, but, clearly, the affordances in question may not necessarily be perceived, or may be perceived but not realized. The concept of domain is, nevertheless, validly interpretable as *a meeting point of affordances*, a space-time where and when a crucially powerful, convergence of affordances favouring the choice of a particular language or languages is at work.

Another value of the concept of affordances lies in its potential effectiveness both as a *means of analysis* and as a *means of appraisal of multilingual phenomena*. Affordances allow both for specification and generalization. Affordances can be treated at any desired degree of detail; they can be identified in any domain and at any level of multilingualism – social, linguistic, stylistic, personal, etc. It would make a huge contribution to the practical management of the vastly diverse aspects of multilingualism if we could measure sociolinguistic factors and material culture artefacts of various degrees of importance, various forms and various levels of tangibility, against each other. On the other hand, if the concept of affordances is employed, the analysis of a particular complex multilingual situation can be rendered clearer and more accurate. Under the unifying rubric of affordance, a variety of diverse elements, material and non-material, social and biological, small-scale and large-scale can be studied. In this process, the various subcategories of affordance – material affordances, natural vs. designed, biological vs. societal, general vs. specific, or distinctions of sure-fire vs. probabilistic; goal vs. happening suggested by Scarantino (2003) – can enable an analysis based on suitably delicate discrimination, classification and assessment. For example, instead of using the traditional general explanatory terms to describe a language as being used in several countries or states, the stability of the status of a given language in a particular country can be related to the quantity and quality of affordances available in its regard. The account offered may be delivered in terms of affordances and each affordance may be associated with a quantitative measure.

With the help of affordances we can analyse situations in more depth exploring and then comparing affordances quantitatively and then qualitatively. In this way broad categories of language behaviour patterns can be looked at in detail using an identification process involving reference to affordances taken up or available.

From the above simple example the potential of the concept of affordances for the study of multilingualism can be appreciated. Unfortunately to date there exist very few studies which have used the concept of affordances in the domain of multiple language learning. The concept of affordances has been applied to the following particular issues. Singleton & Aronin (2007) propose a perspective on multiple language learning based on the theory of affordances. They suggest that multilingual learners tend to exploit the full array of their multilingual affordances in language learning and language use. Van Lier (2007) refers to affordance theory with regard to action-based teaching and learning. He views language learning-as-agency as involving learning to perceive affordances within multimodal communicative events. Otwinowska-Kasztelanic (2009) examines language awareness with respect to the use of cognate vocabulary in teaching English to advanced Polish students through the lens of affordances. She emphasizes the connection between individual language resources, language-learning and language using environments, language awareness and positive lexical transfer from the mother tongue. Dewaele contributes to the affordances approach in his 2010 study, where he investigates the impact of the knowledge of other languages on self-perceived communicative competence and communicative anxiety in French. With the help of the 953 users of French as L1, L2, L3 and L4, Dewaele tested the hypothesis that knowledge of more languages, specifically other Romance languages, strengthens self-perceived communicative competence in French and lead to less communicative anxiety using that language. He found that "when a language is either very strong or very weak in an individual who uses that language, the knowledge of other languages does not play a major role", whereas "at intermediate levels of proficiency, multilingualism and affordances can serve as a crutch in challenging communicative situations" (Dewaele 2010b: 105). The operationalization of affordances as a cumulative score of typologically related languages allowed Dewaele to consider the combined effect of quantity and quality of specific affordances on communicative competence and communicative anxiety in FLA in French L1, L2, L3 and L4 (Dewaele 2010b).

Future research adopting an affordances approach necessitates more exact identification of affordances, that is, deciding what kinds of properties in the sociolinguistic environment qualify as linguistic affordances. Having done that it will be possible to arrive at a classification of linguistic affordances that can be typically found in a community, inventorize in detail the affordances offered in specific sociolinguistic environments for particular languages and analyse and quantify the affordances in particular sociolinguistic environments in terms of types of affordances (e.g., material, ideational affordances, goal/happening, surefire/probability), to assess their degree of perception and take-up, and to identify affordances that are needed but are not in place. This kind of analysis will provide interested parties with criteria for adjusting the language affordances in the context in question, with a view to putting in place optimal configurations for their desired goals. It is for future research to develop a structured taxonomy of linguistic markers of language diversity in terms of different kinds of linguistic affordances with different degrees of impact in different circumstances. With such a taxonomy at their disposal, investigators of language diversity will be able to have greater confidence in his/her analytical, evaluative and predictive endeavours.

Complexity thinking and multilingualism

Of all recent approaches to the study of multilingualism, the complexity perspective is probably the one that is currently developing most widely. Complexity thinking does not consist in one monolithic theory; it is rather an increasingly appreciated perspective in different areas of knowledge, including applied linguistics, using and developing different components and notions of complexity according to the particular interests and preoccupations of the domains in question. Complexity thinking asserts: (i) that the whole is not the sum of its parts, and (ii) that the world around us is characterized by irregularity, fragmentariness, fuzziness and even chaos (cf. Capra 2005; Cilliers 1998; Dent 1999). It includes reference to the concepts *of multiple agents, complex interactions, 'on the verge of chaotic', 'sensitivity to initial conditions',* and *emergent properties.*

Our inference is that multilingualism is inherently complex and is better understood when viewed from a complexity perspective (Aronin & Singleton 2008b; Aronin & Hufeisen 2009b). The essential difference between bilingualism and multilingualism beyond bilingualism, including SLA versus TLA, lies in degree of complexity. For multilingualism beyond bilingualism, complexity is not only one of its characteristics; it is its inherent and key quality (see Chapter 3), a crucial determinant of learning, teaching and social outcomes. Awareness of this fact is vital in language education in all its varieties.

Parallels between the concepts of complexity and recent findings in multilingualism shed important light on the nature of multilingualism. The whole history of multilingualism studies indicates that multilingualism cannot be understood simply by breaking phenomena down into their component parts and cannot be reduced to clear-cut rules, forms and explanations. Rather, multilingualism has been shown to be a dynamic and self-organizing system, displaying *emergent* qualities. It is not only the *multiple agents* – e.g., number of languages, modes of use, variety of speakers, origins of speakers, linguistic abilities and needs of speakers, political and historical nuances, etc. – that make multilingual contact complex. What makes of something merely complicated (having many elements) something truly complex are the *interactions* between those many elements.

The phenomenon whereby interactions create and also result from complexity is labelled *sensitivity to initial conditions.* It is very characteristic of all kinds of multilingualism phenomena. We all see examples of such sensitivity around us constantly; thus, for example, language users and learners differ widely despite a similar education and environment. In the complexity literature this phenomenon is often referred to as the 'butterfly effect'. It was first modelled by the mathematician and meteorologist Edward Lorenz (1917–2008) at the Massachusetts Institute of Technology in his study of weather. The model (see Figure 2) demonstrates sensitive dependence on initial conditions, exemplified and illustrated by noticeable changes occasioned by the infinitesimally tiny effect of a butterfly landing. The extreme sensitivity to initial conditions of chaotic systems means that the very slightest change in those conditions can produce radically different results (see Figure 2).

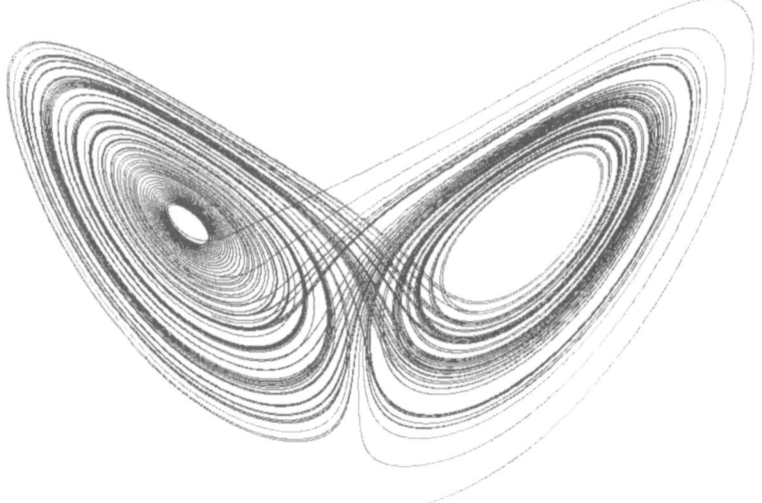

Figure 2. Graphic model of Lorenz Attractor
(the figure is taken from <http://www.zeuscat.com/andrew/chaos/lorenz.html>)

The different outcomes consequent on the interaction of multiple agents in the conditions of sensitivity to initial conditions often result in new *emergent* qualities. Frequent examples of emergent phenomena are metabolism as an emergent property of life; likewise, consciousness is considered to be an emergent property of brain. 'Emergent' in complexity science refers to processes, structures, behaviour or properties which cannot be understood simply by understanding their parts, because they are not merely the sum of their parts. Being the products of the interactions of their parts, emergent phenomena have properties which are the properties of the whole system or entity, but not the properties of any of its parts. Thus, a crowd is other than the sum of the individuals of which it consists (and this is well seen in the unpredictable behaviour of crowds); a traffic jam is other than the sum of the cars comprising it. Other examples of emergent phenomena, processes and structures found in nature are hurricanes and sand dunes, flocks of birds and schools of fish, communities of ants.

To date complexity thinking has been applied to multilingualism by Herdina and Jessner (Jessner 1997; Herdina & Jessner 2002; Jessner 2008b) in the context of investigating language acquisition and psycholinguistics. Their Dynamic Model of Multilingualism (DMM) focuses on 'the variability and dynamics of the individual speaker system' (Herdina & Jessner 2002: 2) and emphasizes a dynamic representation of multilingualism, in particular of multiple language acquisition.

De Bot (2004) has also made use of Dynamic Systems Theory, but for a different purpose – to look at languages in relation to linguistic communities.

Research undertaken from a complexity perspective was presented in a special issue of *Applied Linguistics* edited by Ellis & Larsen-Freeman (2006). The contributors to the issue use the term 'emergentism' and apply the conceptual complexity perspective to a number of areas of language study including syntax and discourse (Cameron & Deignan 2006); multilingual lexicons (Meara 2006); and fluency and accuracy in L2 oral and written production (Larsen-Freeman 2006).

Gabryś-Barker (2005), for her part, takes the complexity of multilingualism and the fuzziness of multilingual lexicon as points of departure in analysing quantitative studies on multilingual development, lexical storage, processing and retrieval.

Increasing awareness and explicit recognition of the complexity of multilingualism allows for a more comprehensive theoretical understanding of multilingualism and yields practical results in the teaching of multiple languages. Thus, recent discussions of multilingualism (see, for example, Herdina & Jessner 2002; Hoffmann 2001a, 2001b) note that:

- the acquisition and use of more than two languages are not only quantitatively but also qualitatively different from bilingualism, exhibiting characteristics not found in bilingualism;
- a bilingual is not the sum of two monolinguals (Grosjean 1985, 1992) and a multilingual is not the sum of multiple monolinguals (Cook 1992, 1993); bilinguals are recognized as possessing a special constellation of language competencies which allow them to communicate in various and multiple social contexts, and users of more than two languages are widely acknowledged to have at their disposal "a configuration of linguistic competences that is distinct from that of bilinguals and monolinguals" (Cenoz & Genesee 1998: 19);
- second, third and subsequent language acquisition processes do not exactly replicate the processes operative in previous language acquisition (Grosjean 1985, 1992);
- trilingual education is not just a simple matter of the mechanical addition of one or more languages in the curriculum but entails an increase in complexity (Cenoz & Genesee 1998; Cenoz & Gorter 2005; Cenoz 2009).

Concluding summary

In this chapter we have briefly described some of the emerging or recently established areas of investigation into multilingualism which attempt to account for multilingualism from a variety of angles.

Thus, we have talked about the concepts of affordances and material culture, as well as referring to more longstanding areas of interest such as linguistic landscape, language ecology and complexity. All of these perspectives, which are increasingly being researched, are seen as promising to lead us to a more comprehensive view of multilingualism.

We have also pointed to some possible avenues of further research in each of these directions. Some of these offer the potential of new modes of measurement, while others present novel explanatory frameworks. All of these new avenues have the capacity to contribute to informing and improving practical aspects of dealing with multilingual diversity.

CHAPTER 10

Concluding thoughts

Multilingualism, as we indicated early in the book, points to an aspect of the specialness of humankind in a way that is not given wide attention. In the domain of communication, researchers have tended to identify as typically human aspects of language such as creativity, arbitrariness and cultural transmission. Usually left out of the picture in this discussion is the human ability to acquire and use a multiplicity of languages, that is, the capacity for multilingualism. Leaving aside the case of working and domestic animals which, alongside their own communication systems, learn to respond to some minimal elements of human language ('whoa!', 'sit!', 'stay!', etc.), this multilingual capacity is uniquely human. Moreover, multilingual competence and behaviour is a highly salient characteristic of human society, and in the modern world it is such an integral and crucial component that without it contemporary global human society simply would not function.

Multilingualism *per se* is obviously not a new phenomenon. Some of its forms may indeed be characteristic principally of societies of the past – for example, forms of multilingualism involving the allocation of important roles to languages which no longer had native speakers (such as Sumerian and Latin). Other forms of multilingualism reflect more recent developments. One thinks, for instance, of the fact that in the present era we are subject to the necessary inclusion across a wide professional range the length and breadth of the entire planet of a specific lingua franca (English). The evolution of different manifestations of multilingualism in human practices, as reflected in recent research, illustrates its quality of *liminality*, in other words, the fact that various processes and features of multilingualism are coming to the surface as its distribution over spaces, populations and functions is changing. Some of these are newly emergent; others are attributes and dynamics which were already existent but which were earlier not clearly discernible, and which are rendered more perceptible by developmental shifts.

We have suggested that, viewed from the perspective of our discussion in this book, three stages are traceable in societal and scientific awareness in respect of language and languages. The first of these, which may be labelled 'monolingual', was not especially focused on multilingualism. During the second, 'bilingual' stage, the acquisition and use of two languages came under the spotlight but often tended to be regarded in a negative manner. In a third, more broadly 'multilingual' (in the sense of 'bilingual plus') stage, awareness has grown of the widespread reality and necessity of living with and through several languages – both among populations at large and in academic circles. Very specific practices aimed at promoting a positive encounter with and response to multilingualism in its various forms have been initiated and supported by international institutions. Thus, for instance, to take a simple but telling example, since 2005 the portfolio of one of the Commissioners of the European Union has explicitly included multilingualism, and a foundation text on multilingualism has been put in place by the Commission of the European Communities (*A new framework strategy for multilingualism*). Innumerable documents and decisions, indeed, address the needs and issues which arise out of the increasing prevalence of multilingual dimensions associated with areas such as economics, social issues, education and culture. There is a proliferation of projects, involving collaboration between various kinds of specialists and various representatives of different social and professional groups, which are aimed at addressing everyday needs in a contemporary world where multilingualism pervades interaction in business, administration, education, health, the law, the media, and so much more. For example, in the educational sphere, the teaching and learning of additional languages is in many countries and regions being extended to practically all ages and population groups, including mature adults via lifelong learning programmes.

It seems that we can now state with some confidence that multilingualism research and public awareness of multilingualism have crossed a second threshold. The first threshold was the reaching of a consensus concerning the importance and the specificities of bilingualism. The second threshold is the growth of an understanding that there is a far-reaching use in the world, by particular societies and by individuals, of more than two languages, and that repertoires of three or more languages may have their own specificities relative to bilingualism. Hence the frequency of the phrase 'beyond bilingualism' in current research and writing in the area – a phrase which in some quarters has become almost a battle cry. In this book we have defined multilingualism as including bilingualism, but our prime focus throughout, in keeping with the spirit of multilingual research in its present orientation, has been on multilingualism in its 'beyond bilingualism' sense and manifestation. The debate which is under way, and to which we hope our discussion here will contribute, while retaining all that has been gained from the classic bilingualism studies, is progressing from a focus on the relationship between bilingualism and monolingualism towards an increasingly intense scrutiny of the question regarding the ways in which going 'beyond bilingualism' might entail a qualitative shift in respect both of monolingualism and bilingualism.

As the conception of multilingualism evolves and expands, new focal topics appear, new classifications and typologies are proposed, and new approaches and models begin to abound. Our own treatment here has reflected the moves that are afoot and has attempted to give some impression of the exciting dynamism of such developments and the paths towards more comprehensive view of multilingualism along which they are leading us. We have in this connection had a particular look at what we consider to be some especially promising domains. Thus, for example, we have entered into the reasoning concerning the potential benefits of the establishment of a fully-fledged philosophy of multilingualism; we have explored the possible role of the notion of affordances in thinking about multilingualism; we have given an account of the uses being made of data deriving from the material culture of multilingualism; and we have examined the suggestion that multilingualism needs to be approached under the auspices of complexity thinking.

Of course, time and space constraints have meant that we have been unable to discuss in the detail they merit an entire swathe of valuable insights and perspectives. For instance, we have said very little about neurobiological perspectives, in which many researchers have invested much and have placed a great deal of hope in regard to the future elucidation of multilingual phenomena. It has to be said with respect to the last point that this is a highly specialized area which lies somewhat beyond our own expertise and, perhaps more importantly, that there is an increasing stock of material on neurolinguistic approaches to multilingualism, with the consequence that the reader with an appetite to for information in this area is unlikely to be left, as the French say, *sur sa faim* ('in a state of hunger').

The current situation with regard to multilingualism research can be likened to the somewhat clichéd but highly apposite metaphor of the unending changes experienced by the walker. At any given stage of his/her progress the walker sees only what the line of the horizon renders visible. With forward motion, however, the horizon also moves, and new sights become accessible. And so it continues. Fresh landscapes and unexpected turns of the road always lie ahead, awaiting simply the next step along the route. So it is with the topics discussed in this book. We have been limited in our purview by the constraints imposed by the current horizon, but as we go forward in our investigations, our horizon will also shift, constantly opening to us previously unperceived vistas, previously unexplored perspectives.

Bibliography

A new framework strategy for multilingualism. 2005. <http://ec.europa.eu/education/languages/archive/doc/com596_en.pdf> (December 3, 2011).

Abu-Rabia, S. 2001. Testing the interdependence hypothesis among native adult bilingual Russian-English students. *Journal of Psycholinguistic Research* 30(4): 437–455.

Adams, J.N. & Swain, S. 2002. Introduction. In *Bilingualism in Ancient Society*, J.N. Adams, M. Janse & S. Swain (eds), 1–20. Oxford: OUP.

Adegbija, E.E. 2004. *Multilingualism: A Nigerian Case Study*. Trenton NJ: Africa World Press.

Aitchison, J. 1998. *Articulate Mammal: Introduction to Psycholinguistics*, 4th edn. London: Routledge.

Ackerman, P. 1988. Determinants of individual differences during skill acquisition: Cognitive abilities and information processing. *Journal of Experimental Psychology: General* 117: 288–318.

Ackerman, P. 1989. Individual differences and skill acquisition. In *Learning and Individual Differences*, P. Ackerman, R. Sternberg & R. Glaser (eds), 165–217. New York NY: Freeman.

Albert, M. & Obler, L. 1978. *Perspectives in Neurolinguistics: The Bilingual Brain: Neuropsychological and Neurolinguistic Aspects of Bilingualism*. San Diego CA: Academic Press.

Alker, H.R., Amin, T., Biersteker, T.J. & Inoguchi, T. 2001. Twelve world order debates which have made our days. Published in the Chicago International studies Association Paper Archive. <http://isanet.ccit.arizona.edu/archive/worldorder.html> (December 3, 2011).

Ammon, U. (ed.). 1989. *Status and Function of Languages and Language Varieties*. Berlin: Mouton de Gruyter.

Ammon, U. 1995. To what extent is German an international language? In *The German Language and the Real World: Sociolinguistic, Cultural and Pragmatic Perspectives on Contemporary German*, P. Stevenson (ed.), 25–53. Oxford: Clarendon Press.

Ammon, U. 2007. Lost in translation. *Nature* 445: 454–455.

Andreesen, W. 1998. New Russian-language newspapers in Berlin. Paper presented at 64th IFLA General Conference, Amsterdam, August 16 – August 21, 1998. <http://www.ifla.org/IV/ifla64/096-116e.htm> (December 3, 2011).

Aronin, L. 2004. Multilinguality and emotions: Emotional and attitudinal experiences of trilingual immigrant students towards themselves and languages in multilingual settings. *Estudios de Sociolinguistica* 5(1): 59–81.

Aronin, L. 2005. Theoretical perspectives of trilingual education. In *The International Journal of the Sociology of Language* 171: 7–22.

Aronin, L. 2006. Dominant language constellations: An approach to multilingualism studies. In *Multilingualism in Educational Settings,* M. Ó Laoire (ed.), 140–159. Hohengehren: Schneider Publications.

Aronin, L. 2007. *Current Multilingualism as a New Linguistic World Order* [CLCS Occasional Paper 67]. Dublin: Trinity College.

Aronin, L., Fishman, J., Singleton, D., & Ó Laoire, M. Under review. Introduction. In *Current Multilingualism: A New Linguistic Dispensation*, D. Singleton, J. Fishman, L. Aronin & M. Ó Laoire (eds). Berlin: Mouton de Gruyter.

Aronin, L. & Hufeisen, B. 2009a. Introduction: On the genesis and development of L3 research, multilingualism and multiple language acquisition. In *The Exploration of Multilingualism: Development of Research on L3, Multilingualism and Multiple Language Acquisition* [AILA Applied Linguisics Series 6], L. Aronin & B. Hufeisen (eds), 1–9. Amsterdam: John Benjamins.

Aronin, L. & Hufeisen, B. 2009b. Methods of research in multilingualism studies: Reaching a comprehensive perspective. In *The Exploration of Multilingualism: Development of Research on L3, Multilingualism and Multiple Language Acquisition* [AILA Applied Linguistics Series 6], L. Aronin & B. Hufeisen (eds), 103–120. Amsterdam: John Benjamins.

Aronin, L. & Hufeisen, B. (eds). 2009c. *The Exploration of Multilingualism: Development of Research on L3, Multilingualism and Multiple Language Acquisition* [AILA Applied Linguistics Series 6]. Amsterdam: John Benjamins.

Aronin, L. & Ó Laoire, M. 2001. Exploring multilingualism in cultural contexts: Towards a notion of multilinguality. Paper presented at the Third International Conference on Third Language Acquisition and Trilingualism, Leewarden-Liouwert, the Netherlands.

Aronin, L. & Ó Laoire, M. 2004. Exploring multilingualism in cultural contexts: towards a notion of multilinguality. In *Trilingualism in Family, School and Community*, C. Hoffmann & J. Ytsma (eds), 11–29. Clevedon: Multilingual Matters.

Aronin, L. & Ó Laoire, M. 2007. The material culture of multilingualism. Paper presented at the Fifth International Conference on Multilingualism and Third Language Acquisition, Stirling, UK.

Aronin, L. & Ó Laoire, M. 2012. The material culture of multilingualism. In *Minority Languages in the Linguistic Landscape*, D. Gorter, L. van Mensel & H.F. Marten (eds), 299–318. Basingstoke: Palgrave.

Aronin, L. & Singleton, D. 2006. Multilingualism as a new linguistic world order. Paper presented at the Sociolinguistics Symposium, Limerick.

Aronin, L. & Singleton, D. 2008a. Multilingualism as a new linguistic dispensation. *International Journal of Multilingualism* 5(1): 1–16.

Aronin, L. & Singleton, D. 2008b. The complexity of multilingual contact and language use in times of globalization. *Conversarii. Studi Linguistici* 2: 33–47.

Aronin, L. & Singleton, D. 2008c. The philosophy of multilingualism. In *Achieving Multilingualism: Wills and Ways*, O. Arnandiz & M.S. Jorda (eds). Proceedings of the 1st International Conference on Multilingualism (ICOM), Universitat Jaume-1.

Aronin, L. & Singleton, D. 2008d. English as a constituent of a dominant language constellation. Paper presented at the GlobEng Conference, Verona, Italy.

Aronin, L. & Singleton, D. 2010. Affordances and the diversity of multilingualism. *International Journal of the Sociology of Language* 205: 105–129. (Special Issue *The Diversity of Multilingualism*, edited by L. Aronin & D. Singleton).

Aronin, L. & Singleton, D. Forthcoming. Multilingualism and philosophy. In *The Encyclopedia of Applied Linguistics*, C.A. Chapelle (ed.). Hoboken NJ: Wiley-Blackwell.

Auer, P. & Li Wei (eds). 2007. *Handbook of Multilingualism and Multilingual Communication*. Berlin: Mouton de Gruyter.

Avgerou, C. 2002. *Information Systems and Global Diversity*. Oxford: OUP.

Backhaus, P. 2007. *Linguistic Landscapes: A Comparative Study of Urban Multilingualism in Tokyo*. Clevedon: Multilingual Matters.

Baetens Beardsmore, H. 1986. *Bilingualism: Basic Principles,* 2nd edn. Clevedon: Multilingual Matters.

Baker, A., Ferguson, S. & Dawson, A. 2003. The perceived value of time: Controls versus shift-workers. *Time and Society* 12(1): 27–39.

Baker, C. 1988. *Key Issues in Bilingualism and Bilingual Education*. Clevedon: Multilingual Matters.

Baker, C. 1993 [1996, 2001, 2006]. *Foundations of Bilingual Education and Bilingualism*. Clevedon: Multilingual Matters.

Baker, C. 2007. Becoming bilingual through bilingual education. In *Handbook of multilingualism and Multilingual Communication*, P. Auer & Li Wei (eds), 131–152. Berlin: Mouton de Gruyter.

Baker, C. & Prys Jones, S. (eds). 1998. *Encyclopedia of Bilingualism and Bilingual Education*. Clevedon: Multilingual Matters.

Baker, W., Trofimovich, P., Mack, M. & Flege, J.E. 2002. The effect of perceived phonetic similarity on non-native sound learning by children and adults. *Proceedings of the Annual Boston University Conference on Language Development* 26(1): 36–47.

Barbour, S. 2002. Language, nationalism and globalism: Educational consequences of changing patterns of language use. In *Beyond Boundaries: Language and Identity in Contemporary Europe*, P. Gubbins & M. Holt (eds), 11–18. Clevedon: Multilingual Matters.

Bardel, C. & Lindqvist, C. 2007. The role of proficiency and psychotypology in lexical cross-linguistic influence. A study of a multilingual learner of Italian L3. In *Atti del VI Congresso Internazionale dell'Associazione Italiana di Linguistica Applicata, Napoli, 9–10 febbraio 2006*, M. Chini, P. Desideri, M.E. Favilla & G. Pallotti (eds), 123–145. Perugia: Guerra Edizioni.

Bardel, C., Falk, Y. & Lindqvist, C. Under review. Multilingualism in Sweden. In *Current Multilingualism: A New Linguistic Dispensation,* D. Singleton, J. Fishman, L. Aronin & M. Ó Laoire (eds). Berlin: Mouton de Gruyter.

Barnes, J.D. 2006. *Early Trilingualism: Focus on Questions*. Clevedon: Multilingual Matters.

Barron-Hauwaert, S. 2003. Trilingualism. A study of children growing up with three languages. In *The Multilingual Mind: Issues Discussed by, for, and about People Living with Many Languages,* T. Tokuhama-Espinosa (ed.), 129–150. Westport CT: Praeger.

Barron-Hauwaert, S. 2004. *Language Strategies for Bilingual Families: The-One-Parent-One-Language Approach*. Clevedon: Multilingual Matters.

Barrett, R. 2003. Models of gay male identity and the marketing of 'gay language' in foreign language phrasebooks for gay men. *Estudios de Sociolinguistica* 4(2): 533–562.

Bauman, Z. 1999. *Globalization: The Human Consequences*. Cambridge: Polity Press.

Beaney, M. 2006. Wittgenstein on language: From simples to samples. In *The Oxford Handbook of Philosophy of Language*, E. Lepore & B. Smith (eds), 40–59. Oxford: Clarendon Press.

Beauvillain, C. & Grainger, J. 1987. Accessing interlexical homographs: Some limitations of a language-selective access. *Journal of Memory and Language* 26(6): 658–672.

Ben Zeev, S. 1977. The Influence of bilingualism on cognitive strategy and cognitive development. *Child Development* 48: 1009–1018.

Bendle, M. 2002. The crisis of 'identity' in high modernity. *The British Journal of Sociology* 53(1): 1–18.

Bergman, C.R. 1976. Interference vs. independent development in infant bilingualism. In *Bilingualism in the Bicentennial and Beyond*, G.D. Keller, R.V. Teschner & S. Viera (eds), 86–96. New York NY: Bilingual Press.

Betteridge, T. (ed.) 2007. *Borders and Travellers in Early Modern Europe*. Aldershot: Ashgate.

Bialystok, E. 1987. Words and things: Development of word concept by bilingual children. *Studies in Second Language Acquisition* 9: 133–140.

Bialystok, E. 1988. Levels of bilingualism and levels of linguistic awareness. *Developmental Psychology* 24(4): 560–567.

Bialystok, E. 1997. The structure of age: In search of barriers to second language acquisition. *Second Language Research* 13: 116–137.

Bialystok, E. 1999. Cognitive complexity and attentional control in the bilingual mind. *Child Development* 70: 636–644.

Bialystok, E. 2001. *Bilingualism in Development: Language, Literacy, and Cognition*. Cambridge: CUP.

Bialystok, E. 2002. Cognitive processes of L2 users. In *Portrait of the L2 user*, V. Cook (ed.), 147–165. Clevedon: Multilingual Matters.

Bialystok, E. 2006. Effect of bilingualism and computer video game experience on the Simon task. *Canadian Journal of Experimental Psychology* 60(1): 68–79.

Bialystok, E. 2009. Bilingualism: The good, the bad, and the indifferent. *Bilingualism: Language and Cognition* 12(1): 3–11.

Bialystok, E., Craik, F.I.M. & Freedman, M. 2007. Bilingualism as a protection against the onset of symptoms of dementia. *Neuropsychologia* 45: 459–464.

Bialystok, E., Craik, F.I.M., Klein, R. & Viswanathan, M. 2004. Bilingualism, aging, and cognitive control: Evidence from the Simon task. *Psychology and Aging* 19(2): 290–303.

Bialystok, E. & Martin, M.M. 2004. Attention and inhibition in bilingual children: Evidence from the dimensional change card sort task. *Developmental Science* 7(3): 325–339.

Bickerton, D. 2009. Recursion: Core of complexity or artifact of analysis? In *Syntactic Complexity: Diachrony, Acquisition, Neuro-cognition, Volution*, T. Givón & M. Shibatani (eds), 531–544. Amsterdam: John Benjamins.

Birdsong, C. 2003. Authenticité de prononciation en français L2 chez des apprenants tardifs anglophones: Analyses segmentales et globales. *AILE* 18: 17–36.

Birdsong, D. & Molis, M. 2001. On the evidence for maturational constraints in second language acquisition. *Journal of Memory and Language* 44: 235–249.

Birdsong, D. 1992. Ultimate attainment in second language acquisition. *Language* 68(4): 706–755.

Björklund, S. & Suni, I. 2000. The role of English as L3 in a Swedish immersion programme in Finland: Impacts on language teaching and language relations. In *English in Europe: The Acquisition of a Third Language*, J. Cenoz & U. Jessner (eds), 198–221. Clevedon: Multilingual Matters.

Bloch, B. & Trager, G.L. 1942. *Outline of Linguistic Analysis*. Baltimore MD: Linguistic Society of America/Waverly Press.

Bloomfield, L. 1933. *Language*. New York NY: Allen & Unwin.

Blommaert, J. 2008. Language, asylum and the national order. Working papers in *Urban Language & Literacies* 50. <http://www.kcl.ac.uk/content/1/c6/04/20/06/50.pdf> (July 9, 2011).

Blommaert, J. 2009. Language, asylum, and the national order. *Current Anthropology* 50(4): 415–441.

Blommaert, J. 2010. *The Sociolinguistics of Globalization*. Cambridge: CUP.

Blommaert, J. & Rampton, B. 2011. Language and Superdiversity: A position paper. *Working papers* [Urban Language & Literacies, Paper 70]. <www.kcl.ac.uk/sspp/departments/education/.../llg/workingpapers/70.pdf>

Bloomfield L. 1933[1914]. *Language,* rev. edn. New York NY: Holt.

Bongaerts, T. 2003. Effets de l'âge sur l'acquisition de la prononciation d'une seconde langue. *Acquisition et Interaction en Langue Étrangère* 18: 79–98.

Boroditsky, L. 2010. Lost in translation. *The Wall Street Journal,* July 24, 2010.

Bosch, L. & Sebastián-Gallés, N. 1997. Native language recognition abilities in four-month-old infants from monolingual and bilingual environments. *Cognition* 65(1): 33–69.

Bosch, L. & Sebastián-Gallés, N. 2003. Simultaneous bilingualism and the perception of a language specific vowel contrast in the first year of life. *Language and Speech* 46: 217–243.

Bossomaier, T. & Green, D. 1998. *Patterns in the Sand: Computers, Complexity, and Everyday Life.* Reading: Perseus Books.

Brann, C.M.B. 1981. Trilingualism in language planning for education in Sub-Saharan Africa. Paris: UNESCO, ref. ED-81/WS/116.

Braudel, F. 1969. Histoire et sciences sociales: La longue durée. In *Ecrits sur l'histoire*, F. Braudel (ed.), 41–83. Paris: Flammarion.

Braun, M. 1937. Beobachtungen zur Frage der Mehrsprachigkeit. *Göttingische Gelehrte Anzeigen* 4: 115–130.

Braun, A. & Cline, T. 2010. Trilingual families in mainly monolingual societies: Working towards a typology. *International Journal of Multilingualism* 7(2): 110–127.

Braunmüller, K. & Ferraresi, G. (eds). 2003. *Aspects of Multilingualism in European Language History* [Hamburg Studies on Multilingualism 2]. Amsterdam: John Benjamins.

Breedveld, K. 1998. The double myth of flexibilization: Trends in scattered work hours, and differences in time sovereignty. *Time & Society* 7(1): 129–143.

Bronfenbrenner, U. 1993. The ecology of cognitive development: Research models and fugitive findings. In *Development in Context: Acting and Thinking in Specific Environments*, R.H. Wozniak & K.W. Fisher (eds), 3–44. Hillsdale NJ: Lawrence Erlbaum Associates.

Bull, H. 1977. *The Anarchical Society: A Study of Order in World Politics.* New York NY: Columbia University press.

Bull, H. & Watson, A. (eds). 1984. *The Expansion of International Society.* Oxford: Clarendon press.

Bybee, J.L. 1988. Morphology as lexical organization. In *Theoretical Morphology*, M. Hammond & M. Noonan (eds), 119–141. San Diego CA: Academic Press.

Cameron, L. & Deignan, A. 2006. The emergence of metaphor in discourse. *Applied Linguistics* 27: 671–690.

Canagarajah, S. 2009. The plurilingual tradition and the English language in South Asia. *AILA Review* 12: 5–22.

Capra, F. 2005. Complexity and life. *Theory, Culture and Society* 22(5): 33–44.

Castells, M. 1997. *The Power of Identity.* Oxford: Blackwell.

Caramazza, A. & Brones, I. 1979. Lexical access in bilinguals. *Bulletin of the Psychonomic Society* 13(4): 212–214.

Carlson, S.M. & Meltzoff, A.N. 2008. Bilingual experience and executive functioning in young children. *Developmental Science* 11(2): 282–298.

Cenoz, J. 1998. Mulilingual education in the Basque Country. In *Beyond Bilingualism: Multilingualism and Multilingual Education*, J. Cenoz & F. Genesee (eds), 175–191. Clevedon: Multilingual Matters.

Cenoz, J. 2000. Research on multilingual acquisition. In *English in Europe: The Acquisition of a Third Language*, J. Cenoz & U. Jessner (eds), 39–53. Clevedon: Multilingual Matters.

Cenoz, J. 2003. The additive effect of bilingualism on third language acquisition: A review. *International Journal of Bilingualism* 7: 71–88.

Cenoz, J. 2009. *Towards Multilingual Education: Basque Educational Research in International Perspective*. Bristol: Multilingual Matters.

Cenoz, J. & Genesee, F. (eds). 1998. *Beyond Bilingualism: Multilingualism and Multilingual Education*. Clevedon: Multilingual Matters.

Cenoz, J. & Gorter, D. 2005. Trilingualism and minority languages in Europe. *The International Journal of the Sociology of Language* 171: 1–5.

Cenoz, J. & Gorter, D. (eds). 2008a. Multilingualism and minority languages: achievements and challenges in education. *AILA Review* 21.

Cenoz, J. & Gorter, D. 2008b. The linguistic landscape as an additional source of input in second language acquisition. *IRAL: International Review of Applied Linguistics* 46: 267–287.

Cenoz, J., Hufeisen, B. & Jessner, U. 2001. *Cross-linguistic Influence in Third Language Acquisition: Psycholinguistic Perspectives*. Clevedon: Multilingual Matters.

Cenoz, J., Hufeisen, B. & Jessner, U. 2008. *Looking Beyond second Language Acquisition: Studies in Tri- and Multilingualism*, 2nd edn. Tübingen: Stauffenburg.

Cenoz, J. & Jessner, U. 2000. *English in Europe: The Acquisition of a Third Language*. Clevedon: Multilingual Matters.

Cenoz, J. & Jessner, U. 2009. The study of multilingualism in educational contexts. In *The Exploration of Multilingualism: Development of Research on L3, Multilingualism and Multiple Language Acquisition* [AILA Applied Linguistics Series 6], L. Aronin & B. Hufeisen (eds), 121–138. Amsterdam: John Benjamins.

Chase-Dunn, C. 1999. Globalization: A world-systems perspective. *Journal of World-Systems Research* 5(2): 165–185.

Chaunu, P. 1966. *La Civilisation de L'Europe Classique*. Paris: Arthaud.

Cheshire, J. 2002. Who we are and where we're going: Language and identities in the new Europe. In *Beyond Boundaries: Language and Identity in Contemporary Europe*, P. Gubbins & M. Holt (eds), 19–34. Clevedon: Multilingual Matters.

Chimombo, M. 1979. An analysis of the order of acquisition of English grammatical morphemes in a bilingual child. *Working Papers on Bilingualism* 18. Toronto: The Ontario Institute for Studies in Education.

Chinchilla, N. 2005. Globalization, international migration, and transnationalism: Some observations based on the Central American experience. In *Critical Globalization Studies*, R. Appelbaum & W. Robinson (eds), 167–176. New-York and London: Routledge.

Chiti-Batelli, A. 2003. Can anything be done about the 'Glottophagy' of English? A bibliographical survey with a political conclusion. *Language Problems and Language Planning* 27(2): 137–153.

Chomsky, N. 1957. *Syntactic Structures*. The Hague: Mouton.

Chomsky, N. 2000. *The Architecture of Language*. New Delhi: OUP.

Chomsky, N. 2006. *Language and Mind*, 3rd edn. Cambridge: CUP.

Cilliers, P. 1998. *Complexity and Postmodernism: Understanding Complex Systems*. London: Routledge.

Cilliers, P. 2005. On the importance of a certain slowness: Stability, memory and hysteresis in complex systems. Paper delivered at the Complexity, Science and Society Conference. Liverpool.

Claiborne, R. 1990. *The Life and Times of the English Language*. London: Bloomsbury.

Clark, E.V. 2009. *First Language Acquisition*, 2nd edn. Cambridge: CUP.

Clyne, M. 1967. *Transference and Triggering*. The Hague: Nijhoff.

Clyne M. 1987. Constraints on code-switching: How universal are they? *Linguistics* 25: 739–764. (Reprinted in 2000 in *The Bilingualism Reader*, Li Wei (ed.), 257–280. New York NY: Routledge).

Clyne, M. 1992a. German as a pluricentric language. In *Pluricentric Languages: Differing Norms in Different Nations*, M. Clyne (ed.), 117–147. Berlin: Mouton de Gruyter.

Clyne, M. 1992b. Pluricentric languages – Introduction. In *Pluricentric Languages: Differing Norms in Different Nations*, M. Clyne (ed.), 1–9. Berlin: Mouton de Gruyter.

Clyne, M. 1992c. Epilogue. In *Pluricentric Languages: Differing Norms in Different Nations*, M. Clyne (ed.), 455–465. Berlin: Mouton de Gruyter.

Clyne, M. 1997. Multilingualism. In *The Handbook of Sociolinguistics*, F. Coulmas (ed.), 301–314. Oxford: Blackwell.

Clyne, M. 2003. *Dynamics of Language Contact: English and Immigrant Languages*. Cambridge: CUP.

Cook, V. 1991. The poverty-of-the-stimulus argument and multicompetence. *Second Language Research* 7: 103–117.

Cook, V. 1992. Evidence for multi-competence. *Language Learning* 42(4): 557–591.

Cook, V. 1993. *Linguistics and Second Language Acquisition*. London: Macmillan.

Cook, V. 1995. Multicompetence and effects of age. In *The Age Factor in Second Language Acquisition*, D. Singleton & Z. Lengyel (eds), 51–56. Clevedon: Multilingual Matters.

Cook, V. 1996. Competence and multi-competence. In *Performance and Competence in Second Language Acquisition*, G. Brown, K. Malmkjaer & J. Williams (eds), 57–69. Cambridge: CUP.

Cook, V. 1999. Going beyond the native speaker in language teaching. *TESOL Quarterly* 33(2): 185–209.

Cook, V. 2001. Requirements for a multilingual model of language production. <http://homepage.ntlworld.com/vivian.c/Writings/Papers/RequirementsForMultilingualModel.htm> (December 3, 2011).

Cook, V. 2002. Background to the L2 user. In *Portraits of the L2 User*, V. Cook (ed.), 1–28. Clevedon: Multilingual Matters.

Cook, V. Second Language Acquisition Topics. <http://homepage.ntlworld.com/vivian.c/SLA/index.htm> (December 3, 2011).

Cook, V. 2003a. Introduction: The changing L1 in the L2 user's mind. In *Effects of the Second Language on the First*, V. Cook (ed.). Clevedon: Multilingual Matters.

Cook, V. (ed.). 2003b. *The Effects of the Second Language on the First*. Clevedon: Multilingual Matters.

Cook, V. Evidence for Multicompetence. <http://homepage.ntlworld.com/vivian.c/SLA/Multicompetence/MCEvidence.htm> (July 26, 2009).

Cook, V. 2008. ELF: Central or atypical second language acquisition? Paper presented at AILA (International Association of Applied Linguistics) Congress 2008, Essen, Germany, 24–29 August.

Cook, V. 2010. The relationship between first and second language acquisition revisited. In *The Continuum Companion to Second Language Acquisition*, E. Macaro (ed.), 137–157. London: Continuum.

Cook, V. Forthcoming a. ELF: Central or atypical second language acquisition? In *Current Multilingualism: A New Linguistic Dispensation*, D. Singleton, J. Fishman, L. Aronin & M. Ó Laoire (eds). Berlin: Mouton de Gruyter.

Cook, V. Forthcoming b. Multi-competence. In *The Encyclopedia of Applied Linguistics*, C.A. Chapelle (ed.). Hoboken NJ: Wiley Blackwell.

Cook, V., Bassetti, B., Kasai, C., Sasaki, M. & Takahashi, J.A. 2006. Do bilinguals have different concepts? The case of shape and material in Japanese L2 users of English. *International Journal of Bilingualism* 10: 137–152.

Cook, V. & Newson, M. 2007. *Chomsky's Universal Grammar: An Introduction*, 3rd edn. Oxford: Blackwell.

Cooper, D.E. 1973. *Philosophy and the Nature of Language*. London: Longman.

Corder, S.P. 1967. The significance of learners' errors. *International Review of Applied Linguistics* 5(4): 161–170.

Corder, S.P. 1971. Idiosyncratic dialects and error analysis. *International Review of Applied Linguistics* 9(2): 147–159.

Cotton, H.M., Millar, F. & Rogers, G.M. 2002. *The Roman Republic and the Augustan Revolution*. Chapel Hill NC: University of North Carolina Press.

Coulmas, F. 1992. *Language and Economy*. Oxford: Blackwell.

Coulmas, F., Backhaus, P. & Shikama, A. 2002. Monolinguistic Assumptions under pressure – perspectives on the languages of Tokyo from the points of view of the economics of language and social psychology. *ASIEN* 84: 8–18.

Council of Europe. Education and Languages. <http://www.coe.int/t/dg4/linguistic/division_EN.asp> (October 15, 2010).

Coupland, N. & Garrett, P. 2010. Linguistic landscapes, discursive frames and metacultural performance: The case of Welsh Patagonia. *International Journal of the Sociology of Language* 205: 7–36. (Special Issue edited by L. Aronin & D. Singleton).

Cristoffanini, P., Kirsner, K. & Milech, D. 1986. Bilingual lexical representation: The status of Spanish-English cognates. *Quarterly Journal of Experimental Psychology* 38A: 367–393.

Crystal, D. 1981. Review of R. Harris, *The Language Myth*. *The Listener*, 2727, 17 September 1981.

Crystal, D. 1985. How many millions? The statistics of English today. *English Today* 1: 7–10.

Crystal, D. 1997. *The Cambridge Encyclopedia of Language*, 2nd edn. Cambridge: CUP.

Crystal, D. 2000. *Language Death*. Cambridge: CUP.

Crystal, D. 2003. *English as a Global Language*, 2nd edn. Cambridge: CUP.

Cummins, J. 1977. A comparison of reading skills in Irish and English medium schools. In *Studies in Reading*, V. Greaney (ed.), 128–134. Dublin: Educational Co. of Ireland. (Reprinted in *Oideas* 26: 21–26, 1982).

Cummins, J. 1983. Language proficiency, biliteracy and French immersion. *Canadian Journal of Education* 8(2): 117–138.

Cummins, J. 1984. *Bilingualism and Special Education: Issues in Assessment and Pedagogy*. Clevedon: Multilingual Matters.

Cummins, J. 1991. Language development and academic learning. In *Language, Culture and Cognition*, L. Malave & G. Duquette, 161–175. Clevedon: Multilingual Matters.

Cummins, J., Swain, M., Nakajima, K., Handscombe, J., Green, D. & Tran, C. 1984. Linguistic interdependence among Japanese and Vietnamese immigrant students. In *Communicative Competence Approaches to Language Proficiency Assessment: Research and Application*, C. Rivera (ed.), 60–81. Clevedon: Multilingual Matters.

Dalby, A. 2003. *Language in Danger*. New York NY: Columbia University Press.

Das Gupta, J. 1970. *Language Conflict and National Development: Group Politics and National Language Policy in India*. Berkeley CA: University of California Press.

Daulton, F.E. 2008. *Japan's Built-in Lexicon of English-based Loanwords*. Clevedon: Multilingual Matters.

DeGraff, M. 2005. Linguists' most dangerous myth. The fallacy of Creole Exceptionalism. *Language in Society* 34(4): 533–591.

De Angelis, G. 2005. Multilingualism and non-native lexical transfer: An identification problem. *International Journal of Multilingualism* 2(1): 1–25.

De Angelis, G. 2007. *Third or Additional Language Acquisition*. Clevedon: Multilingual Matters.

De Angelis, G. & Dewaele, J.-M. 2009. The development of psycholinguistic research on cross-linguistic influence. In *The Exploration of Multilingualism: Development of Research on L3, Multilingualism and Multiple Language Acquisition* [AILA Applied Linguistics Series 6], L. Aronin & B. Hufeisen (eds), 63–77. Amsterdam: John Benjamins.

De Angelis, G. & Selinker, L. 2001. Interlanguage transfer and competing linguistic systems in the multilingual mind. In *Cross-linguistic Aspects of L3 Acquisition*, U. Jessner, B. Hufeisen & J. Cenoz (eds), 42–58. Clevedon: Multilingual Matters.

de Bot, K. 1992. A bilingual production model: Levelt's 'speaking' model adapted *Applied Linguistics* 13(1): 1–24.

de Bot, K. 2004. The multilingual lexicon: Modelling selection and control. *International Journal of Multilingualism* 1(1): 17–32.

de Bot, K. 2010. Rethinking multilingual processing: From a static to a dynamic approach. Paper presented at the Summer 2010 Obermann Research Seminar, 'Third Language Acquisition: Developing a Research Base'.

de Bot, K., Lowie, W. & Verspoor, M. 2007. A Dynamic Systems Theory approach to second language acquisition. *Bilingualism: Language and Cognition* 10 (1): 7–21.

de Bot, K. & Makoni, S. 2005. *Language and Aging in Multilingual Contexts*. Clevedon: Multilingual Matters.

de Bot, K. & Schreuder, R. 1993. Word production and the bilingual lexicon. In *The Bilingual Lexicon* [Studies in Bilingualism 6], R. Schreuder & B. Weltens (eds), 191–214. Amsterdam: John Benjamins.

De Graff, M. 2005. Linguists' most dangerous myth. The fallacy of Creole Exceptionalism. *Language in Society* 34(4): 533–591.

de Groot, A. 1995. Determinants of bilingual lexicosemantic organization. *Computer Assisted Language Learning* 8(2–3): 151–180.

De Houwer, A. 1995. Bilingual language acquisition. In *The Handbook of Child Language*, P. Fletcher & B. MacWhinney (eds), 219–250. Oxford: Blackwell.

De Houwer, A. 2005. Early bilingual acquisition: Focus on morphosyntax and the separate development hypothesis. In *The Handbook of Bilingualism*, J. Kroll & A. de Groot (eds), 30–48. Oxford: OUP.

De Houwer, A. 2009. *Bilingual First Language Acquisition*. Clevedon: Multilingual Matters.

De Mejía, A.-M. 2002. *Power, Prestige and Bilingualism: International Perspectives on Elite Bilingual Education*. Clevedon: Multilingual Matters.

Demick, B. 2002. A snip of the tongue and English is yours! *Los Angeles Times*, April 8, 2002. <http://www.tomcoyner.com/a_snip_of_the_tongue_and_english.htm> (February 20, 2009).

Dent, E. 1999. Complexity science: A worldview shift. <http://polaris.umuc.edu/~edent/emergence/emerge2-r.htm> (May 2007).

Dercon, C. 2001. Speed-space. In *Virilio Live*, John Armitage (ed.), 69–81. London: Sage.

de Swaan, A. 1988a. A political sociology of the world language system, 1: The dynamics of language spread. *Language Problems and Language Planning* 22(1): 63–75.

de Swaan, A. 1988b. A political sociology of the world language system, 2: The unequal exchange of texts. *Language Problems and Language Planning* 22(2): 109–128.

de Swaan, A. 1999. The constellation of languages. Which languages for Europe? Report of the Conference Held in Oegstgeest. Oegstgeest: European Cultural Foundation.

de Swaan, A. 2001. *The Words of the World: The Global language System*. Cambridge: Polity Press.

Deuchar, M. & Quay, S. 2000. *Bilingual Acquisition: Theoretical Implications of a Case Study*. Oxford: OUP.

Dewaele, J.-M. 2004. Blistering barnacles! What languages do multilinguals swear in?! *Estudios de Sociolinguistica* 5(1): 83–105.

Dewaele, J.-M. 2007. The effect of multilingualism, sociobiographical, and situational factors on communicative anxiety and foreign language anxiety of mature language learners. *International Journal of Bilingualism* 11(4): 391–409.

Dewaele, J.-M. 2010a. *Emotions in Multiple Languages*. Basingstoke: Palgrave.

Dewaele, J.-M. 2010b. Multilingualism and affordances: Variation in self-perceived communicative competence and communicative anxiety in French L1, L2, L3 and L4. *IRAL* 48: 105–129.

Diaz, R. & Klinger, C. 1991. Towards an exploratory model of the interaction between bilingualism and cognitive development. In *Language Processing in Bilingual Children*, E. Bialystok (ed.), 167–192. Cambridge: CUP.

Diebold, A.R. 1961. Incipient bilingualism. *Language* 37: 97–112.

Dijkstra, T. 2003. Lexical processing in bilinguals and multilinguals. In *The Multilingual Lexicon*, J. Cenoz, B. Hufeisen & U. Jessner (eds), 11–26. Dordrecht: Kluwer.

Dittmar, N. & Steckbauer, P. Under review. Emerging and conflicting forces of polyphony in the Berlin speech community after the fall of the wall: On the social identity of adolescents. In *Current Multilingualism: A New Linguistic Dispensation*, D. Singleton, J. Fishman, L. Aronin & M. Ó Laoire (eds). Berlin: Mouton de Gruyter.

Doepke, F. 1996. *The Kinds of Things: A Theory of Personal Identity Based on Transcendental Argument*. Chicago IL: Open Court.

Dörnyei, Z. & Ushioda, E. (eds). 2009. *Motivation, Language Identity and the L2 Self*. Bristol: Multilingual Matters.

Doyle, A.-B., Champagne, M. & Segalowitz, N. 1978. Some issues in the assessment of the consequences of early bilingualism. In *Aspects of Bilingualism*, M. Paradis (ed.), 13–21. Columbia SC: Hornbeam Press.

Duncan, S.E. & De Avila, E.A. 1979. Bilingualism and Cognition: Some Recent Findings. *NABE Journal* 4(1): 5–50.

Dylan. Language Dynamics and Management of Diversity. <www.dylan-project.org/Dylan_en/home/home.php> (December 5, 2011).

Edwards, J. 1991. Socio-educational issues concerning indigenous minority languages: Terminology, geography and status. In *European Lesser-used Languages in Primary Education*, J. Sikma & D. Gorter (eds), 207–226. Leeuwarden: Friske Akademy/Mercator Education.

Edwards, J. 1992. Sociopolitical aspects of language maintenance and loss. Towards a typology of minority language situations. In *Maintenance and Loss of Minority Languages* [Studies in Bilingualism 1], W. Fase, K. Jaspaert & S. Kroon (eds), 37–54. Amsterdam: John Benjamins.

Edwards, J. 1994. *Multilingualism*. London: Routledge.

Edwards, J. 2007. Societal Multilingualism: Reality, recognition and response. In *Handbook of Multilingualism and Multilingual Communication*, P. Auer & Li Wei (eds), 447–467. Berlin: Mouton de Gruyter.

Edwards, J. 2010. *Minority Languages and Group Identity: Cases and Categories* [IMPACT: Studies in Language and Society 27]. Amsterdam: John Benjamins.

Ellis, R. 1994. *The Study of Second Language Acquisition*. Oxford: OUP.

Ellis, N. & Larsen-Freeman, D. 2006. Introduction. Language emergence: Implications for applied linguistics. *Applied Linguistics* 27(4): 558–589.

Encyclopaedia of National Languages of Russia. 2002. Moscow: Academia.
Государственные и титульные языки России. Энциклопедический словарь-справочник\Под общ.ред. проф. В.П. Нерознака. М.: Academia, 2002.

Ennaji, M. Under review. Multilingualism in Morocco and the linguistic features of the Casablanca variety. In *Current Multilingualism: A New Linguistic Dispensation,* D. Singleton, J. Fishman, L. Aronin & M. Ó Laoire (eds). Berlin: Mouton de Gruyter.

Eriksen, T. 2001. *Tyranny of the Moment: Fast and Slow Time in the Information Age*. London: Pluto Press.

Euro Com Center. The Eurocom Research Group. <http://www.eurocomcenter.com/index2.php?lang=uk&main_id=3&sub_id=3> (December 5, 2011).

European Commission. 2009. Study on the contribution of multilingualism to creativity: Final report. Brussels: European Commission.

Extra, G. Under review. Mapping increasing linguistic diversity in European and non-European countries. In *Current Multilingualism: A New Linguistic Dispensation,* D. Singleton, J. Fishman, L. Aronin & M. Ó Laoire (eds). Berlin: Mouton de Gruyter.

Extra, G. & Yağmur, K. (eds). 2004a. *Urban Multilingualism in Europe: Immigrant Minority Languages at Home and School*. Clevedon: Multilingual Matters.

Extra, G. & Yağmur, K. 2004b. Demographic perspectives. In *Urban Multilingualism in Europe: Immigrant Minority Languages at Home and School*, G. Extra & Y. Kutlay (eds), 25–72. Clevedon: Multilingual Matters.

Fabbro, F. 1999. *The Neurolinguistics of Bilingualism: An Introduction*. Hove: Psychology Press.

Fabbro, F. 2002. The neurolinguistics of L2 users. In *Portraits of the L2 User*, V. Cook (ed.), 197–218. Clevedon: Multilingual Matters.

Fantini, A.E. 1985. *Language Acquisition of a Bilingual Child: A Sociolinguistic Perspective*. Clevedon: Multilingual Matters.

Ferguson, C.A. 1959. Diglossia. *Word* 15: 325–340.

Fill, A. & Mühlhäusler, P. (eds). 2001. *The Ecolinguistics Reader. Language, Ecology and Environment*. London: Continuum.

Fischer, S.R. 2004. *A History of Language*. Globalities Series. Reaktion books Ltd.

Fishman, J.A. 1964. Language maintenance and language shift as fields of inquiry. *Linguistics* 9: 32–70.

Fishman, J.A. 1965. Who speaks what language to whom and when? *La Linguistique* 2: 67–88. (Also reproduced in 2000, *The Bilingualism Reader*, Li Wei (ed.), 89–106. London: Routledge).

Fishman, J.A. 1966. *Language Loyalty in the United States. The maintenance and perpetuation of Non-English Mother Tongue by American Ethnic and Religious groups.* The Hague: Mouton.

Fishman, J.A. 1967. Bilingualism with and without diglossia; diglossia with or without bilingualism. *Journal of Social Issues* 23: 29–38.

Fishman, J.A. 1972 [1972, rev. edn. 1986). Domains and the relationship between micro-and macrosociolinguistics. In *Directions in Sociolinguistics: The Ethnography of Communication*, J.J. Gumperz & D. Hymes (eds), 435–453. Oxford: Basil Blackwell.

Fishman, J.A. 1989. *Language and Ethnicity in Minority Sociolinguistics Perspective.* Clevedon: Multilingual Matters.

Fishman, J.A. 1998. The new linguistic order. *Foreign Policy* 113(Winter): 26–40.

Fishman, J.A. (ed.). 1999. *Handbook of Language & Ethnic Identity.* Oxford: OUP.

Fishman, J.A. 2001. *Can Threatened Languages Be Saved?* Clevedon: Multilingual Matters.

Flaherty, M. & Seipp-Williams, L. 2005. Sociotemporal rhythms in e-mail: A case study. *Time and Society* 14(1): 39–49.

Flege, J. 1999. Age of learning and second language speech. In *Second Language Acquisition and the Critical Period Hypothesis*, D. Birdsong (ed.), 101–131. Mahwah NJ: Lawrence Erlbaum Associates.

Flege, J.E. & MacKay, I.R.A. 2011. What accounts for 'age' effects on overall degree of foreign accent? In *Achievements and Perspectives in the Acquisition of Second Language Speech: New Sounds 2010*, Vol. 2, M. Wrembel, M. Kul & K. Dziubalska-Kołaczyk (eds), 65–82. Bern: Peter Lang.

Fouser, R. 2001. Too close for comfort? Sociolinguistic transfer from Japanese into Korean as an L3. In *Cross-linguistic Influence in Third Language Acquisition: Psycholinguistic Perspectives*, J. Cenoz, B. Hufeisen & U. Jessner (eds), 149–169. Clevedon: Multilingual Matters.

Franceschini, R. 2009. Genesis and development of research in multilingualism: Perspectives for future research. In *The Exploration of Multilingualism: Development of Research on L3, Multilingualism and Multiple Language Acquisition* [AILA Applied Linguistics Series 6], L. Aronin & B. Hufeisen (eds), 27–61. Amsterdam: John Benjamins.

Frege, G. 1972. *Gottlob Frege: Conceptual Notation and Related Articles*, translated and edited by T. Bynum. Oxford: OUP.

Friedman, L. 1999. *The Horizontal Society.* Newhaven CT: Yale University Press.

Furlong, A. 2009. The relation of plilingualism/culturalism to creativity: A matter of perception. *International Journal of Multilingualism* 6(4): 343–368.

Fussman, G. 1996. Southern Bactria and Northern India before Islam: A review of archaeological reports. *Journal of the American Oriental Society* 116: 243–259.

Gabryś-Barker, D. 2005. *Aspects of Multilingual Storage, Processing and Retrieval.* Katowice: Wydawnictwo Uniwersitetu Śląskiego.

Gabryś-Barker, D. 2009. The role of transfer of learning in multilingual instruction and development. In *Multidisciplinary Perspectives on Second Language Acquisition and Foreign Language Learning*, J. Arabski & A. Wojtaszek (eds), 152–169. Katowice: University of Silesia Press.

Gafaranga, J. 2009. Code-switching as a conversational strategy. In *Handbook of Multilingualism and Multilingual Communication*, P. Auer & Li Wei (eds), 279–314. Berlin: Mouton de Gruyter.

García, O. (ed.). 2008. *Bilingual Education in the 21st Century: A Global Perspective.* Chichester: Wiley-Blackwell.

García, O. 1997. Bilingual Education. In *The Handbook of Sociolinguistics*, F. Coulmas (ed.), 405–420. Oxford: Basil Blackwell.

García, O. Reimagining bilingualism in education for the 21st century. Keynote Address at NALDIC (National Association for Language Development in the Curriculum), November 14, 2009. <www.naldic.org.uk/docs/events/documents/NQ7.2.3.pdf> (July 17, 2011).

García, O. Under review. Informal bilingual acquisition: Dynamic spaces for language education. In *Current Multilingualism: A New Linguistic Dispensation*, D. Singleton, J. Fishman, L. Aronin & M. Ó Laoire (eds). Berlin: Mouton de Gruyter.

Gardner, R.C. 2006. The socio-educational model of Second Language Acquisition: A research paradigm. *The EUROSLA Yearbook* 6: 237–260.

Gardner, R.A. & Gardner, B.T. 1969. Teaching sign language to a chimpanzee. *Science* 165: 664–672.

Gardner, B.T. & Gardner, R.A. 1971. Two-way communication with an infant chimpanzee. In *Behavior of Nonhuman Primates*, A.M. Schrier & F. Stollnitz (eds), 117–184. New York NY: Academic Press.

Garhammer, M. 1995. Changes in working hours in Germany. *Time & Society* 4(2): 167–203.

Garipov, Y. & Solnyshkina, M. 2006. Language reforms in Tatarstan's education system and the ethnolinguistic orientation of young people. In *Voices Diversae: Lesser-Used Language Education in Europe. Belfast Studies in language, Culture and Politics*, D. Ó Riagáin (ed.), 15: 131–137. Belfast: Cló Ollscoil na Banríona.

Genesee, F. 1989. Early bilingual development: One language or two. *Journal of Child Language* 16: 161–179. (Reproduced in 2000, *The Bilingual Reader*, Li Wei (ed.), 327–343. London: Routledge).

Genesee, F. 2000. Early bilingual language development: One language or two? In *The Bilingualism Reader*, Li Wei (ed.), 327–343. London: Routledge. (Originally published in *Journal of Child Language* 16(1): 161–179).

Genesee, F. 2009. Preface. In *Towards Multilingual Education: Basque Educational Research from an International Perspective*, J. Cenoz (ed.), ix–xii. Bristol: Multilingual Matters.

Genesee, F., Nicoladis, E. & Paradis, J. 1995. Language differentiation in early bilingual development. *Journal of Child Language* 22(3): 611–631.

Gibson, J.J. 1977. The theory of affordances. In *Perceiving, Acting, and Knowing*, R.E. Shaw & J. Bransford (eds), 67–82. Hillsdale NJ: Lawrence Erlbaum Associates.

Gibson, J.J. 1979. *The Ecological Approach to Visual Perception*. Boston MA: Houghton Mifflin.

Gibson, M. & Hufeisen, B. 2003. Investigating the role of prior foreign language knowledge. In *The Multilingual Lexicon*, J. Cenoz, B. Hufeisen & U. Jessner (eds), 87–192. Dordrecht: Kluwer.

Giddens, A.1991. *Modernity and Self-Identity*. Cambridge: Polity Press.

Goldin-Meadow, S. 1996. Book review of *Kanzi: The Ape at the Brink of the Human Mind* by Savage-Rumbaugh, S. & Lewin, R. *International Journal of Primatology* 17: 145–148.

Gloning, I. & Gloning, K. 1965. Aphasien bei polyglotten. Beitrag zur dynamik des sprachabbaus sowie zur lokalisationsfrage dieser storungen. *Wiener Zeitschrift für Nervenheilkunde* 22: 362–397.

Goodz, N.S. 1994. Interactions between parents and children in bilingual families. In *Educating Second Language Children: The Whole Child, the Whole Curriculum, the Whole Community*, F. Genesee (ed.), 61–81. Cambridge: CUP.

Goral, M., Levy, E. & Obler, L. 2002. Neurolinguistic aspects of bilingualism. *The International Journal of Bilingualism* 6(4): 411–440.

Gorter, D. 2006. *Linguistic Landscape: A New Approach to Multilingualism*. Clevedon: Multilingual Matters.

Gorter, D., van Mensel, L. & Marten, H.F. (eds). 2012. *Minority Languages in the Linguistic Landscape*. Basingstoke: Palgrave.

Graddol, D. 1997. *The Future of English?* London: The British Council.

Graddol, D. 2006. *English Next*. London: British Council.

Green, D.W. 1986. Control, activation and resource: A framework and a model for the control of speech in bilinguals. *Brain and Language* 27: 210–223.

Green, D.W. 1993. Towards a model of L2 comprehension and production. In *The Bilingual Lexicon* [Studies in Bilingualism 6], R. Schreuder & B. Weltens (eds), 249–277. Amsterdam: John Benjamins.

Green, D.W. 1998. Mental control of the bilingual lexico-semantic system. *Bilingualism: Language and Cognition* 1: 67–81.

Grin, F. 1999. Economics. In *Handbook of Language and Ethnic Identity*, J. Fishman (ed.), 9–24. Oxford: OUP.

Grosjean, F. 1982. *Life with Two Languages: An Introduction to Bilingualism*. Cambridge MA: Harvard University Press.

Grosjean, F. 1985. The bilingual as a competent but specific speaker-hearer. *Journal of Multilingual and Multicultural Development* 6: 467–477.

Grosjean, F. 1989. Neurolinguists, beware! The bilingual is not two monolinguals in one person. *Brain and Language* 36: 3–15.

Grosjean, F. 1992. Another view of bilingualism. In *Cognitive Processing in Bilinguals*, R. Harris (ed.), 51–62. Amsterdam: North-Holland.

Grosjean, F. 1997. Processing mixed language: Issues, findings and models. In *Tutorials in Bilingualism: Psycholinguistic Perspectives*, A. de Groot & J. Kroll (eds), 225–254. Mahwah NJ: Lawrence Erlbaum Associates.

Grosjean, F. 2001. The bilingual's language modes. In *One Mind, Two Languages: Bilingual Language Processing*, J. Nicol (ed.), 1–22. Oxford: Blackwell. (Also in Li Wei (ed.), *The Bilingual Reader*, 2nd edn. London: Routledge, 2007).

Grosjean, F. 2010. *Bilingual Life and Reality*. Cambridge MA: Harvard University Press.

Gross, D.C., Stanney, K.M. & Cohn, J. 2005. Evoking affordances in virtual environments via sensory-stimuli substitution. *Presence: Teleoperators and Virtual Environments* 14(4): 482–491. Cambridge MA, USA: MIT Press.

Gumperz, J. 1964. Linguistic and social interaction in two communities. *American Anthropologist* 66(6): 137–153.

Gumperz, J. 1968. Types of linguistic communities. In *Readings in the Sociology of Language*, J. Fishman (ed.), 460–472. The Hague: Mouton.

Gumperz, J.J. 1971. Some remarks on regional and social language differences in India. In *Language in Social groups: Essays by John J. Gumperz*, A.S. Dil (ed.), 1–11. Stanford CA: Stanford University Press.

Gumperz, J.J. 1982a. *Discourse Strategies*. Cambridge: CUP.

Gumperz, J.J. 1982b. *Language and Social Identity*. Cambridge: CUP.

Gurvitch, G. 1964. *The Spectrum of Social Time*. Dordrecht: Reidel.

Haarmann, H. 1979. *Quantitative Aspekte des Multilingualismus: Studien zur Gruppenmehrsprachigkeit ethnisher Minderheiten in der Sowjetunion*. Hamburg: Buske.

Haberland, H. 2005. Domains and domain loss. In *The consequences of mobility*, B. Preisler, A. Fabricius, H. Haberland, S. Kjærbeck & K. Risager (eds), 227–237. Roskilde: Roskilde University.

Hagen, R.-M. & Hagen, R. 2003. *What Great Paintings Say*, Vol. 2. Köln: Taschen.

Hakuta, K. & Diaz, R. 1984. The relationship between bilingualism and cognitive ability: A critical discussion and some new longitudinal data. In *Children's Language*, K.E. Nelson (ed.), Vol. 5, 319–344. Hillsdale NJ: Lawrence Erlbaum Associates.

Hall, A.R. 1952. Bilingualism and applied linguistics. *Zeitschrift für Phonetik und allgemeine Sprachwissencshaft* 6: 13–30.

Hamers, J.F. & Blanc, M.H.A. 1989. *Bilinguality and Bilingualism*. Cambridge: CUP.

Hamers, J.F. & Blanc, M.H.A. 2000. *Bilinguality and Bilingualism*, 2nd edn. Cambridge: CUP.

Hammarberg, B. (ed.). 2009. *Processes in Third Language Acquisition*. Edinburgh: Edinburgh University Press.

Hammarberg, B. 2010. The languages of the multilingual: Some conceptual and terminological issues. *IRAL* 48(2–3): 91–104. (Special Issue *Approaches to Third Language Acquisition*, edited by C. Bardel & C. Lindqvist).

Harding, E. & Riley, P. 1986. *The Bilingual Family: A Handbook for Parents*. Cambridge: CUP.

Harjanne, P. & Tella, S. 2008. Strong signals in foreign language education, with a view to future visions. In *From Brawn to Brain: Strong Signals in Foreign Language Education. Proceedings of the ViKiPeda-2007 Conference in Helsinki, May 21–22, 2007* [Research Report 290], S. Tella (ed.), 55–84. Helsinki: University of Helsinki. Department of Applied Sciences of Education.

Harris, R. 1981. *The Language Myth*. London: Duckworth.

Harris, R. 1998. *Introduction to Integrational Linguistics*. Oxford: Pergamon.

Harvey, D. 1989. *The Condition of Postmodernity*. Oxford: Blackwell.

Haugen, E. 1953. *The Norwegian Language in America: A Study in Bilingual Behavior*. Philadelphia PA: University of Pennsylvania Press.

Haugen, E. 1956. *Bilingualism in the Americas: A Bibliography and Research Guide* [Publication of the American Dialect Society 26]. Tuscaloosa AL: University of Alabama Press.

Haugen, E. 1972. *The Ecology of Language*, edited by A.S. Dill. Stanford CA: Stanford University Press.

Haugen, E. 1987. *Blessings of Babel: Bilingualism and Language Planning*. Berlin: Mouton de Gruyter.

Hauser, M., Chomsky, N. & Fitch, T. 2002. The faculty of language: What is it, who has it, and how did it evolve. *Science* 198: 1569–1579.

Hawkins, E. 1999. Foreign language study and language awareness. *Language Awareness* 3–4: 124–142.

Hayes, C. 1951. *The Ape in Our House*. New York NY: Harper.

Herdina, P. & Jessner, U. 2000a. Multilingualism as an ecological system. The case for language maintenance. In *ECOnstructing Language, Nature and Society. The Ecolinguistic Project Revisited Essays in Honour of Alwin Fill*, B. Kettemann & H. Penz (eds), 131–144. Tübingen: Stauffenburg.

Herdina, P. & Jessner, U. 2000b. The dynamics of third language acquisition. In *English in Europe: The Acquisition of a Third Language*, J. Cenoz & U. Jessner (eds), 84–98. Clevedon: Multilingual Matters.

Herdina, P. & Jessner, U. 2002. *A Dynamic Model of Multilingualism: Perspectives of Change in Psycholinguistics*. Clevedon: Multilingual Matters.

Hernandez, A., Bates, E. & Avila, L. 1994. On-line sentence interpretation in Spanish-English bilinguals: What does it mean to be 'in between'? *Applied Psycholinguistics* 15: 417–446.

Hess, E. 2008. *Nim Chimpsky: The Chimp who would be human*. New York NY: Bantam.

Heugh, K. Under review. Slipping between policy and management: (de)centralized responses to linguistic diversity in Ethiopia and South Africa. In *Current Multilingualism: A New Linguistic Dispensation,* D. Singleton, J. Fishman, L. Aronin & M. Ó Laoire (eds). Berlin: Mouton de Gruyter.

Hockett, C.F. 1963. The problem of universals in language. In *Universals of Language,* J.H. Greenberg (ed.), 1–22. Cambridge MA: The MIT Press.

Hoffmann, C. 2000. The spread of English and the growth of multilingualism with English in Europe. In *English in Europe: The Acquisition of a Third Language,* J. Cenoz & U. Jessner (eds), 1–21. Clevedon: Multilingual Matters.

Hoffmann, C. 2001a. The status of trilingualism in bilingualism studies. In *Looking Beyond Second Language Acquisition: Studies in Tri- and Multilingualism,* J. Cenoz, B. Hufeisen & U. Jessner (eds), 13–25. Tubingen: Stauffenburg.

Hoffmann, C. 2001b. Towards a description of trilingual competence. *The International Journal of Bilingualism* 5(1): 1–17.

Holmes, G. 2001. *The Oxford History of Medieval Europe*. Oxford: Oxford University Press.

Horenczyk, G. 2000. Conflicted identities: Acculturation attitudes and immigrants' construction of their social worlds. In *Language, Identity and Immigration*, E. Olstain & G. Horenczyk (eds), 13–30. Jerusalem: Magnes press.

Hornberger, N. 2002. Multilingual language policies and the continua of biliteracy: An ecological approach. *Language Policy* 1(1): 27–51.

Hornberger, N. 2009. Multilingual education policy and practice: Ten cenrtainties (grounded in indigenous experience). *Language Teaching* 42(2): 197–211.

Hornberger, N. & Pütz, M. (eds). 2006. *Language Loyalty, Language Planning and Language Revitalization: Recent Writings and Reflections from Joshua A. Fishman,* 29–47. Clevedon: Multilingual Matters.

Hufeisen, B. 1998. L3-Stand der Forschung- Was bleibt zu tun? In *Tertiärsprachen. Theorien, Modelle, Methode,* B. Hufeisen & B. Lindemann (eds), 169–183. Tübingen: Stauffenburg.

Hufeisen, B. 2005. Multilingualism: Linguistic models and related issues. In *Introductory Readings in L3,* B. Hufeisen & R.J. Fouser (eds), 31–45. Tübingen: Stauffenburg.

Hufeisen, B. 2010. Theoretische Fundierung multiplen Sprachenlernens – Factorenmodell 2.0. *Jahrbuch Deutsch als Fremdsprache* 36: 191–198.

Hufeisen, B. & Marx, N. 2003. Multilingualism: Theory, research methods and didactics. In *New Visions in Foreign and Second Language Education,* G. Bräuer & K. Sanders (eds), 178–203. San Diego CA: LARC Press.

Hufeisen, B. & Marx, N. 2007. How can *DaFnE* and *EuroComGerm* contribute to the concept of receptive multilingualism? In *Receptive Multilingualism* [Hamburg Studies on Multilingualism 6], J.D. ten Thije & L. Zeevaert (eds), 307–321. Amsterdam: John Benjamins.

Hufeisen, B. & Neuner, G. (eds). 2004. *The Plurilingualism Project: Tertiary Language Learning – German after English*. Strasbourg: Council of Europe Publishing.

Hui-chi Lee. 2004. A survey of language ability, language use and language attitudes of young aborigines in Taiwan. In *Trilingualism in Family, School and Community,* C. Hoffmann & J. Ytsma, 101–117. Clevedon: Multilingual Matters.

von Humboldt, W. 1936. *On Language: The Diversity of Human Language Structure and Its Influence on the Mental Development of Mankind.* English translation – 1988. Trans. by P. Heath. Cambridge: CUP.

Hung Cam Thai. 2005. Globalization as a gender strategy: Respectability, masculinity, and convertibility across the Vietnamese diaspora. In *Critical Globalization Studies*, R. Appelbaum & W. Robinson (eds), 313–322. London: Routledge.

Hutchby, I. 2003. Affordances and the analysis of technologically mediated interaction. *Sociology* 37(3): 581–589.

Hyltenstam, K. & Abrahamsson, N. 2000. Who can become native-like in a second language? All, some, or none? On the maturational controversy in second language acquisition. *Studia Linguistica* 54(2): 150–166.

Hyltenstam, K. & Obler, L. (eds). 1989. *Bilingualism across the Lifespan: Aspects of Acquisition, Maturity and Loss.* Cambridge: CUP.

Hymes, D. 1972. On communicative competence. In *Sociolinguistics: Selected Readings*, J.B. Pride & J. Holmes (eds), 269–293. Harmondsworth: Penguin.

Ianco-Worrall, A. 1972. Bilingualism and cognitive development. *Child Development* 43: 1390–1400.

Indefrey, P. & Gullberg, M. 2006. Introduction. In *The cognitive Neuroscience of Second Language Acquisition*, M. Gullberg & P. Indefrey (eds), 1–8. Oxford: Blackwell.

Ingman, M. 2001. Mitochondrial DNA Clarifies Human Evolution. American Institute of Biological Sciences. http://www.actionbioscience.org/evolution/ingman.html

The Irish Times. From Acholi to Zulu, Ireland a land of over 167 languages. March 25, 2006. <http://www.irishtimes.com/newspaper/frontpage/2006/0325/1142365526361.html> (December 5, 2011).

Jakobovits, L.A. 1970. *Foreign Language Learning: A Psycho-linguistic Analysis of the Issues.* Rowley MA: Newbury House.

James, C. 1971. The exculpation of contrastive linguistics. In *Papers in Contrastive Linguistics*, G. Nickel (ed.), 53–68. Cambridge: CUP.

Jarvis, S. & Pavlenko, A. 2008. *Crosslinguistic Influence in Language and Cognition.* NewYork NY: Routledge.

Jedynak, M. 2009. *Critical Period Hypothesis Revisited: The Impact of Age on Ultimate Attainment in the Pronunciation of a Foreign Language.* Frankfurt: Peter Lang.

Jescheniak, J.D. & Levelt, W.J.M. 1994. Word frequency effects in speech production: Retrieval of syntactic information and of phonological form. *Journal of Experimental Psychology: Learning, Memory, and Cognition* 20(4): 824–843.

Jessner, U. 1997. Towards a dynamic view of multilingualism. In *Language Choices: Conditions, Constraints and Consequences* [IMPACT: Studies in Language and Society 1], M. Putz (ed.), 17–30. Amsterdam: John Benjamins.

Jessner, U. 2003. The nature of cross-linguistic interaction. In *The Multilingual Lexicon*, J. Cenoz, B. Hufeisen & U. Jessner (eds), 45–55. Dordrecht: Kluwer.

Jessner, U. 2006. *Linguistic Awareness in Multilinguals: English as a Third Language.* Edinburgh: Edinburgh University Press.

Jessner, U. 2008. Teaching third languages: Findings, trends and challenges. *Language Teaching* 41(1): 15–56.

Jia, G. & Aaronson, D. 1999. Age differences in second language acquisition. The dominant language switch and maintenance hypothesis. *Proceedings of the 23rd Annual Boston University Conference on Language Development*, 301–312. Sommerville MA: Cascadilla.

Jia, G. & Aaronson, D. 2003. A longitudinal study of Chinese children and adolescents learning English in the United States. *Applied Psycholinguistics* 24: 131–161.

Jones, B.L. 1981. Welsh: linguistic conservation and shifting bilingualism. In *Minority Languages Today*, E. Haugen, J.D. McClure & D. Thompson (eds), 40–51. Edinburgh: Edinburgh University Press.

Johnson, C.E. & Wilson, I.L. 2002. Research evidence for early language differentiation: Research issues and some preliminary data. *International Journal of Bilingualism* 6: 271–289.

Johnson, R.K. & Swain, M. 1997. *Immersion Education: International Perspectives.* Cambridge: CUP.

Kachru, B.B., Kachru, Y. & Sridhar, S.N. 2008. *Language in South Asia.* Cambridge: CUP.

Kaneko, K. & Tsuda, I. 2001. *Complex Systems: Chaos and Beyond. A Constructive Approach with Applications in Life Sciences.* Berlin: Springer.

Kang, C. To know you is to love you. *LA Times story*, July 28, 2006. <http://www.languagehat.com/archives/002431.php> (December 5, 2011).

Kanno, Y. 2003. *Negotiating Bilingual and Bicultural Identities: Japanese Returnees Betwixt Two Worlds.* Mahwah NJ: Lawrence Erlbaum Associates.

Kasper, G. 1984. Perspectives on language transfer. *BAAL Newsletter* 22: 3–23.

Katz, J. J. 1972. *Linguistic Philosophy: The Underlying Reality of Language and its Philosophical Import.* London: Allen and Unwin.

Kellerman, E. 1977. Towards a characterization of the strategy of transfer in second language learning. *Interlanguage Studies Bulletin* 2: 58–145.

Kellerman, E. 1979. Transfer and non-transfer: Where are we now? *Studies in Second Language Acquisition* 2: 37–57.

Kellerman, E. 1983. Now you see it, now you don't. In *Language Transfer in Language Learning*, S. Gass & L. Selinker (eds), 112–134. Rowley MA: Newbury House.

Kellogg, W.N. & Kellogg, L.A. 1933. *The Ape and the Child: A Comparative Study of the Environmental Influence Upon Early Behavior.* New York NY: McGraw-Hill Book Co.

Kemp, C. 2007. Strategic processing in grammar learning: Do multilinguals use more strategies? *International Journal of Multilingualism* 4(4): 241–261.

Kemp, C. 2009. Defining multilingualism. In *The Exploration of Multilingualism: Development of Research on L3, Multilingualism and Multiple Language Acquisition* [AILA Applied Linguistics Series 6], L. Aronin & B. Hufeisen (eds), 11–26. Amsterdam: John Benjamins.

Kecskés, I. & Papp, T. 2000. *Foreign Language and Mother Tongue.* Mahwah NJ: Lawrence Erlbaum Associates.

Kinsella, C. 2009. An Investigation into the Proficiency of Successful Late Learners of French. PhD dissertation, Trinity College Dublin.

Kirk-Greene, C.W.E. 1981. *French False Friends.* London: Routledge & Kegan Paul.

Kirsner, K., Lalor, E. & Hird, K. 1993. The bilingual lexicon: Exercise, meaning and morphology. In *The Bilingual Lexicon* [Studies in Bilingualism 6], R. Schreuder & B. Weltens (eds), 215–248. Amsterdam: John Benjamins.

Kloss, H. 1966. Types of multilingual communities: A discussion of ten variables. *Sociological Inquiry* 36(2): 135–145.

Kloss, H. 1978. *Die Entwicklung neuer germanischer Kultursprachen seit 1950,* 2nd edn. Dusseldorf: Schwann.

Kong, L. 1996. Popular music in Singapore: Local cultures, global resources and regional identities. *Environment and Planning D: Society and Space* 14: 273–292.

Kopečková, R. 2011. Learning vowel sounds in a migrant setting: The case of Polish children and adults in Ireland. In *Achievements and Perspectives in SLA of Speech: New Sounds 2010* Vol. 2, M. Wrembel, M. Kul & K. Dziubalska-Kołaczyk (eds), 137–148. Frankfurt: Peter Lang.

Kouritzin, S.G. 1999. *Face(t)s of First Language Loss*. Mahwah NJ: Lawrence Erlbaum Associates.

Kramer, S.N. 1963. *The Sumerians: Their History, Culture, and Character*. Chicago IL: University of Chicago Press.

Kramsch, C. 2008. Ecological perspectives on foreign language education. *Language Teaching* 41(3): 389–408.

Kroll, J.F. & Dijkstra, A. 2005. The bilingual lexicon. In *The Oxford Handbook of Applied Linguistics*, R.B. Kaplan (ed.), 301–321. Oxford: OUP.

Lacey, A.R. 2001. *A Dictionary of Philosophy*, 3rd edn. London: Routledge.

Lamarre, P. & Dagenais, D. 2004. Language practices of trilingual use in two Canadian cities. In *Trilingualism in Family, School and Community*, C. Hoffmann & J. Ytsma (eds), 53–74. Clevedon: Multilingual Matters.

Lambert, W. 1975. Culture and language as factors in learning and education. In *Education of immigrant students*, A. Wolfgang (ed.), 55–83. Toronto: OISE.

Lanza, E. 1997. *Language Mixing in Infant Bilingualism: A Sociolinguistic Perspective*. Oxford: Clarendon Press.

Larsen-Freeman, D. 2002. Language acquisition and language use from a chaos/complexity theory perspective. In *Language Acquisition and Language Socialization, Ecological Perspectives*, C. Kramsch (ed.), 33–46. London: Continuum.

Larsen-Freeman, D. 2006. The emergence of complexity, fluency, and accuracy in the oral and written production of five Chinese learners of English. *Applied Linguistics* 27(4): 590–619.

Larsen-Freeman, D. & Long, M. 1997. *An Introduction to Second Language Acquisition Research*. London: Longman.

Le Goff, J. 1964. *La civilisation de l'occident medieval*. Paris: Arthaud.

Lemmon, C.R. & Goggin, J.P. 1989. The measurement of bilingualism and its relationship to cognitive ability. *Applied Psycholinguistics* 10(2). 133–155.

Lenneberg, E.N. 1967. *Biological Foundations of Language*. New York: Wiley.

Leopold, W.F. 1939–1949. *Speech Development of a Bilingual Child: A Linguist's Record*, 4 Vols. Evanston IL: Northwestern University Press.

Levelt, W.J.M. 1989. *Speaking: from Intention to Articulation*. Cambridge MA: The MIT Press.

Levine, R. 1997. *A Geography of Time: The Temporal Misadventures of a Social Psychologist*. New York NY: Basic Books/Harper Collins.

Li Wei. 2000. Dimensions of bilingualism. In *The Bilingualism Reader*, Li Wei (ed.), 3–25. London: Routledge.

Li Wei. 2011. Moment analysis and translanguaging space: Discursive construction of identities by multilingual Chinese youth in Britain. *Journal of Pragmatics* 43: 1222–1235.

Lightbown, P. & Spada, N. 2006. *How Languages are Learned*, 3rd edn. Oxford: OUP.

Lin, A.M.Y. 2007. *Problematizing Identity: Everyday Struggles In Language, Culture and Education*. Mahwah NJ: Lawrence Erlbaum Associates.

Lodge, R.A. 1993. *French: From Dialect to Standard*. London: Routledge.

Lüdi, G. 2008. Mapping immigrant languages in Switzerland. In *Mapping Linguistic Diversity in Multicultural Contexts*, M. Barni & G. Extra (eds), 195–216. Berlin: Mouton de Gruyter.

Lyons, J. 1963. *Structural Semantics: An Analysis of Part of the Vocabulary of Plato*. Oxford: Blackwell/The Philological Society.

Lytra, V. 2007. Teasing in contact encounters: Frames, participant positions and responses. *Multilingua* 26(4): 381–408.

Mackey, W.F. 1957. The Description of Bilingualism. *Canadian Journal of Linguistics* 7: 51–85.

Mackey, W.F. 1970. A typology of bilingual education. *Foreign language Annals* 3: 596–608.

Mackenzie, J.M. 2005. *Peoples, Nations and Cultures*. London: Weidenfeld & Nicolson.

Macnamara, J. 1966. *Bilingualism and Primary Education*. Edinburgh: Edinburgh University Press.

Macnamara, J. 1967. The bilingual's linguistic performance: A psychological overview. *Journal of Social Issues* 23: 121–135.

Macrory, G. 2006. Bilingual language development: What do early years practitioners need to know? *Early Years* 26(2): 159–169.

Maggipinto, A. 2000. Multilanguage acquisition, new technologies, education and global citizenship. *Italian Culture* 18(2): 147–149.

Maines, D.R. 1978. Bodies and selves: Notes on a fundamental dilemma in demography. *Studies in Symbolic Interaction* 1: 241–265.

Maneva, B. 2004. 'Maman, je suis polyglotte' (Mommy, I'm a polyglot): A case study of multilingual language acquisition from 0 to 5 years. *The International Journal of Multilingualism* 1(1): 109–122.

Mar-Molinero, C. 2000. *The Politics of Language in the Spanish-Speaking World: From Colonisation to Globalisation*. London: Routledge.

Marshall, J.C. 1970. The biology of communication in man and animals. In *New Horizons in Linguistics*, J. Lyons (ed.), 229–241. Harmondsworth: Penguin.

Marx, N. & Hufeisen, B. 2003. Multilingualism: Theory, research methods and didactics. In *New Visions in Foreign and Second Language Education*, G. Bräuer & K. Sanders (eds), 178–203. San Diego CA: LARC Press.

Matthews, P., Adcock, J., Chen, Y., Fu, S., Devlin, J., Rushworth, M., Smith, S., Beckmann, C. & Iversen, S. 2003. Towards understanding language organization in the brain using fMRI. *Human Brain Imaging* 18: 239–247.

Maurais, J. 2003. Towards a new linguistic world order. In *Languages in a Globalizing World*, J. Maurais & M. Morris (eds), 13–36. Cambridge: CUP.

McArthur, T. & Gachelin, J.-M. 1992. Romance. In *The Oxford Companion to the English Language*, T. McArthur (ed.), 872–874. London: BCA/Oxford University Press.

McLaughlin, B. 1978. *Second-language Acquisition in Childhood*. Hillsdale NJ: Lawrence Erlbaum Associates.

Meara, P. 2006. Emergent properties of multilingual lexicons. *Applied Linguistics* 27(4): 620–644.

Mesthrie, R, Swann, J., Deumert, A. & Leap, W.L. 2009. *Introducing Sociolinguistics*, 2nd edn. Edinburgh: Edinburgh University Press.

Meisel, J.M. (ed.). 1990. *Two First Languages: Early Grammatical Development in Bilingual Children*. Dordrecht: Floris.

Milroy, L. & Muysken, P. (eds). 1995. *One Speaker, Two Languages: Cross-Disciplinary Perspectives on Code-Switching*. Cambridge: CUP.

Mishina-Mori, S. 2002. Language differentiation of the two languages in early bilingual development. *IRAL* 40(3): 211–233.

Morris, M. 2007. *An Introduction to the Philosophy of Language*. Cambridge: CUP.

Mühlhäusler, P. 1996. *Linguistic Ecology. Language Change and Linguistic Imperialism in the Pacific Region*. London: Routledge.

Müller-Lancé, J. 2003. A strategy model of multilingual learning. In *The Multilingual Lexicon*, J. Cenoz, B. Hufeisen & U. Jessner (eds), 117–132. Dordrecht: Kluwer.

Muñoz, C. & Singleton, D. 2007. Foreign accent in advanced learners: Two successful profiles. *The EUROSLA Yearbook* 7: 171–190.

Muñoz, C. & Singleton, D. 2011. A critical review of age-related research on L2 ultimate attainment, state of the art article. *Language Teaching* 44(1): 1–35.

Myers-Scotton, C. 2003. Code-switching: Evidence for both flexibility and rigidity in language. In *Bilingualism: Beyond Basic Principles*, J.-M. Dewaele, A. Housen & Li Wei (eds), 189–203. Clevedon: Multilingual Matters.

Nemser, W. 1971. Approximative systems of foreign language learners. *International Review of Applied Linguistics* 9: 115–123.

Nesse, A. 2003. Written and spoken languages in Bergen in the Hansa era. In *Aspects of Multilingualism in European Language History* [Hamburg Studies on Multilingualism 2], K. Braunmüller & G. Ferraresi (eds), 61–84. Amsterdam: John Benjamins.

Neuner, G. 2004. The concept of plurilingualism and tertiary language didactics. In *The Plurilingualism Project: Tertiary Language Learning – German after English*, B. Hufeisen & G. Neuner (eds), 13–34. Strasbourg: European Centre for Modern languages, Council of Europe Publishing.

Ng, S.H. & He, A. 2004. Code-switching in tri-generational family conversations among Chinese immigrants in New Zealand. *Journal of Language and Social Psychology* 23(1): 28–48.

Nicoladis, E. 1998. First clues to the existence of two input languages: pragmatic and lexical differentiation in a bilingual child. *Bilingualism: Language and Cognition* 1(2): 105–116.

Nicoladis, E. & Genesee, F. 1997. Language development in pre-school bilingual children. *Journal of Speech-Language Pathology and Audiology* 21(4): 258–270.

Nicoladis, E. & Secco, G. 2000. The role of a child's productive vocabulary in the language choice of a bilingual family. *First Language* 58(1): 3–28.

Norman, Donald A. 2002. *The Design of Everyday Things*. New York NY: Basic Books.

O'Brien, J.M. 1994. *Alexander the Great: The Invisible Enemy. A Biography* London: Routledge.

Odlin, T. 1989. *Language Transfer: Cross-linguistic Influence in Language Learning*. Cambridge: CUP.

OED. 2011. *Oxford English Dictionary*. Oxford: OUP. <www.oed.com>.

Oflazer, K. (ed.). 2003. *Language Engineering for Lesser-studied Languages*. Amsterdam: IOS Press.

Ó Laoire, M. & Aronin, L. 2005. Thinking of multilinguality – 'my self' or 'my various selves'?: An exploration of the identity of multilinguals. Paper presented at the Fourth International Conference on Multilingualism and Multilingual Acquisition, Fribourg, Switzerland September 8–10 2005.

Ó Laoire, M. & Singleton, D. 2009. The role of prior knowledge in L3 learning and use: Further evidence of psychotypological dimensions. In *The Exploration of Multilingualism: Development of Research on L3, Multilingualism and Multiple Language Acquisition* [AILA Applied Linguistics Series 6], L. Aronin & B. Hufeisen (eds), 63–77. Amsterdam: John Benjamins.

Oller, D.K. & Eilers, R.E. (eds). 2002. *Language and Literacy in Bilingual Children*. Clevedon: Multilingual Matters.

Ó Riagáin, P. 1997. *Language Policy and Social Reproduction: Ireland 1893–1993*. Oxford: OUP.

O'Rourke, B. & Carson, L. (eds). 2010. *Language Learner Autonomy: Policy, Curriculum, Classroom. A Festschrift in Honour of David Little*. Bern: Peter Lang.

Otwinowska-Kasztelanic, A. 2009. Language awareness in using cognate vocabulary: The case of polish advanced students of English in the light of the theory of affordances. In *Neurolinguistics and Psycholinguistic Perspectives on SLA*, 175–190. Bristol: Multilingual Matters.

Padilla, A.M. & Liebman, E. 1975. Language acquisition in the bilingual child. *The Bilingual Review/La Revista Bilingüe* 2: 34–55.

Panayiotou, A. 2004. Bilingual emotions: The untranslatable self. *Estudios de Sociolinguistica* 5(1): 1–19.

Papdaki-D'Onofrio, E. 2003. Bilingualism/multilingualism and language acquisition theories. *Child Care Information Exchange* September/October: 34–39.

Paradis, J. 2008. Are simultaneous and early sequential bilingual acquisition fundamentally different? Paper presented at the conference 'Models of Interaction in Bilinguals', University of Wales, Bangor, October 2008.

Paradis, M. (ed.). 1978. *Aspects of Bilingualism*, Columbia SC: Hornbeam Press.

Paradis, M. 1981. Neurolinguistic organization of a bilingual's two languages. In *The Seventh LACUS Forum*, J. Copeland & P. Davis (eds), 486–494. Columbia SC: Hornbeam Press.

Paradis, M. 2004. *A Neurolinguistic Theory of Bilingualism* [Studies in Bilingualism 18]. Amsterdam: John Benjamins.

Paradis, M. & Goldblum, M.C. 1989. Selective crossed aphasia in a trilingual aphasic patient followed by reciprocal antagonism. *Brain and Language* 36: 62–75.

Parker, A.R. 2011. Evolving the narrow language facullty: Was recursion the pivotal step? In *The Evolution of Language: Proceedings of the 6th International Conference (EVOLANG 6)*, A. Cangelosi, A.D.M. Smith & K. Smith (eds), 239–246. London: World Scientific.

Parker, D. & Stacey, R. 1994. Chaos, management and economics: The implications of non-linear thinking. *IEA Hobart Paper* 125. London: The Institute of Economic Affairs.

Pattanayak, D.P. (ed.). 1990. *Multilingualism in India*. Clevedon: Multilingual Matters.

Patterson, J. & Zurer-Pearson, B. 2004. Bilingual lexical development: Influences, contexts, and processes. In *Bilingual Language Development and Disorders in Spanish-English Speakers*, G. Goldstein (ed.), 77–104. Baltimore MD: Paul Brookes.

Paulston, C.B. 1994. *Linguistic Minorities in Multilingual Settings: Implications for Language Policies* [Studies in Bilingualism 4]. Amsterdam: John Benjamins.

Pavlenko, A. 2003. 'Languages of the enemy': Foreign Language education and national identity. *International Journal of Bilingual Education and Bilingualism* 6(5): 313–331.

Pavlenko, A. 2005. *Emotions and Multilingualism*. Cambridge: CUP.

Pavlenko, A. 2006. *Bilingual Minds: Emotional Experience, Expression and Representation*. Clevedon: Multilingual Matters.

Pavlenko, A. (ed.). 2008. *Multilingualism in Post-Soviet Countries*. Bristol: Multilingual Matters.

Pavlenko, A. (ed.). 2010. *Thinking and Speaking in Two Languages*. Clevedon: Multilingual Matters.

Peal, E. & Lambert, W.E. 1962. The relation of bilingualism to intelligence. *Psychological Monographs* 76(27): 1–23.

Pei, M. 1967. *The Story of the English Language*. London: George Allen & Unwin.

Pettito, L.A., Katerelos, M., Bronna, G., Levy, K.G., Tétreault, K. & Ferraro, V. 2001. Bilingual signed and spoken language acquisition from birth: implications for the mechanisms underlying early bilingual language acquisition. *Journal of Child Language* 28(2): 453–496.

Picard, J.M. 2003. The French language in medieval Ireland. In *The Languages of Ireland*, M. Cronin & C. Ó Cuilleanáin (eds), 57–77. Dublin: Four Courts Press.

Pintner, R. & Keller, R. 1922. Intelligence tests for foreign children. *Journal of educational Psychology* 13: 214–222.

Polka, L. & Sundara, M. 2003. Word segmentation in monolingual and bilingual infant learners of English and French. *Proceedings of the International Congress of Phonetic Sciences* 15: 1021–1024.

Poplack, S. 1980. 'Sometimes I'll start a sentence in Spanish y termino en español': Toward a typology of code-switching. *Linguistics* 18(7–8): 581–618.

Poplack, S. 1987. Contrasting patterns of code-switching in two communities. In *Aspects of Multilingualism*, E.Wande, J. Anward, B. Nordberg, L. Steensland & M. Thelander (eds), 51–77. Uppsala: Borgströms, Motala.

Postgate, J.P. 1922. *Translation and Translations: Theory and Practice*. London: Bell.

Premack, D. 1970. Education of Sarah – A chimp learns language. *Psychology Today* 4(4): 54–58.

Premack, D. 1971. Language in Chimpanzee. *Science* 172(3985): 808–822.

Protassova, E. 2004. *Fennorossy: Life and the Use of Language*. St. Petersburg: Zlatoust. (Протасова, Е.Ю. Феннороссы: жизнь и употребление языка. – СПб.: Златоуст, 2004. – 308с).

Pütz, M. 2004. Linguistic repertoire/Sprachrepertoire. In *An International Handbook of the Science of Language and Society / Ein internationales Handbuch zur Wissenschaft von Sprache und Gesellschaft*, 2nd edn, U. Ammon, N. Dittmar, K.J. Mattheier & P. Trudgill (eds), 226–231. Berlin: Walter de Gruyter.

Quay, S. 1995. The bilingual lexicon: Implications for studies of language choice. *Journal of Child Language* 22(2): 369–87.

Quist, P. & Jørgensen, J.N. 2007. Crossing – negotiating social boundaries. In *Handbook of Multilingualism and Multilingual Communication*, P. Auer & Li Wei (eds), 371–389. Berlin: Mouton de Gruyter.

Redlinger, W.E. & Park, T.-Z. 1980. Language mixing in young bilinguals. *Journal of Child Language* 7: 337–352.

Reichle, R.V. 2010a. The Critical Period Hypothesis: Evidence from information structural processing in French. In *Neurolinguistic and pycholinguistic perspectives on SLA*, J. Arabski & A. Wojtaszek (eds), 17–29. Bristol: Multilingual Matters.

Reichle, R.V. 2010b. Judgments of information structure in L2 French: Nativelike performance and the Critical Period Hypothesis. *International Review of Applied Linguistics in Language Teaching* 48(1): 53–85.

Riley, P. 2010. Reflections on identity, modernity and the European language portfolio. In *Language Learner Autonomy: Policy, Curriculum, Classroom. A Festschrift in Honour of David Little*, B. O'Rourke & L. Carson (eds), 373–385. Bern: Peter Lang.

Ringbom, H. 1987. *The Role of the First Language in Foreign Language Learning*. Clevedon: Multilingual Matters.

Ringbom, H. 2007. *Cross-linguistic Similarity in Foreign Language Learning*. Clevedon: Multilingual Matters.

Risk, H. 1969. French loan-words in Irish. *Études Celtiques* 12: 585–655.

Robertson, S. 1954. *Development of Modern English*. New York NY: Prentice-Hall.

Romaine, S. 1989/1995. *Bilingualism*. London: Wiley-Blackwell.

Ronjat, J. 1913. *Le Développment du Langage Observé chez un Enfant Bilingue*. Paris: Champion.

Rosier, P. & Farella, M. 1976. Bilngual education at Rock Point – Some early results. *TESOL Quarterly* 10: 379–388.

Russell, C. & Russell, W.S. 1973. Language and animal signals. In *Linguistics at Large*, N. Minnis (ed.), 159–192. St. Albans: Paladin.

Saer, O.J. 1923. The effects of bilingualism on intelligence. *British Journal of Psychology* 14: 25–28.

Safont Jordà, M.P. 2005. *Third Language Learners: Pragmatic Production and Awareness*. Clevedon: Multilingual Matters.

Safont Jordà, M.P. 2007. Language use and language attitudes in the Valencian community. In *Multilingualism in European Bilingual Contexts: Language Use and Attitudes*, D. Lasagabaster & A. Huguet (eds), 90–113. Clevedon: Multilingual Matters.

Saunders, G. 1982. *Bilingual Children: Guidance for the Family*. Clevedon: Multilingual Matters.

de Saussure, F. 1916. *Cours de Linguistique Générale*. Paris: Payot. English translation: *Course in General Linguistics*. New York NY: McGraw, 1959.

Savage-Rumbaugh, S. & Lewin, R. 1994. *Kanzi: The Ape at the Brink of the Human Mind*. New York NY: John Wiley and Sons.

Scarantino, A. 2003. Affordances explained. *Philosophy of Science* 70: 949–961.

Schachter, J. 1974. An error in error analysis. *Language Learning* 24(2): 205–214.

Schelleter, C., Sinka, I. & Garman, M. 1997. Latvian/English and German/English bilingual acquisition: New light on universal grammar. In *Proceedings of the First International Symposium on Bilingualism*, 442–452. Vigo: University of Vigo.

Schiffmann, H. 1996. *Linguistic Culture and Language Policy*. London: Routledge.

Schilling, H. 2008. *Early Modern European Civilization and its Political and Cultural Dynamism*. Waltham MA: Brandeis University Press.

Schlereth, T.J. (ed.). 1985a. *Material Culture: A Research Guide*. Lawrence KS: University Press of Kansas.

Schlereth, T.J. 1985b. Material culture and cultural research. In *Material Culture: A Research Guide*, T.J. Schlereth (ed.), 1–34. Lawrence KS: University Press of Kansas.

Schmid, M.S. 2004. Identity and first language attrition: A historical approach. *Estudios de Sociolinguistica* 5(1): 41–58.

Scott, S., Blank, C., Rosen, S. & Wise, R. 2000. Identification of a pathway for intelligible speech in the left temporal lobe. *Brain* 123: 2400–2406.

Secada, W.G. 1991. Degree of bilingualism and arithmetic problem solving in Hispanic first graders. *Elementary School Journal* 92: 213–231.

Segalowitz, N. 1997. Individual differences in second language scquisition. In *Tutorials in Bilingualism: Psycholinguistic Perspectives*, A. de Groot & J. Kroll (eds), 85–112. Mahwah NJ: Lawrence Erlbaum Associates.

Segalowitz, N. 2001. On the evolving connections between psychology and linguistics. *Annual Review of Applied Linguistics* 21: 3–22.

Selinker, L. 1972. Interlanguage. *International Review of Applied Linguistics* 10(3): 209–231.

Selinker, L. 1992. *Rediscovering Interlanguage*. New York NY: Longman.

Sharwood Smith, M. & Kellerman, E. (eds). 1986. *Crosslinguistic Influence in Second Language Acquisition*. New York NY: Pergamon Institute of English.

Sharwood Smith, M. 1994. *Second Language Learning: Theoretical Foundations*. London: Longman.

Silverstein, M. 2003. Indexical order and the dialectics of sociolinguistic life. *Language and Communication* 23: 193–229.

Singleton, D. 1987. Mother and other tongue influences on learner French. *Studies in Second Language Acquisition* 9(3): 327–345.

Singleton, D. 1992. *French: Some Historical Background*. Dublin: Authentik.

Singleton, D. 1996. Crosslinguistic lexical operations and the L2 mental lexicon. In *Language, Education and Society in a Changing World*, T. Hickey & J. Williams (eds), 246–252. Clevedon: IRAAL/Multilingual Matters.

Singleton, D. 1999. *Exploring the Second Language Mental Lexicon*. Cambridge: CUP; Beijing: Beijing World Publishing.

Singleton, D. 2003. Perspectives on the multilingual lexicon: A critical synthesis. In *The Multilingual Lexicon*, J. Cenoz, U. Jessner & B. Hufeisen (eds), 167–176. Dordrecht: Kluwer.

Singleton, D. 2005. The Critical Period Hypothesis: A coat of many colours. *International Review of Applied Linguistics in Language Teaching (IRAL)* 43: 269–285.

Singleton, D. 2006. Lexical transfer: Interlexical or intralexical? In *Cross-linguistic Influences in the Second Language Lexicon*, J. Arabski (ed.), 130–143. Clevedon: Multilingual Matters.

Singleton, D. 2007a. How integrated is the integrated mental lexicon? In *Second Language Lexical Processes: Applied Linguistic and Psycholinguistic Processes*, Z. Lengyel & J. Navracsics (eds), 3–16. Clevedon: Multilingual Matters.

Singleton, D. 2007b. *Globalization, Language and National Identity: The Case of Ireland* [CLCS Occasional Paper 68]. Dublin: Trinity College, Centre for Language and Communication Studies.

Singleton, D. In press. Multilingual lexical operations: Keeping it all together … and apart. In *Third Language Acquisition in Adulthood*, S. Flynn & J. Rothman (eds). Amsterdam: John Benjamins.

Singleton, D. & Aronin, L. 2007. Multiple language learning in the light of the theory of affordances. *Innovation in Language Teaching and Learning* 1(1): 83–96.

Singleton, D. & Leśniewska, J. In press. Age and SLA: Research highways and byeways. In *New perspectives on Individual Differences in Language Learning and Teaching*, M. Pawlak (ed.). Berlin: Springer.

Singleton, D. & Little, D. 1984/2005. A first encounter with Dutch: Perceived language distance and transfer as factors in comprehension. In *Introductory Readings in L3*, B. Hufeisen & R.J. Fouser (eds), 101–109. Tübingen: Stauffenberg. (First published in *Language across Cultures*, L. Mac Mathúna & D. Singleton (eds), 259–269. Dublin: Irish Association for Applied Linguistics).

Singleton, D. & Kopečková, R. In press. Second language phonology: A critical perspective on critical period perspectives. In *Anthologie: Fremdsprachen in der Perspektive lebenslangen Lernens/Anthology: Foreign Languages in the Perspective of Lifelong Learning*, A. Berndt (ed.). Oxford: Peter Lang.

Singleton, D. & Muñoz, C. 2011. Around and beyond the Critical Period Hypothesis. In *Handbook of Research in Second Language Teaching and Learning*, Vol. 2, E. Hinkel (ed.), 407–425. London: Routledge.

Singleton, D. & Ó Laoire, M. 2006a. Psychotypologie et facteur L2 dans l'influence translexicale. Une analyse de l'influence de l'anglais et de l'irlandais sur le français L3 de l'apprenant. *Acquisition et Interaction en Langue Étrangère* 24: 101–117.

Singleton, D. & Ó Laoire, M. 2006b. Psychotypology and the 'L2 factor' in cross-lexical interaction: An analysis of English and Irish influence in learner French. In *Språk, Lärande och Utbildning i Sikte*, M. Bendtsen, M. Björklund, C. Fant & L. Forsman (eds), 191–205. Vasa: Faculty of Education, Åbo Akademi.

Singleton, D. & Ryan, L. 2004. *Language Acquisition: The Age Factor,* 2nd edn. Clevedon: Multilingual Matters.

Singleton, D. & Ryan, L. 2009. Child language development in a multilingual environment. In *Tanulmányok a mentális lexikonról. Studies on the Mental Lexicon*, Z. Lengyel & J. Navracsics (eds), 83–96. Budapest: Tinta Kiadó.

Singleton, D., Skrzypek, A., Kopečková, R. & Bidzińska, B. 2007. Attitudes towards and perceptions of English L2 acquisition among Polish migrants in Ireland. In *Cultures in Contact: Contemporary Issues in Language Use and Language Learning*, B. Geraghty & J.E. Conacher (eds). London: Continuum.

Singleton, D., Smyth, S. & Debaene, E. 2009. 'Second language Acquisition and native language maintenance in the Polish diaspora in Ireland and France' and 'Our languages: Who in Ireland speaks and understands Russian?': The rationale, structure and aims of two Dublin-based research projects. In *Contemporary Migrations: Dilemmas of Europe and of Poland*, M. Duszczyk & M. Lesinska (eds), 196–220. Warsaw: Centre of Migration Research.

Sinka, I., Garman, M. & Schelleter, C. 2000. Early verbs in bilingual acquisition. *Reading Working Papers in Linguistics* 4: 175–187.

Sinka, I. & Schelleter, C. 1998. Morphosyntactic development in bilingual children. *Journal of Bilingualism* 2(3): 301–326.

Sjöholm, K. 1976. A comparison of the test results in grammar and vocabulary between Finnish- and Swedish-speaking applicants for English. In *Errors Made by Finns and Swedish-speaking Finns in the Learning of English*, H. Ringbom & R. Palmberg (eds), 54–137. Åbo: Åbo Academy, Publications of the Department of English.

Sjöholm, K. 1979. Do Finns and Swedish-speaking Finns use different strategies in the learning of English as a foreign language? In *Perceptions and Production of English: Papers on Interlanguage* [AFTIL Vol. 6], R. Palmberg (ed.). Åbo: Åbo Academy, Publications of the Department of English.

Sklair, L. 1999. Competing conceptions of globalization. *Journal of World-Systems Research* 5(2): 143–162.

Skutnabb-Kangas, T. 1981. *Bilingualism or Not: The Education of Minorities.* Clevedon: Multilingual Matters.

Skutnabb-Kangas, T. 1995. *Multilingualism for All.* Lisse: Swets & Zeitlinger.

Skutnabb-Kangas, T. 2000. *Linguistic Genocide in Education – Or Worldwide Diversity and Human Rights?* Mahwah NJ: Lawrence Erlbaum Associates.

Skutnabb-Kangas, T. 2001. The globalisation of (educational) language rights. *International Review of Education/Internationale Zeitschrift für Erziehungswissenschaft/Revue internationale l'éducation* 47(3–4): 201–219.

Slobin, D.I. 1973. Cognitive prerequisites for the development of grammar. In *Studies of Child Language Development*, C.A. Ferguson & D.I. Slobin (eds), 175–208. New York NY: Holt, Rinehart & Winston.

Sorace, A. & Ladd, D.R. 2004. *Raising Bilingual Children.* Washington DC: Linguistic Society of America.

Southerton, D. 2003. 'Squeezing time'. Allocating practices, coordinating networks and scheduling society. *Time and Society* 12(1): 5–25.

Spolsky, B. 1999. Second language learning. In *Handbook of Language and Ethnic Identity*, J.A. Fishman (ed.), 181–192. Oxford: OUP.

Spolsky, B. 2009. *Language Management.* Cambridge: CUP.

Starr, C.G. 1991. *A History of the Ancient World*, 4th edn. Oxford: OUP.

Stemberger, J.P. & MacWhinney, B. 1988. Are inflected forms stored in the lexicon? In *Theoretical Morphology: Approaches in Modern Linguistics*, M. Hammond & M. Noonan (eds), 101–116. San Diego CA: Academic Press.

Stewart, W. 1968. A sociolinguistic typology for describing national multilingualism. In *Readings in the Sociology of Language*, J. Fishman (ed.), 531–545. The Hague: Mouton. (This is a revised version of the author's 1962 'Outline of Linguistic Typology for Describing Multilingualism' in *Study of the Role of second Languages in Asia, Africa and Latin America*, F.A. Rice (ed.), 15–25. Washington DC: Center for Applied Linguistics).

Swain, M. 1981. Bilingual education for majority and minority language students. *Studia Linguistica* 35(1–2): 15–32.

Swain, M. & Lapkin, S. 1982. *Evaluating Bilingual Education: A Canadian Case Study*. Clevedon: Multilingual Matters.

Swain, S. 2002. Bilingualism in Cicero: Evidence of code-switching. In *Bilingualism in Ancient Society*, J.N. Adams, M. Janse & S. Swain (eds), 129–167. Oxford: OUP.

Tabouret-Keller, A. 1998. Language and identity. In *Handbook of Sociolinguistics*, F. Coulmas (ed.), 315–326. Oxford: Blackwell.

Taeschner, T. 1983. *The Sun is Feminine: A Study on Language Acquisition in Bilingual Children*. Berlin: Springer.

Tandefelt, M. 2003. Vyborg: Free trade in four languages. In *Aspects of Multilingualism in European Language History* [Hamburg Studies in Multilingualism 2], K. Braunmüller & G. Ferraresi (eds), 85–104. Amsterdam: John Benjamins.

ten Thije, J. & Zeevaert, L. (eds). 2007. *Receptive Multilingualism: Linguistic Analyses, Language Policies and Didactic Concepts* [Hamburg Studies in Multilingualism 6]. Amsterdam: John Benjamins.

Terrace, H.S. 1979. *Nim*. New York NY: Knopf.

Terrace, H.S. 1983. Apes who 'talk': Language or projection of language by their teachers? In *Language in Primates: Perspectives and Implications*, J. de Luce & H.T. Wilder (eds), 22–39. Berlin: Springer.

Thackara, J. 2005. *In the Bubble: Designing in a Complex World*. Cambridge MA: The MIT Press.

Thody, P. & Evans, H. 1985. *Faux Amis and Key Words – A Dictionary-Guide to French Language, Culture and Society through Lookalikes and Confusables*. London: The Athlone Press.

Thomas, J. 1988. The role played by metalinguistic awareness in second and third language learning. *Journal of Multilingual and Multicultural Development* 9: 235–246.

Thomas, W. & Collier, V. 1997. *School Effectiveness for Language Minority Students* [NCBE. Resource Collection Series 9]. Washington DC: Clearing House for English Language Acquisition.

Titone, R. 1972. *Le bilinguisme précoce*. Bruxelles: Dessart.

Todeva, E. & Cenoz, J. (eds). 2009. *The Multiple Realities of Multilingualism: Personal Narratives and Researchers' Perspectives*. Berlin: Mouton de Gruyter.

Tomasello, M. 1999. *The Cultural Origins of Human Cognition*. Cambridge MA: Harvard University Press.

Tomasello, M. 2008. *Origins of Human Communication*. Cambridge MA: The MIT Press.

Tomasello, M. & Call, J. 1997. *Primate Cognition*. Oxford: OUP.

Toolan, M. 2008. Introduction: Language teaching and integrational linguistics. In *Language Teaching: Integrational Linguistic Approaches*, M. Toolan (ed.), 1–23. London: Routledge.

Turner, V. 1974. Passages, margins, and poverty: Religious symbols of communitas. In *Dramas, Fields, and Metaphors: Symbolic Action in Human Society,* 231–271. Ithaca NY: Cornell University Press.

Trotter, D. 2003. Oceano vox: You never know where a ship comes from: On multilingualism and language-mixing in medieval Britain. In *Aspects of Multilingualism in European Language History* [Hamburg Studies on Multilinguism], K. Braunmüller & G. Ferraresi (eds), 15–33. Amsterdam: John Benjamins.

Tucker, G.R. 1998. A global perspective on multilingualsim and multilingual education. In *Beyond Bilingualism: Multilingualism and Multilingual Education,* J. Cenoz & F. Genesee (eds), 3–15. Clevedon: Multilingual Matters.

Trudgill, P. & Cheshire, J. (eds). 1998. *The Sociolinguistics Reader.* Vol. 1: *Multilingualism and Variation,* 1–4. London: Arnold.

Turell, T. 2001. *Multilingualism in Spain: Sociolinguistic and Psycholinguistic Aspects of Linguistic Minority Groups.* Clevedon: Multilingual Matters.

Umbel, V.M., Zurer-Pearson, B., Fernandez, M.C. & Oller, D.K. 1992. Measuring bilingual children's receptive vocabularies. *Child Development* 63(4): 1012–1020.

Urry, J. 2000. *Sociology beyond Societies: Mobilities for the Twenty- First Century.* London: Routledge.

Urry, J. 2003. *Global Complexity.* Cambridge: Polity Press.

Valdés, G. Multilingualism. Linguistic Society of America. <http://www.lsadc.org/info/ling-fields-multi.cfm> (July 28, 2009).

Valdés, G. & Figueroa, R. 1994. *Bilingualism and Testing: A Special case of Bias.* Norwood NJ: Ablex.

Valenty, S. & Good, J.M. 1991. Social affordances and interaction I: Introduction. *Ecological Psychology* 3: 77–98.

van Heuven, W.J.B., Schriefers, H., Dijkstra, T. & Hagoort, P. 2008. Language conflict in the bilingual brain. *Cerebral Cortex* 18(11): 2706–2716.

Van Lier, Leo. 2007. Action-based teaching, autonomy and identity. *Innovation in Language Teaching and Learning* 1(1): 46–65.

van Roey, J., Granger, S. & Swallow, H. 1988. Introduction générale. *Dictionnaire des faux amis français~anglais.* Paris-Gembloux: Duculot.

Verhoeven, L. 2006. Sociocultural variation in literacy achievement. *British Journal of Educational Studies* 54: 189–211.

Vertovec, S. 2007. Super-diversity and its implications. *Ethnic and Racial Studies* 29(6): 1024–1054.

Vertovec, S. 2010. Super-diversity and its implications. *Ethnic and Racial Studies* 30(6): 1024–1054.

Vila i Morena, F.X. 2008. Language-in-Education policies in the Catalan language area. *AILA Review* 21: 31–48.

Vildomec, V. 1963. *Multilingualism.* Leiden: A.W. Sythoff.

Volterra, V. & Taeschner, T. 1978. The acquisition and development of language by bilingual children. *Journal of Child Language* 5(2): 311–326.

von Frisch, K. 1962. *Dialects in the Lnguage of the Bees.* New York NY: W.H. Freeman.

Waldrop, M.M. 1992. *Complexity.* New York NY: Touchstone Books, Simon & Shuster.

Walker, U. 2006. The role of bi/multilingual selves among multilingual migrants on Aotearoa/ New Zealand: Implications for language learning and teaching. In *Multilingualism in Educational Settings,* M. Ó Laoire (ed.), 1–19. Hohengehren: Schneider.

Warren, R & Owen, D.H. 1982. Functional optical invariants: A new methodology for aviation research. *Journal of Aviation, Space and Environmental Medicine* 53: 977–983.

Waterworth, S. 2003. Temporal reference frameworks and nurses' work organization. *Time & Society* 12(1): 41–54.

Weinreich, P. 1953. *Languages in Contact.* The Hague: Mouton.

Weinreich, P. 2000. Ethnic identity and 'acculturation': Ethnic stereotyping and identification, self-esteem and identity diffusion in a multicultural context. In *Language, Identity and Immigration*, E. Olshtain & G. Horenczyk (eds), 31–63. Jerusalem: Magnes Press.

Wells, G. 1979. Influences of the home on language development. *Bristol Working Papers in Language 1.* Bristol: University of Bristol.

Werker, J.F. 2003. The acquisition of language specific phonetic categories in infancy. *Proceedings of the International Congress of Phonetic Sciences* 15: 21–25.

Wesche, M.B. & Paribakht, T.S. 2010. *Lexical Inferencing in a First and Second Language: Cross-Linguistic Dimensions.* Bristol: Multilingual Matters.

Whitaker, H. 1978. Bilingualism: A neurolinguistics perspective. In *Second Language Acquisition Research: Issues and Implications*, W. Ritchie (ed.), 21–32. New York NY: Academic Press.

White, P. 1991. Geographical aspects of minority language situations in Italy. In *Linguistic Minorities, Society and Territory*, C. Williams (ed.), 44–65. Clevedon: Multilingual Matters.

Whorf, B.L. 1956. *Language, Thought and Reality: Selected Writings*, J.B. Carrol (ed.), 246–270. Cambridge MA: The MIT Press & New York NY: Wiley.

Wieszbicka, A. 1999. *Emotions across Languages and Cultures: Diversity and Universals.* Cambridge: CUP.

Williams, C.J.F. 1989. *What is Identity?* Oxford: Clarendon Press.

Williams, S. & Hammarberg, B. 1998. Language switches in L3 production: Implications for a polyglot speaking model. *Applied Linguistics* 19(3): 295–333.

Ytsma, J. 2001. Towards a typology of trilingual primary education. *Journal of Bilingual Education and Bilingualism* 4: 11–22.

Zhang, H.-Q. 2006. Bilingual Sibling Interaction: A Case Study of Linguistic Features and their Social Functions. MPhil. dissertation. Trinity College Dublin.

Zierer, E. 1977. Experiences in the bilingual education of a child of pre-school age. *IRAL* 15: 144–149.

Zipf, G.K. 1949[1965]. *Human Behavior and the Principle of Least Effort. An Introduction to Human Ecology.* New York NY: Hafner.

Zurer-Pearson, B. 2002. Bilingual infants: Mapping the research agenda. In *Latinos: Remaking America*, M.M. Páez & M.M. Suárez-Orozco (eds), 306–320. Berkeley CA: University of California Press.

Language index

A

African American Vernacular English (AAVE) 41
African languages 18
Afrikaans 41, 43, 140
Akkadian 47
Algerian Arabic 72
American Sign Language 14
Amharic 43, 62
ancient languages 47
Anglo-Norman 48
Arabic 23, 36, 40, 43, 53, 59–60, 65, 69, 72, 135, 138, 142, 150, 171–172, 179

B

Bantu language 138
Bashkir 177
Basque 41, 55, 70, 101, 108, 144, 176–177
Bayerisch 135
Bengali 138, 142
Bhojpuri 61
Brazilian 96
Byelorussian 61, 175

C

Casablanca variety of Moroccan Arabic 43
Catalan 41, 50, 55, 65, 70, 154
Celtic 140, 161
Chakesang 138
Chinese 36, 65, 73, 107, 122, 137–139, 142, 147, 159
Chuvash 177
Cockney 135
Corsican 138
creole 41, 135
Croatian 175
Czech 66, 96

D

Danish 40
Dari 65
Deori 138
Duri 149
Dutch 41, 60, 96, 100, 118, 136, 138–139, 144, 158, 175

E

English 5, 18, 28, 39, 41–43, 45–49, 51, 54–56, 60–61, 63–66, 68–70, 90, 94–96, 99–101, 105–109, 112–114, 129, 136–140, 142–143, 145–151, 155–161, 168, 171–172, 176, 179, 181, 187
Esperanto 78, 135

F

Finnish 5, 47, 63, 69, 73, 148–150, 159, 175
Finno-Permic (branch of languages, language) 177
Finno-Ugric language family 177
Finno-Volgaic (branch of languages, language) 177
Francien 18
French 5, 18, 21, 28, 41, 43, 48, 60–61, 65, 68–69, 86, 96, 100, 109, 111–112, 118, 135, 138–140, 142, 145–146, 148, 150–151, 156–158, 160–161, 172, 175–176, 182
Frisian 55, 61
Fusha (or Al-Fusha) 23

G

German 2, 12, 18, 21, 23, 41, 43, 47–48, 60–61, 64–67, 69, 79, 88, 92–93, 96, 100, 105–106, 118, 137–139, 142, 146, 148, 151, 158, 179

Germanic language 161
Greek 29, 46, 48, 65, 148
Guarani 23

H

Haitian Creole 135
Hakka 60
Han 73
Hausa 77
Hebrew 41, 51, 61, 65, 72–73, 171–172, 179
High German 64, 148
Hindi 40, 45, 61, 138–139, 142
Hindustani 40
Hokkien 100
Huave 2
Hungarian 60

I

Iberian 96
Indian English 41
Indo-European languages 108, 148
Iraqi Arabic 72
Irish 18, 39, 41–42, 47, 50, 70, 101, 109, 156, 161
Irish English 41
Italian 2, 40–41, 43, 64–65, 96, 100, 105, 122, 138, 142, 144, 148, 157, 172, 175

J

Japanese 69, 106, 112, 138, 142, 151, 157, 159–160

K

Kannada 139
Kazakh 67
Khezha 138
Kinyarwanda 68
Kiswahili (Swahili) 45

Korean   40, 56, 94–95, 139,
   159–160
Kuwaiti Arabic   23

L
L1   29, 61, 64–65, 87, 101,
   112–114, 122–124, 130, 146,
   148–149, 152–154, 157, 159, 161,
   164, 182
L2   29, 64–65, 86–87, 90, 112,
   114, 122–124, 129–130, 139,
   146, 152–153, 157–159, 161, 164,
   182, 185
L3   5, 64, 66, 86–88, 90, 122–
   124, 146, 164, 182
L4   64, 87, 122, 124, 164, 182
Ladin   64
Lahauli   138
languages of the Pacific
   Northwest   24
Latin   46–47, 52, 72, 148, 156–
   157, 161, 187
Latvian   61, 106
Lebanese Arabic   23
Letzebuergesch   100
Lingala   45
Lithuanian   61, 69
Low German   48

M
Maithili   61
Malagasy   148
Malay   100–101, 138, 142
Malayalam   139
Mandarin   39, 48, 60, 69, 73,
   100–101
Māori   41
Mari   177
Modern Hebrew   179
Modern Standard Arabic   23,
   59, 72
Moldovan   40
Mordvin   177
Moroccan Arabic   43, 72

N
Neomelanesian   135
Nguni group of languages   140
Norwegian   22, 40, 48

O
Occitan   138
Old Church Slavonic   72

P
Parthian   48
Persian   48, 60, 69, 179
pidgin   135
Polish   18, 39, 47–48, 61, 69–70,
   118, 181
Portuguese   18, 43, 96, 138, 142
Putonghua (standardized
   Mandarin)   73

R
Rinkeby Swedish   43
Romance language   161
Romanian   40, 158
Romansch   41
Runyankole   68
Russian   36, 39, 47–48, 51,
   61–62, 64–67, 69, 72–73,
   137–138, 142, 144, 171–172, 175,
   177–179

S
Sanskrit   72
Singapore English   100
Slavic languages   175
Sotho   140
Sotho family (of languages)
   140
Southern Min   60, 69
South Tyrol dialect   64
Spanish   2, 5, 18, 23, 27, 43, 45,
   65, 70, 93, 96, 100–101, 105,
   107–108, 114, 122, 138–139, 142,
   154, 156–157, 172, 175–176
Sumerian   47, 187

T
Tamil   100, 155
Tatar   177–178
Tok Pisin   41
Tswana   140
Tulu   139
Turkic Altai language family
   177
Turkish   43, 53, 60, 179

U
Udmurt   92, 177
Ukrainian   36, 61, 64–65, 172,
   175
urban dialect   40
Urdu   40, 142
Uzbek   67

V
Venetian   148
Veronese   148

W
Welsh   41, 49
Wolof   137
World Englishes   41

X
Xhosa   140

Y
Yiddish   61, 72, 93–94, 179

Z
Zhuang   73
Zulu   140

Name index

A

Abrahamsson 102–103
Abu-Rabia 112
Ackerman 91
Adams 43
Adcock 27
Adegbija 91
Aitchison 11, 15
Albert 27
Alker 42
Ammon 55, 139–141
Anchimbe 18
Andreesen 67
Aronin 6–7, 17–18, 31, 42–43,
 45, 49–52, 54, 59, 62–63,
 79–83, 89, 91, 119, 163–166,
 168–169, 172–173, 175–176,
 179–181, 183
Auer 31
Avgerou 35
Avila 112, 152

B

Backhaus 94, 165
Baetens Beardsmore 4–5, 25
Baker, A. 34
Baker, C. 7, 28, 41, 101–102, 105,
 110–111, 129, 131
Baker, W. 152
Barbour 54
Bardel 43, 157
Barnes 108
Barrett 96
Barron-Hauwaert 125, 128
Bassetti 151
Bates 152
Bauman 35, 38
Beaney 19
Beauvillain 151
Beckmann 27
Bendle 38
Ben-Yehuda 179

Ben Zeev 28, 109
Bergman 21
Betteridge 37
Bialystok 28, 104, 109–111, 114
Bickerton 14
Bidzińska 18
Birdsong 12–13, 102
Björklund 54
Blanc 7, 25, 28–29, 31, 109, 111,
 113, 119, 123
Blank 27
Bloch 20
Blommaert 36, 39, 67–68, 96,
 164
Bloomfield 2, 59
Bongaerts 102
Bosch 104
Bossomaier 91–92
Brann 18, 77–78
Braudel 35
Braun, A. 126–128
Braun, M. 2
Braunmüller 43
Breedveld 34
Brones 151
Bronfenbrenner 165
Bull 43
Bybee 147

C

Call 16
Cameron 185
Canagarajah 155
Capra 52, 183
Caramazza 151
Carlson 110
Cenoz 5, 31, 54–55, 81–82, 91,
 94, 101, 122, 131, 164–165,
 176–177, 185
Champagne 104
Chase-Dunn 40
Chaunu 37

Chen 27
Cheshire 41, 54
Chimombo 21
Chinchilla 37
Chiti-Batelli 49
Chomsky 14, 20, 24
Cilliers 34–35, 183
Claiborne 161
Clark 106
Cline 126–128
Clyne 26, 83–84, 100, 139
Collier 113
Cook 20, 30, 54, 81–82, 88, 103,
 137, 147, 150–152, 164, 185
Cooper 11, 20
Corder 25
Cotton 48
Coulmas 94
Coupland 169
Craik 110
Cristoffanini 151
Cross 153
Crystal 6, 45, 48–49, 153
Cummins 28 29, 109, 111 114

D

Dagenais 91
Dalby 48
Das Gupta 131–132
Daulton 160
De Angelis 6, 157, 164
De Avila 112
Debaene 18
De Bot 84, 94, 124, 153
De Graff 135
De Groot 157
De Houwer 91, 104, 108
Deignan 185
De Mejia 120–121
Demick 56
Dent 183
Dercon 36

De Swaan 72–74, 137–138
Deuchar 108
Devlin 27
Dewaele 6, 82, 124, 181–182
Diaz 28, 110, 112
Diebold 2
Dijkstra 150, 152–153
Dittmar 43
Doepke 38
Dörnyei 91
Doyle 104
Duncan 95, 112

E
Edwards 2, 17, 31, 117–118, 122, 140–141, 165
Eilers 27
Ellis, N. 185
Ellis, R. 91
Ennaji 43
Eriksen 34
Evans 161
Extra 31, 36, 38, 53, 137

F
Fabbro 148
Falk 43
Fantini 105
Farella 112
Ferguson 21–23, 118, 134
Fernandez 104
Ferraresi 43
Figueroa 121
Fill 165
Fischer 37
Fishman 21, 23–24, 38, 40–43, 48–49, 73–74, 78, 93–94, 134, 173, 180
Fitch 14
Flaherty 34
Fouser 159–160
Franceschini 6–7, 64, 124, 164
Freedman 110
Frege 19
Friedman 38, 78
Fu 27
Furlong 110
Fussman 45

G
Gabryś-Barker 147, 165, 185
Gachelin 161
Gafaranga 26, 154
Garcia 130–131
Gardner 14, 91
Garhammer 34
Garipov 178
Garman 106
Garrett 169
Genesee 21, 31, 82, 104–105, 108, 128, 185
Gibson, J. 174
Gibson, M. 158
Giddens 38
Glonings 27
Goggin 112
Goldblum 148
Goldin-Meadow 16
Good 124, 174
Goodz 101, 104
Goral 27
Gorter 54–55, 165, 169, 185
Graddol 41, 48, 139, 142–144
Grainger 151
Grammont 92
Granger 161
Green 31, 83–85, 91–92, 112, 150
Grimm 133
Grin 94
Grosjean 29–30, 54, 81, 84, 86, 88, 103, 148, 151, 185
Gullberg 26
Gumperz 17, 21, 24, 60, 62
Gurvitch 35

H
Haarman 67
Haberland 180
Hagen 45
Hagoort 152
Hakuta 112
Hall 2
Hamers 7, 25, 28–29, 31, 109, 111, 113, 119, 123
Hammarberg 146, 164
Handscombe 112
Hannifin 42
Harding 120
Harjanne 53

Harris 153, 162
Haugen 4, 21–22, 118, 140, 165
Hauser 14
Hawkins 56
Hayes 14
He 101
Herdina 5–6, 22, 31, 41, 81, 83, 88, 145, 164, 184–185
Hernandez 152
Hess 15
Heugh 43
Hockett 11
Hoffmann 5, 30–31, 49, 55, 124–125, 185
Holmes 37
Ho-min Sohn 95
Horenczyk 38
Hornberger 22, 94, 165
Hufeisen 6, 31, 82–83, 86–88, 90–91, 119, 158, 163, 165, 183
Hui-chi Lee 91
Humboldt 77, 133
Hung Cam Thai 96
Hutchby 174
Hyltenstam 27, 102–103
Hymes 24

I
Ianco-Worrall 28, 109
Indefrey 26
Ingman 37
Iversen 27

J
Jakobovits 27–28, 109
Jarvis 103
Jedynak 102
Jescheniak 83
Jessner 3, 5–6, 22, 31, 41, 49, 54–56, 81–83, 88–90, 124, 145, 159, 164–165, 184–185
Jia 114, 120
Johnson 104, 114
Jones 41, 49
Jørgensen 53

K
Kachru 91
Kang 94
Kanno 151

Kasai 151
Katz 20
Kecskés 103
Keller 27, 79
Kellerman 6, 22, 147
Kellogg 14
Kemp 5–6, 82, 164
Kinsella 102
Kirk-Greene 161
Kirsner 151, 157–158
Klein 110
Klinger 28, 110
Kloss 132, 139
Kopečková 18, 152
Kouritzin 38, 148
Kramer 47
Kramsch 165
Kroll 153

L
Lacey 19, 167
Ladd 104
Lamarre 91
Lambert 28–29, 109, 111
Lanza 108
Lapkin 109, 113
Larsen-Freeman 31, 52, 185
Le Goff 37
Lemmon 112
Leśniewska 102
Lenneberg 26
Leopold 21, 93, 105
Levelt 31, 83–84
Levine 35
Lewin 15
Liebman 27
Lightbown 91
Lindquist 43
Little 6, 147, 158
Li Wei 4, 28, 31, 110, 120, 149
Lodge 18
Long 31
Louis Ronjat's son 21, 93
Lowie 84, 154
Lüdi 42

M
Mack 152
MacKay 152
Mackenzie 149

Mackey 4, 128–129
Macnamara 3, 27, 109
Macrory 107
MacWhinney 147
Maggipinto 40
Maines 38
Makoni 18, 94
Maneva 26
Mar-Molinero 49
Marshall 13
Marten 169
Martin 110
Marx 31, 86, 165
Matthews 27
Maurais 42, 48
McArthur 161
McLaughlin 21
Meara 185
Meinhof 18
Meisel 104
Meltzoff 110
Mesthrie 60, 133
Milech 151
Millar 48
Milroy 26
Mishina-Mori 106
Molis 102
Müller-Lancé 158
Muñoz 91, 94, 102
Muysken 26
Myers-Scotton 150

N
Nakajima 112
Nemser 25
Nesse 48
Neuner 6, 90, 165
Newson 20
Ng 101
Nicoladis 104, 107–108
Norman 48, 161, 174

O
Obler 27
O'Brien 45
Odlin 22
Ó Laoire 7, 43, 49, 59, 63,
    79–81, 83, 89, 133, 147, 160,
    164, 168–169, 172–173
Oller 27, 104

Ó Riagáin 49
Otwinowska-Kasztelanic 181
Owen 174

P
Padilla 27
Panayiotou 82
Papdaki-D'Onofrio 105
Papp 81, 103, 151
Paradis 27, 102, 108, 148, 150,
    158
Paribakht 159
Park 107
Parker 180
Parker, A. R. 14
Pattanayak 31, 91
Patterson 104
Paulston 31, 38, 120
Pavlenko 71, 82, 91, 103, 151
Peal 28, 109
Pei 161
Penfield 26
Pettito 107
Picard 161
Pintner 27
Polka 104
Poplack 26
Postgate 145
Premack 15
Protassova 73
Prys Jones 41
Pütz 62, 94

Q
Quay 107–108
Quist 53

R
Rampton 36
Redlinger 107
Reichle 102
Riley 77, 99, 121
Ringbom 5, 63, 81, 147
Risk 161
Robertson 161
Rogers 48
Romaine 25, 126–127
Ronjat 21, 92, 101
Rosen 27
Rosier 112

Rushworth 27
Russell 11
Ryan 26, 73, 91, 101

S
Saer 27
Safont Jordà 50, 147
Sasaki 151
Saunders 21
Saussure 20
Savage-Rumbaugh 15
Scarantino 181
Schelleter 106
Schiffmann 132
Schilling 37
Schleicher 133
Schlereth 170
Schmid 71, 82
Schreuder 84, 150
Schriefers 152
Scott 27
Sebastián-Gallés 104
Secco 107
Segalowitz 91, 104, 175–176
Seipp-Williams 34
Selinker 6, 25, 164
Sharwood Smith 4, 22
Shikama 94
Silverstein 65
Singleton 6, 18, 22, 26, 39,
    42–43, 50–52, 54, 73, 84, 91,
    94, 101–102, 133, 146–147, 150,
    152, 156, 158, 160–166, 175–176,
    179–181, 183
Sinka 106
Sjöholm 6, 147, 159
Sklair 35
Skrzypek 18
Skutnabb-Kangas 3, 25, 29,
    31, 49
Slobin 105–106
Smith 4, 22, 27
Smyth 18
Solnyshkina 178
Sorace 104

Southerton 34
Spada 91
Spolsky 53, 132
Sridhar 91
Stacey 180
Starr 47
Steckbauer 43
Stemberger 147
Stewart 118, 134–136
Sundara 104
Suni 54
Swain 43, 47, 109, 111–114
Swallow 161

T
Tabouret-Keller 79
Taeschner 21, 106
Takahashi 151
Tandefelt 47
Tella 53
ten Thije 3
Terrace 15
Thackara 35
Thody 161
Thomas 5, 113
Titone 3
Tèo Ñòan 96
Tòan Phầm 96
Todeva 91, 94
Tomasello 16
Toolan 153
Trager 20
Tran 112
Trofimovich 152
Trotter 48
Trudgill 41
Tucker 41
Turell 31, 91
Turner 52

U
Umbel 104
Urry 35–36, 38
Ushioda 91

V
Valdés 41, 121
Valenty 174
Van Heuven 152
Van Lier 175, 181
Van Mensel 169
Van Roey 161
Verhoeven 112
Verspoor 84, 154
Vertovec 36
Vildomec 146
Virilio 36
Viswanathan 110
Volterra 106
Von Frisch 13
Vygotsky 111

W
Walker 90
Warren 174
Waterworth 34
Watson 43
Weinreich 4, 21–22, 38, 120
Werker 104
Wesche 159
Whitaker 148
White 140
Whorf 20
Wieszbicka 82
Williams, C. 38
Williams, S. 146
Wilson 104
Wise 27

Y
Yağmur 31, 36, 38
Ytsma 55, 131

Z
Zierer 93
Zipf 69
Zurer-Pearson 104–105

Subject index

A

accuracy 185
acquisition 3–6, 8–9, 17, 20–21, 25–27, 31, 77, 80, 83, 86–91, 97, 99, 101–103, 105–106, 112–115, 121–126, 139, 145, 151, 157–158, 163–164, 175–176, 179, 184–185, 187
acquisitional stages 22
activation/inhibition 27, 29, 31, 84–86, 152–153
additional language 3, 6–7, 30, 45, 47, 50, 54, 57, 87–88, 90, 101–103, 106, 109, 111–114, 121, 123–124, 146–147, 150, 152–153, 157, 159
additive bilingualism 120, 129
additive multilingualism 29
affordances 38, 55, 174–182, 186
African multilingualism 18
African sociolinguistics 18
age factor 25, 115
alphabet 40
Anglophone 109, 114, 158
aphasia 148
aphasic 27, 85
approximative system 25
arbitrariness 12, 187
awareness 3, 28, 30–31, 70, 80, 82, 88–89, 108–109, 111, 159–160, 162, 164, 175, 178, 181

B

balanced bilingualism 6, 120
Basic Interpersonal Communicative Skills (BICS) 112–114
beyond bilingualism 110, 120, 122, 128, 183, 188
bilingual 2–4, 6–7, 19–22, 24, 26–31, 39, 42, 47, 50, 62, 77–78, 81, 84–86, 90–91, 93, 99–101, 104–105, 107–110, 112–113, 117–118, 120–122, 124–132, 144, 151–152, 154–155, 158, 185, 187–188
bilingual development 21, 27
bilingual first language acquisition (BFLA) 21, 91
bilingualism 1–7, 16–17, 20–31, 79, 83, 102, 110–111, 117–123, 126–130, 132, 151, 164, 167, 183, 185, 188
bilinguality 7, 79, 109, 111
bilingual programmes 112–113
bilingual stage 19–20, 31, 187
borrowing 22, 26, 156, 159–161
brain-imaging 26–27

C

classifications 8, 117–121, 124–125, 128, 133, 136, 138, 141, 143–144, 163, 173, 188
classifications in education 128
classifications of languages 136, 138, 141–142
classifications of multilinguals 8, 117
code-switching 24, 26, 62, 85, 150, 154, 159
cognates 70, 157–161
Cognitive-Academic Language Proficiency (CALP) 112–114
coinage 22
communication 11–16, 18, 23–24, 26, 28, 35, 41, 43, 46–49, 59, 62, 82, 88, 93, 110, 114, 135, 137–139, 163, 175–176, 179–180, 187
communication in other species/ animal communication 11–12, 163
communication systems 11, 13–14, 187

communicative competence 24, 182
communicative sensitivity 28, 110
community multilingualism 168
compartmentalization 23
complexity 5, 9, 39, 51–52, 54, 57, 66, 88, 91, 93, 117–119, 122–123, 126, 128, 131, 141, 166, 168, 180, 182–186, 189
compound bilinguals 22, 120
comprehension 3, 17, 148–149
conceptualization of multilingualism 163
conceptualizer 31, 84
consecutive bilinguality 7
consecutive multilinguality 7
constructs (theoretical constructs) 79, 163–164
convergence 84
co-ordinate bilinguals 22, 120
creativity (or open-endedness or productivity) 13–14, 187
Critical Period Hypothesis 91, 99, 102
cross-linguistic influence 22, 55, 103, 133, 146–147, 153
cross-linguistic interaction 6, 22, 89, 147, 153
cross-linguistic operation 22
cultural transmission 12, 187
current multilingualism 43, 50, 52, 56–57, 165
curriculum 6, 49–50, 109, 112, 128–129, 185

D

design features of human language 11, 14
dialect 23, 40, 120, 134–135
diglossia 22–23, 43, 132, 134

diglossic [situation] 22–23, 132
displacement 13
diversity 5, 28, 30, 36, 39, 43, 46, 49, 55, 65, 91, 94, 118, 122–123, 131, 139, 182, 186
domain 23–24, 100, 114, 180
dominance configuration 73–74
Dominant Language Constellation (DLC) 8, 59–75, 164, 171
double monolingualism hypothesis 29
duality 12–13
dynamic model of multilingualism (DMM) 88–89, 184

E
early bilingual 120
ecological approach to language 22
ecology of language 22
emergentism 185
emergent 183–184
endangered languages 136
ESL 129
ethnicity 17, 36, 53, 60, 65, 71, 77–78, 96–97
Ethnologue 41

F
Factor Model 86, 88
first foreign language 5, 88
first language 3–4, 21–22, 29, 87–88, 91, 109, 111–114, 120–121, 157, 164
fluency 2, 80, 148, 185
foreign language 5–6, 53, 65–66, 87–88, 100, 113, 121, 124, 130, 156, 176
foreign language anxiety 124
Functional Magnetic Resonance Imaging (fMRI) 27

G
galactic model 73, 137–138
globalization 1, 18–19, 32–33, 36, 39–40, 42, 48, 56–57, 68, 74, 126, 132, 136, 167
glocalization 39

H
heritage language 35, 50, 61, 67, 70, 71, 130, 168
hierarchy of languages 137, 143
historical multilingualism 43–46, 57
holistic perspective 30
home language 3, 101, 124, 127–128, 131, 148
human language 8, 19, 11–14, 16–17, 88, 163, 179, 187
hypercentral language 137–138

I
identity 17–18, 33, 38–39, 43, 55, 57, 59, 61–62, 64–65, 71–72, 77–80, 83, 90–91, 94–97, 136, 151, 155, 163, 167–168, 170, 174
idiolect 60
immersion 25, 109, 111–114, 129–130
immigration 17, 68, 125
indexicality 65–66
indigenous languages 132, 144, 168–169
indigenous populations 38
individual differences 90–91
individual language affordances 176, 178
individual multilingualism 7–8, 77–78, 89, 96–97
input 16, 25–26, 88, 91, 106, 108
integration of languages (in multilingual mind) 106–107, 115, 147, 150, 152–153, 157–158, 162
interference 22, 145
interlanguage 25, 164
international language 39, 43, 49, 55, 60, 136

L
language as ability 17
language as a tool 11, 17
language as a unique human possession 11
language attitudes 140
language behaviour 13, 23, 181
language choice 24, 62, 89, 108, 180

language community 50, 59–60
language constellation 8, 59, 61, 64, 66–67, 73–75, 163–164
language-defined object 171–172
language development 8, 27, 99, 109, 113, 129
language disorder 27
language diversity 49, 182
language education 43, 167, 183
language majority 129–130
language minority 113, 129–130
language mode 29–30, 86, 88
language of instruction 128, 176
language of wider communication 13, 43, 45, 55, 72, 94, 135–136
language practices 126, 130–131
language processing 83, 85–86, 151
language proficiency 9, 54, 112, 114, 157
language revitalization 50, 173
language separation 149–150, 154
language shift 38, 101, 132, 168, 177
language skills 1, 3, 45, 57, 91, 95, 112
language teaching 6, 22, 52–54, 70, 82, 92
language types 134–136
language variety 16, 18, 22–23, 26, 40, 43, 46, 55, 59–60, 132, 136, 139, 143
late bilingual 120
learning strategies 5, 80, 82, 87
lesser-used languages 136, 177
lexicon 31, 84, 102, 107, 148, 150, 157, 159, 161, 185
liminal 50, 52–53
liminality 51–54, 57, 187
lingua franca 42–43, 60, 72, 137, 143, 187
linguistic awareness 70, 164
linguistic distance 71, 131–132
linguistic diversity 36, 139
linguistic landscape 165, 169, 186

linguistic repertoire 5, 24,
    62–64, 68, 70, 82, 96
linguistic system 134–135, 147
listening comprehension 3
loanwords 160–161
local languages 100
Lorenz butterfly 92, 183–184

M
malleability 54, 56–57
material culture 166, 168–175,
    181, 186, 189
material culture of
    multilingualism 166,
    168–171, 189
materialities 169–171, 173–175
matrix language 150, 155
medium of instruction 129, 178
mental lexicon 150, 157
metalinguistic awareness 3, 30,
    80, 82, 109, 164, 175, 178
metaphors 16, 164–165
M-factor 89
migration 18, 36–39, 41, 53, 71,
    77, 96, 132
minority language 55, 90, 94,
    111–112, 129–130, 136–137,
    140–141, 154, 169
mobility 33, 36–39, 42–45, 49,
    56–57, 96, 125, 136
models of multilingual
    acquisition and processing
    8, 77
models of multilingualism 83
monolingual 2, 5–6, 19–20, 23,
    27–30, 41–42, 54, 59–60, 62,
    64, 74, 83–84, 86, 103–105,
    108–109, 115, 118, 126, 128–129,
    131–132, 141, 168, 187
monolingual perspective 60
monolingual stage 19
morphosyntax 104, 108, 114
mother tongue 3, 23, 25, 38, 80,
    88, 92, 95, 111, 113, 139, 181
multicompetence 9, 20, 30, 88,
    147, 150–151, 153, 164, 166
multidialectalism 148
multilingual 1–9, 18–19, 24, 29,
    31, 36, 41–48, 51–52, 54–56,
    59–60, 63–64, 69–71, 73–74,
    77–78, 80–81, 83, 85–86,

88–91, 96–97, 99–107, 115,
    117–118, 121, 126, 128, 131–134,
    136, 138, 141, 143–150, 154,
    156, 162–168, 170–174, 176,
    180–181, 183, 185–189
multilingual cities 36
multilingual communities 9,
    45, 69, 126, 131–132, 149, 180
multilingual education 54, 128,
    131, 164, 176
multilingual environment 55,
    59, 117, 170, 172
multilingual families 55, 101,
    126
multilinguality 7–8, 77, 79–81,
    83–84, 89–90, 94–95, 97, 99,
    101–102, 105–106, 109–111,
    115, 145
multilingual language
    knowledge 156, 162
multilingual lexicon 83, 185
multilingual perspective 8
multilingual's languages 3, 9,
    80, 83, 103, 107, 145, 147–148,
    150, 162
multilingual transfer 147
multiple language acquisition
    83, 86, 99, 103, 122, 124, 126,
    158, 184
mutual intelligibility 40

N
native language 3, 55, 66, 106,
    113, 126–127, 135, 150
native speakers 2, 49, 54–55,
    103, 112, 134, 139, 141–142, 150,
    161, 187
negative transfer 22, 146
neuroscience 26
new linguistic dispensation
    42–43, 50, 54, 56–57
non-human communication
    11, 13–14
number of languages 4, 7,
    19–20, 40–41, 44–45, 48–49,
    63, 65, 69, 71, 111, 124, 132, 183

O
official language 40, 61, 72,
    100, 135, 148, 176

'one parent, one language'
    strategy OPOL 21
open-endedness (or creativity or
    productivity) 13–14, 111, 187
order of acquisition 3

P
parents 15, 21, 56, 68, 91–93,
    101, 104–105, 124–127, 129,
    148–149, 154, 173
peripheral language 73, 137–138
philosophy of language 19,
    165–167
philosophy of multilingualism
    165–167, 189
phonology 102, 104, 108, 114,
    153
pluricentric languages 136, 139
plurilingualism 4, 7
positive transfer 22
Positron Emission Tomography
    (PET) 27
primary language 67, 113, 164
production 17, 31, 84–85, 153,
    185
productivity (or open-endedness
    or creativity) 13–14, 111, 187
proficiency 1–4, 8–9, 25–26,
    29–30, 50, 54, 56, 61–62, 68,
    80, 85, 89, 91, 94, 102, 110,
    112–114, 120–121, 155–157, 162,
    177, 182
pronunciation 102, 140, 153, 158
properties of contemporary
    multilingualism 54

Q
quadilingualism 117
quadrilingual 7

R
receptive multilingualism 155
recursive bilingualism 130
recursivity 14
regional languages 43, 49, 55,
    94, 136

S
script 40, 160, 172
secondary language 164

second language   2–4, 6, 21–22,
   25–26, 31, 61, 90–91, 109,
   113–114, 120–123, 151, 157, 160,
   164, 178
second language acquisition
   (SLA)   4, 26, 30–31, 90–91,
   122, 183
semanticity   12, 14
semilingualism   29
separation/intergration of
   languages   101, 106, 150
sequential bilingualism   21,
   25–26, 29, 102
sequential bilinguality   7, 111
sequential multilinguality   99,
   102, 111, 115
shifts in norms   54
sign languages   12
simultaneous bilingual
   development   21
simultaneous bilinguality   7
simultaneous multilinguality
   106, 115
social language affordances
   176–177, 179
societal awareness   19–20, 31, 95
societal bilingualism   7
societal diglossia   23
societal multilingualism   7,
   97, 126
source language   25, 160

speaking   3, 50, 123
speech community   22–23,
   59–60, 135
standardization   134
status (of a language)   23,
   40–41, 43, 49, 53, 56, 60, 128,
   132–133, 135–136, 143, 156, 168,
   175–176, 181
submersion   111, 114, 129
subordinative bilinguals   22,
   120
subtractive bilingualism   120,
   129
subtractive multilingualism   29,
   129–130
successive bilingualism   21
suffusive   50–51
suffusiveness   51, 54, 57
supercentral languages   72, 138
super-diversity   36
syntax   102, 140, 185

T
target language   25, 85, 102,
   112, 159
terminology   1, 22, 78, 117, 122
tertiary language   164
thesaurus of multilingualism
   163–164
third language   5, 64, 90,
   123–125, 147, 164

third language acquisition
   (TLA)   64, 90, 123–124, 183
transfer   22, 87, 146–147, 152–
   153, 156, 164, 181
transitional competence   25
translanguaging   149
transversion   84
triglossic   43
trilingual   7, 86, 100, 105,
   124–128, 131–132, 148, 185
trilingual children   124–125
trilingual education   128, 131,
   185
trilingual families   125–128
trilingualism   7, 117, 126, 128
truncated multilingualism   164
two trends   48
typological closeness   122, 175
typologies   71, 117–121, 123, 125,
   128–131, 133, 136, 138–139,
   144, 188

V
verbal repertoire   62
vitality (language vitality)   72,
   134
vocabulary   113, 157, 174, 181
vocal-auditory channel   11–12

W
writing systems   12